Contract Law in Belgium

Contract Law in Belgium

Ilse Samoy
Tâm Dang Vu
Tom Hick

This book was originally published as a monograph in the International Encyclopaedia of Laws/Contracts.

Founding Editor: Roger Blanpain
General Editor: Frank Hendrickx
Volume Editor: Jacques Herbots

Wolters Kluwer

Published by:
Kluwer Law International B.V.
PO Box 316
2400 AH Alphen aan den Rijn
The Netherlands
E-mail: lrs-sales@wolterskluwer.com
Website: www.wolterskluwer.com/en/solutions/kluwerlawinternational

Sold and distributed by:
Wolters Kluwer Legal & Regulatory U.S.
7201 McKinney Circle
Frederick, MD 21704
United States of America
E-mail: customer.service@wolterskluwer.com

ISBN 978-94-035-4480-9

e-Book: ISBN 978-94-035-4490-8
web-PDF: ISBN 978-94-035-4500-4

The Authors

Prof. Dr Ilse Samoy (born on 9 March 1974) studied Law at the FUNDP Namur, the KULeuven in Belgium and the Heidelberg University (1992–1997). After being a member of the bar from 1997 to 2001, she obtained her doctoral degree in 2005 as Fellow of the Research Foundation – Flanders, with a Ph.D. thesis on indirect representation under the supervision of Prof. Dr Sophie Stijns. From 2005 until 2008, she was a postdoctoral researcher of the Research Foundation – Flanders. She was appointed as a professor at the KULeuven in 2008 and teaches Contract, Tort and Evidence Law. Her research focuses on tort and evidence law.

Dr Tâm Dang Vu (born on 20 November 1979) studied Law at the KULeuven in Belgium (1997–2002). She started her professional career as a member of the bar. In 2008, she became a research and teaching assistant at the KULeuven, where she obtained her doctoral degree in 2017, with a Ph.D. thesis on linked contracts. Since 2019, she is a judge in the Tribunal of First Instance of Brussels. She has worked on the update from 2011.

The Authors

Dr Tom Hick (born on 30 March 1995) studied Law at the Université Saint Louis de Bruxelles (2013–2016) and the KULeuven (2016–2018). In 2018, he became a research and teaching assistant at the Institute for the Law of Obligations, KULeuven where he is preparing a Ph.D. thesis on pre-contractual liability for the breaking off of contractual negotiations.

He worked on the latest update.

Bieke Cornelissen, since 2019 assisting academic staff at the Institute for the Law of Obligations, KULeuven, helped work on the latest update.

Table of Contents

The Authors 3

List of Abbreviations 13

Preface 15

General Introduction 17

§1. The General Background of the Country 17
I. Geography 17
II. Cultural Composition 17
III. Political System 17
A. The Constitution and the Three Powers 18
B. Constitutional Reforms 18
C. Provinces 20
D. Political Parties 20
IV. Social and Cultural Values 21

§2. Belgian Law Belongs to the French Legal Family 22

§3. Primacy of Legislation as a Characteristic of the Belgian System 22

§4. The Position of the Judiciary 23

§5. Distinction Between Public and Private Law ('Administrative Contracts') 24

§6. Distinction Between Civil Law and Commercial Law ('Commercial Contracts') 25

Introduction to the Law of Contracts 27

§1. Introductory Concept: Definition of Patrimonial Obligation 27
I. Definition 27
II. Characteristics 28
A. A Legal Bond Between Persons: Rights in Personam and Rights in Rem 28
B. Sources of Obligations 28

C. Object of the Patrimonial Obligation 30
1. Obligations to Do Something, to Abstain from Something or to Give Something 30
2. Duty of Best Efforts Versus Duty to Achieve a Specific Result 31
D. Enforcement of the Obligation 32

§2. Definition of Contract 33
I. Definition 33
II. Characteristics of a Patrimonial Contract 33
A. The Meeting of Minds 33
B. Between Two or More Parties 34
C. A Juridical Act 34

§3. Historical Background and Basic Principles of the Law of Contracts 34
I. Autonomy of Will and Its Restrictions 34
A. Autonomy of Will 34
B. Principle of Contractual Freedom 35
C. Restrictions on Contractual Freedom 36
II. Binding Power of Contracts 37
III. Consensualism 38

§4. Classification of Contracts 39
I. Consensual, Real and Solemn Contracts 39
II. Unilateral and Synallagmatic Contracts 39
III. Onerous and Gratuitous Contracts 41
IV. Commutative and Aleatory Contracts 41
V. *Intuitu Personae* and *Intuitu Pecuniae* Contracts 41
VI. Nominate, Innominate and 'Mixed' Contracts 42
VII. Contracts with an Instantaneous Execution, Fixed-Term Contracts, Open-Ended Contracts and Long-Term Contracts 42
VIII. Main Contracts and Accessory Contracts 43
IX. Frame-Contracts and Preliminary Contracts 43
X. Negotiated and Adhesion Contracts and the Use of Standard Terms 43
XI. Commercial Contracts and Contracts with Consumers 44

§5. Contract and Torts 45
I. Tort Law and Contract Law 45
A. The Difference Between Tortious, Contractual and Criminal Liability 45
B. The Concepts of Concurrence and Coexistence 46
II. Concurrence of Contractual and Tortious Liability 47
A. Concurrence of Civil and Criminal Liability 47
B. Concurrence of Contractual and Tortious Liability 48
III. Coexistence of Claims in Contract and Tort 49

A. Active Coexistence: The Contractual Auxiliary Performer 49
B. Passive Coexistence 49

§6. Contract and Quasi-Contracts 49
I. *Negotiorum Gestio* 50
II. Restitution of Undue Payments 50
III. Unjustified Enrichment 51

§7. Contract and the Law of Property 52

§8. Contract and Trust 53

§9. Good Faith and Fair Dealing 53
I. Complementing the Contract 53
II. Moderation of the Exercise of Contractual Rights 54

§10. Drafting Style 56

§11. Sources of the Law of Contracts 56
I. Legislation 56
II. Jurisprudence 57
III. Doctrine 57

Part I. General Principles of the Law of Contract 59

Chapter 1. Formation 59

§1. Phases in the Formation Process 59
I. The Negotiation Phase 59
A. General Principles 59
B. Preliminary Documents 60
II. Offer and Acceptance 62
A. Offer 62
B. Acceptance 63
III. Consideration 63
A. Does this Requirement Exist in Your Legal System? 63
B. Gratuitous Promise 65
C. 'Natural Obligations' (Do They Exist in Your Legal System?) 65

§2. Liability and Negotiations: Precontractual Liability 65
I. Definitions 65
II. Precontractual Fault 66
III. Causal Link 67
IV. Loss and Compensation 67

§3. Formal and Evidential Requirements 68
I. Formal Requirements 68

A. Contracts Under Seal: Does This Term of Art Exist in Your Legal System? 68
B. 'Solemn' Contracts: Do They Exist in Your Legal System? 68
II. Evidential Requirements 69
A. The Parol Evidence Rule 69
B. Function of the Notary: Does the 'Notaire' Exist in Your Legal System? If Not, Which Legal Profession Assumes This Role? 69
III. Proof 71
A. Introductory Concepts 71
B. Basic Principles in the Context of Court Proceedings 72
C. Object of Proof 73
D. Burden of Proof 74
1. Rule and Role of the Parties and the Judge 74
2. Exceptions 75
E. Standard of Proof 76
F. Probative Instruments 76
1. Written Proof 76
2. Testimony 79
3. Presumptions 79
4. Admissions 80
5. Party-Oath 80
G. Hierarchy of Probative Instruments 81
1. Article 8.9 of the Civil Code: Priority of Written Proof 81
2. Legal Exceptions on Article 8.9 of the Civil Code 81
3. Hierarchy of Probative Instruments and Their Probative Effect 82

Chapter 2. Conditions of Substantive Validity 84

§1. Capacity of the Parties 84
I. Capacity to Hold Rights and Capacity to Participate in Legal Transactions 84
II. Categories of People Incapable of Holding Rights 85
A. Aliens 85
B. Certain Categories of Criminally Condemned Persons 86
III. Categories of People Incapable of Participating in Legal Transactions 86
A. Minors 86
B. Certain Categories of Persons with a Mental Disorder 88

§2. The Meeting of Minds 88
I. Concept and Scope 88
II. Defects of Consents 90
A. Mistake 90
B. Misrepresentation (Deceit) 91
C. Improper Pressure (Violence) 92

D. Gross Disparity *(Laesio)* 93

§3. Cause 95

§4. Object 96
I. Concept 96
II. Requirements 97
III. Consequences 98
IV. Theory of the Dissolution in Case of Disappearance of the Object 98
V. Initial Impossibility 98

§5. Consequences of a Defect of Consent or a Lack of Substantive Validity: Nullity 98
I. Concept and Characteristics 98
II. Modulations of the Nullity Sanction 99
III. Damages 101

Chapter 3. The Contents of a Contract 102

§1. Different Clauses 102
I. Ascertaining Express Terms 102
II. Implied Terms 102
III. Exemption Clauses 102
A. Concept and Qualification of Exemption Clauses 102
B. Acceptance 103
C. Interpretation 104
D. Validity 104
E. Abuse of Exemption? 105
IV. Penalty Clauses 105
A. Concept and Function 105
B. Qualification: Difference with Termination Clauses 106
C. Legality and Restriction of Exaggerate Penalty Clauses 107
D. Penalty Reduction in Case of Partial Performance and Control on Abuse of Rights 108
V. Arbitration Clauses 108
VI. Replacement Clauses 109

§2. Interpretation 109
I. Point of Departure: Article 1156 of the Civil Code 110
II. Other Interpretation Rules 111

§3. Conditional Contracts 111
I. Concept 111
II. The Resolutive Condition 112
A. Concept 112
B. Validity 112

C. Effects 113
III. The Suspensive Condition 114
A. Concept 114
B. Validity 114
C. Effects 114

Chapter 4. Privity of Contract 116

§1. The Rule of Privity of Contract 116
I. Third Parties and the Contract: Main Principles and Concepts 116
A. Internal and External Effects of a Contract 116
B. Parties and Third Parties 117
II. Opposability of the External Effects of a Contract to Third Parties 119
A. Conditions 119
B. Complicity of a Third Party to Breach of a Contract 119
C. Exceptions 120
1. The Paulian Action 120
2. Simulation 122
III. Relativity of the Internal Effects of a Contract Towards Third Parties 123
A. One May Not Lay a Burden on a Third Party 123
B. One May Contract for the Benefit of a Third Party 124
1. Stipulation for the Benefit of a Third Party 124
2. Direct Actions 125
3. Oblique Actions 126

§2. Transfer of Obligations 127
I. Transfer of Contractual Rights 127
II. Transfer of Contractual Debts 130
A. Concept 130
B. Complete Transfer of Debt 130
C. Incomplete Transfer of Debt 130
D. Delegation of Debt 131
III. Transfer of Reciprocal Contracts 132

§3. Subcontracting 132
I. Liability of the Main Contractor for the Defective Performance of the Subcontractor 133
II. The Employer: Subcontractor Relationship: Quasi-Immunity of the Subcontractor 133

Chapter 5. The End of the Contract 135

§1. Performance and Breach 135
I. Performance 135
A. Payment 135

1. Introductory Concepts 135
2. Simple Payment 136
3. Payment with Subrogation 145
B. Novation 149
1. Concept 149
2. Conditions 150
3. Consequences 151
C. Compensation or Set-off 151
1. Concept and Types 151
2. Legal Compensation 151
3. Judicial Compensation 152
4. Contractual Compensation 153
D. Confusion 153
E. Discharge by Agreement 153
F. Extinctive Prescription (Period of Limitation) 154
G. Renunciation and *'Rechtsverwerking'* 155
H. Termination 156
II. Breach of Contract 157
A. Faulty Behaviour of the Debtor 158
1. Personal Faulty Behaviour of the Debtor 158
2. Persons and Objects for which the Debtor Is Responsible 159
3. Proof of the Fault 160
B. Defence of Non-performance by the Debtor 161

§2. Impossibility, Frustration and Hardship 161
I. Impossibility 161
A. Concept 161
B. Conditions 162
C. Consequences of Extraneous Cause and Contractual Risk 163
II. Doctrine of Unforeseen Circumstances 164
A. Concept 164
B. Rejection of the Doctrine of Unforeseen Circumstances 164
III. Contractual Allocation of Liability 166

Chapter 6. Remedies 167

§1. General Provisions 167

§2. Formal Requisition of Putting the Debtor in Delay 167
I. Putting the Debtor in Delay: A General Principle of Law 167
II. Form and Contents 168
III. Consequences 169

§3. General Remedies in Case of Faulty Behaviour 169
I. Performance in Kind 169
A. Definition and Priority Rule 169
B. Performance in Kind by the Debtor 170

C. Performance in Kind by a Third Party 170
1. Replacement of the Debtor by a Judge 170
2. Extrajudicial Replacement 171
D. Enforced Performance Against the Government 171
II. Performance by Equivalent: Damages 172
A. Principle and Scope 172
B. Payment of a Compensation in Case of a Late Payment of a Sum of Money 173
1. General Rules 173
2. Specific Rules Applicable to Contracts Between Enterprises 174
III. Penalty Clauses 174
IV. Astreinte 174

§4. Additional Remedies in Synallagmatic Contracts 175
I. The Right to Choose 175
A. The Right to Choose Between Performance and Termination 175
B. Cumulation Prohibition and Change of Choice 176
II. Termination 176
A. Three Ways to Terminate 176
B. Judicial Termination 176
C. Extrajudicial Termination due to an Express Resolutive Clause 177
D. Extrajudicial Termination upon Notification 179
E. Consequences of Termination and Partial Termination 179
III. Suspension 181
A. Exceptio Non Adimpleti Contractus 181
B. Suspension of the Duty to Perform in Case of Irresistible Force 182

Selected Bibliography 183

Index 187

List of Abbreviations

CC	Belgian Civil Code
(O)CC	(Old) Civil Code
CEL	Code of Economic Law

List of Abbreviations

Preface

This monograph is intended for the use of foreign lawyers desiring information about the Belgian law of contracts. In addition, it aims to offer an overview of the most important principles of contract law and an uniform terminology for the translation of Belgian law terms into English, which can be used by both Belgian and foreign lawyers and authors.

A previous version of the IEL contracts for Belgium by Prof. Dr J. Herbots provided a lot of inspiration regarding the contents and structure of this contribution, as well as its terminology. We also wish to thank our predecessor for his kind remarks and keen observations regarding the adaptations we suggested in our previous version and in this version. In some places, where contract law evolved at a smaller pace, the initial contents of the IEL were left unaltered. Of course, this will be indicated where applicable.

The main source of inspiration for this contribution was provided by Prof. Dr S. Stijns' handbooks (*Leerboek Verbintenissenrecht 1* (Brugge: die Keure, 2016), 284 p.; *Leerboek Verbintenissenrecht 2* (Brugge: die Keure, 2020), 193 p.), and S. Stijns and I. Samoy (*Leerboek Verbintenissenrecht 1 bis* (Brugge: die Keure, 2020), 192 p.), which serve as textbooks for the law students at the universities of Leuven, Hasselt and Brussels. This was complemented with the handbooks on contract law by Prof. Dr P. Wéry (*Droit des obligations, I, Théorie générale du contrat* (Brussels: Larcier, 2011), 1044 p.) and Prof. Dr W. van Gerven and Prof. Dr A. Van Oevelen (*Verbintenissenrecht* (Leuven: Acco, 2015), 728 p).[1]

In between the finalisation of the present monograph and its publication a new handbook on contract law has been published by Prof. Dr I. Claeys and Dr T. Tanghe, namely *Algemeen contractenrecht* (Antwerp: Intersentia 2021) 872 p. The same is true for the update of Prof. Dr Wérys handbook *Droit des obligations – Volume 1* (Brussels: Larcier, 2021) 1085 p. as well as Prof. Dr B. Tilleman, Prof. Dr S. Lierman and Prof. Dr V. Sagaerts *De Valks Juridisch Woordenboek* (Antwerpen: Intersentia, 2020) 824 p. By consequence those books could not be integrated in the present update.

---

1. Other recent handbooks on contract law are, among others: I. Claeys & T. Tanghe, *Algemeen contractenrecht* (Antwerp: Intersentia 2021) 872; L. Cornelis, *Algemene theorie van de verbintenis* (Antwerp: Intersentia, 2000), 997; R. Dekkers & A. Verbeke, *Handboek Burgerlijk Recht*, III (Antwerp: Intersentia: 2007), 820; P. Van Ommeslaghe, *Les obligations vol. 1* in *Traité de droit civil, tome II* (Brussels: Bruylant, 2013), 3 parts; T. Vansweevelt & B. Weyts, *Handboek Verbintenissenrecht* (Antwerpen: Intersentia, 2019) 1214.

Preface

The Belgian Civil Code (CC) is currently undergoing reform. Property law (book 3) and evidentiary law (book 8) have already been voted. By consequence, the CC comprises at present two books. The parts of the Civil Code that have not yet successfully been reformed are still part of the so-called Old Civil Code (OCC).

General Introduction

§1. The General Background of the Country

I. Geography

1. Belgium is a state in Europe, adjacent to the North Sea. It shares borders with France, Germany, Luxembourg and the Netherlands. It covers an area of 30,528 square kilometres (11,787 sq mi), and it has a population of about 11.4 million people. It has a maritime temperate climate with significant precipitation in all seasons.

II. Cultural Composition

2. Belgium has three official languages: Dutch, French and German. The Dutch Region counts 6. 59 million inhabitants, for 3. 63 million inhabitants in the Walloon Region and 1.2 million inhabitants for the bilingual region of Brussels-Capital. The German-speaking Community counts 77.527 inhabitants.[2] Among the non-Belgian citizens residing in Belgium, the greatest number of them are French, Dutch and Italian citizens.[3]

III. Political System

3. In 1830, the Belgian Revolution led to the secession of the southern provinces from the United Kingdom of the Netherlands and established an independent Kingdom of Belgium. Since the installation of Leopold I as king in 1831, Belgium has been a constitutional monarchy and parliamentary, representative democracy, with a laicist constitution based on the Napoleonic Code.

4. The Belgian Constitution (BC) of 1831 set up a centralised state. However, friction between French-speaking Walloons and Dutch-speaking Flemish led to several state reforms (*see* Nos 7–10 *infra*) and to the constitutional establishment of

2. Statbel report on the Structure of the Belgian Population from 22 May 2020, https://statbel.fgov.be/en/themes/population/structure-population#news (consulted on 31 Jul. 2020).
3. Statista report on foreign population of Belgium in 2019 from October 2019, https://www-statista-com.kuleuven.ezproxy.kuleuven.be/statistics/517235/foreign-population-of-belgium-by-origin// (consulted on 31 Jul. 2020).

four linguistic regions (the Dutch, bilingual, French and German language areas), three (cultural) communities (the Dutch, the French and the German Community) and three (economic) regions (the Flemish, the Walloon and the Brussels-Capital Region) in 1970, which now coexist with the federal level.

A. *The Constitution and the Three Powers*

5. The BC sets out the principle of separation between the three powers of the state. At the federal level, the legislative power is wielded collectively by the King and Parliament (Articles 36 and 74 of the BC);[4] the executive power is vested in the King and the ministers (Article 37 BC) and the judicial power is exercised by the courts and tribunals (Article 40 BC). This separation however is not absolute, as some organs of state are partially involved in other state functions than their own (e.g., the King may convene the Parliament for an exceptional assembly, Article 44 BC), and there are several mechanisms for mutual control between powers of state (e.g., the courts and tribunals must refuse the application of illegal administrative decisions, Article 159 BC).

6. The Parliament consists of two Houses, namely the House of Representatives (*Kamer/Chambre*) and the Senate (*Senaat/Sénat*). The House of Representatives has 150 members who are elected by universal suffrage of men and women aged 18 years and over (Article 63 BC). The Senate has 60 members. Fifty of those senators are elected by the regional and community parliaments. The remaining 10 senators are co-opted by the 50 other senators. Eligibility requirements are a minimum age of 21, citizenship, and residency in Belgium (Articles 64 & 69 BC). Parliamentary elections must take place at least every four years (Articles 65 & 70 BC), although they can be dissolved earlier in a limited number of circumstances (*see* Article 46 BC).

Originally, the Chamber of Representatives and the Senate did the same parliamentary work on an equal footing, but the competences of the Senate have been diminished since the constitutional reform of 1993. Now there are three different legislative procedures that can be followed: the unicameral procedure, for the matters listed in Article 74 BC (e.g., budget control); the mandatory bicameral procedure, for the matters listed in Article 77 BC (e.g., constitutional reforms); and the optional bicameral procedure for all matters that do not fall within the former two categories.

B. *Constitutional Reforms*

7. Tensions between the two main linguistic communities of the country, the Flemish and the Walloons, led to state reforms that changed Belgium from a unitary

4. Coordinated Constitution of 17 Feb. 1994, *Belgian Official Gazette* 17 Feb. 1994.

state to a federal state with communities, regions and linguistic regions (*see* No. 4 *supra*). There have been five state reforms, which have brought fundamental changes to the BC.

8. An important step towards the state reforms was the official establishment of the linguistic frontiers and the division of the country into four linguistic regions (the Dutch, bilingual, French and German language areas) in 1962.[5] The first state reform in 1971 established three 'Cultural Communities' (the Dutch, the French and the German Cultural Community) and three 'Regions' (the Flemish, the Walloon and the Brussels-Capital Region). The second state reform in 1980 transformed the 'Cultural Communities' into 'Communities' and extended their powers to the 'matters relating to the person' such as health and education and the acquisition of their own executive bodies. The third state reform in 1988–1989 established the Brussels-Capital Region with its own regional institutions, as well as Dutch and French institutions for community matters. The competences of the regions and the communities were expanded. The fourth state reform, which took place in 1993, turned Belgium into a full-fledged federal state, by rewriting the first article of the Constitution as: 'Belgium is a federal state, composed of communities and regions.' The responsibilities of the communities and regions were expanded again, their resources were increased and they were given more fiscal responsibilities.

9. The different regions and communities have their own institutions. The revisions of the Constitution established a Flemish Council, combining the Council of the Flemish Community and the Council of the Flemish Region, as well as a Council of the French Community, a Walloon Regional Council and the Council of the Brussels-Capital Region. The members of the Councils are elected directly. Each council has its own government: the Flemish Executive, the French Community Executive, the Walloon Regional Executive and the Brussels-Capital Executive.

All Councils with exception to the Council of the Brussels-Capital Region can enact decrees (*decreet/décret*) which have the same legal standing as laws (*wet/loi*) issued by the National Parliament. The Council of the Brussels-Capital Region issues 'ordinances' (*ordonnantie/ordonnance*) which are, contrary to decrees and laws, subject to limited judicial review by the ordinary courts.

10. The 1980 constitutional reform also gave birth to the Court of Arbitration (*Arbitragehof/Cour d'Arbitrage*). Its original purpose was to settle competence disputes between the different legislative bodies. However, in 1988, its powers of judicial review were extended to the control of the compliance of legislation with three fundamental rights: the principle of equality (Article 10 BC), the principle of non-discrimination (Article 11 BC), and freedom of education (Article 24 BC). In 2003,

5. Law of 8 Nov. 1962 and Law of 2 Aug. 1963, coordinated by the royal decree of 18 Jul. 1966, *Belgian Official Gazette* 2 Aug. 1966.

this competence was extended to the whole of Title II of the Constitution, 'Belgians and their rights'.[6] Its name was changed to Constitutional Court (*Grondwettelijk Hof/Cour Constitutionelle*) in 2010.[7]

C. Provinces

11. Belgium is composed of ten provinces, five in the Flemish Region – Antwerp, Flemish-Brabant, West-Flanders, East-Flanders and Limburg – and five in the Walloon Region – Walloon-Brabant, Hainaut, Liège, Luxembourg and Namur. Each province is headed by a Provincial Council (*Provincieraad/Conseil Provincial*), which is elected by universal suffrage for a term of office of six years, a governor, and an executive council called the Permanent Deputation (*Bestendige Deputatie*) in Flanders and Provincial College (*Collège Provincial*) in Wallonia. The Permanent Deputation and the Provincial College consist of seven members: the governor and six deputies elected by the Provincial Council among its members.

D. Political Parties

12. Until the middle of the 1960s, the political arena was dominated almost entirely by three 'national' parties which constituted respectively the political expression of the Christian, socialist and liberal ideologies.[8] However, since around 1970, these parties have split into distinct representations for each communities' interests, besides their initial ideologies. These traditional parties are currently:

- the Christian-Democratic parties: CD&V (*Christian Democratic and Flemish*) in Flanders and CDH (*Humanist Democratic Centre*) in Wallonia;
- the liberal parties: Open-VLD (*Open Flemish Liberals and Democrats*) and MR (*Reformist Movement*) in Wallonia;
- the socialist parties: sp.a (*Socialist Party – Differently*) in Flanders and PS (*Socialist Party*) in Wallonia.

13. After the French protests of May 1968, which had repercussions in Belgium as well, the environmental and left-wing movement gave birth to the ecological parties *Groen!* (Green!, initially AGALEV) in Flanders and *Ecolo* in Wallonia. The sixties and seventies also saw the rise of the VU (*People's Union*), a Flemish nationalistic party. In 1978, following the entrance of the party in a coalition government led by the CD&V, a faction split off and became the *Vlaams Blok* (VA), now *Vlaams Belang* (*Flemish Interest*). VB became one of the largest parties of Flanders in the 1990s, while the VU went in decline and eventually dissolved into the N-VA (*New Flemish Alliance*-the right-wing) and *Spirit* (the left-wing) in 2001.

6. Law of 9 Mar. 2003, *Belgian Official Gazette* 11 Apr. 2003.
7. Law of 21 Feb. 2010, *Belgian Official Gazette* 26 Feb. 2010.
8. This paragraph has largely been inspired by the previous contribution to the IEL Contracts: Belgium by Prof. Dr J. Herbots.

Spirit fused with *Groen!* in 2009, thus ceasing to exist. However, the N-VA (*New Flemish Alliance*), which campaigns for Flemish independence, became the largest party in Flanders as of the 2010 federal elections. Since the 2014 elections, the party has been the largest party in the country.

IV. Social and Cultural Values

14. The social and cultural values, which co-determine the nature of the law of contracts in Belgium, largely coincide with the legal foundations of economic power in a free enterprise economy.[9] Economic power in Western society rests mainly on four fundamental options, which will supposedly remain sacrosanct for our generation. The first three of these options enable individuals or groups of individuals to obtain decision-making power over goods. The fourth gives the same individuals or groups of individuals power over people (employees). The first fundamental option relates to the freedom of commerce and industry, which was introduced in Belgium in 1791 when the medieval guilds and corporations were being abolished during the French Revolution. This freedom means that any person can freely engage in commerce, industry or any other activity of his choosing. The third option relates to the freedom of association, which enables individuals to associate with others in order to engage in industry or commerce, and to that end, to use their own capital to maximise any profit which may ensue for eventual division. Property, freedom of commerce and industry and freedom of association still constitute the legal basis for the free enterprise system in our society and will, unless there is a revolution, undoubtedly continue to do so. The fourth option involves the freedom of labour: thus, the employee is free to choose his job and his employer, and has the consequent freedom to conclude an individual labour contract. By means of this contract, the employee engages himself to work in a position of subordination: that is, under the command, authority and the control of the employer. So the employer gains power over his workers, and the workers have to carry out – within given limits of course – his orders. It is unnecessary to illustrate that in the name of individual freedom, with the employee at the mercy of the labour market forces and the (often) economically stronger employer, much suffering has been caused: child labour, long hours of work, dangerous and unhealthy workplaces, and low wages were all characteristic of the nineteenth and early twentieth centuries. Although protective labour laws and trade union action, resulting from collective bargaining as well as from the direct intervention of the state in a mixed economy, have had a dramatic impact upon the Belgian scene, these basic values are still the pillars of the social system, and fundamentally determine the development of the labour relations system.

The Belgian economic system can adequately be described as a market economy with active government intervention in its cyclical and structural evolution. The economy is very open to the rest of the world, and two-thirds of all exports are destined for EEC (Common Market) countries. While the 'system', and especially the

9. This paragraph was borrowed from the previous contribution to the IEL Contracts: Belgium by Prof. Dr J. Herbots.

profit motive, has been challenged less now, than in the past, its existence has, at the same time, been repeatedly and explicitly recognised and legitimatised.

§2. Belgian Law Belongs to the French Legal Family

15. The territory which later became known as Belgium was annexed by the French First Republic, following the campaigns of 1794 in the French Revolutionary Wars, ending Austrian rule in the region. The French Napoleonic Code, established in 1804, remained in force despite the fall of Napoleon and the unification of Holland and Belgium by the Congress of Vienna. When Belgium became independent after the revolution of 1830, its new constitution contained a provision that the French codes, the Civil Code and the Commercial Code of 1807, should be fundamentally revised as soon as possible. However, this provision has remained unimplemented to the present day, and although several dispositions of the Civil Code were annulled and modified over the years, the parts pertaining to the general principles of contract law are still largely the same as in 1804.[10] Under the initiative of the Minister of Justice Koen Geens, a vast reform project of Belgian codes has been launched. The Belgian Civil Code (CC) was also subject to revision. To date, succession law, evidentiary law and property law have been revised. The expert commissions have submitted reform projects on contract and liability law. While contract law has been submitted to the Parliament,[11] liability law has not.

16. As for the legal scholarship (*rechtsleer/doctrine*), the whole body of French interpretation and legal tradition was taken in together with the Codes in 1830. Initially, the Belgian doctrine was very much oriented towards French law. However, although its evolution often parallels French law, it has also often gone its own way in several matters. The divergences have increased with the steady growth of the availability and influence of international sources.[12]

§3. Primacy of Legislation as a Characteristic of the Belgian System

17. As a civil law system belonging to the French legal family, the Belgian legal system is characterised by primacy of legislation.[13] It is extensively codified and systematised.[14] Belgian law does not recognise the authority of binding precedent.

---

10. P. Wéry, *Droit des obligations, I, Théorie générale du contrat* (Brussels: Larcier, 2010), 43.
11. Law proposal containing book 5 'Obligations' of the Civil Code of 24 Feb. 2021, 1806/001, 55th legislature.
12. M. Van Hoecke en S. Vandenbogaerde, 'Basic Features of the Belgian Legal System' in M. Kruithof en W. De Bondt (eds), *Introduction to Belgian Law* (Alphen aan de Rijn: Wolters Kluwer, 2017) 25.
13. This paragraph was largely inspired by the previous contribution to the IEL Contracts: Belgium by Prof. Dr J. Herbots.
14. J. Smits, *The Making of European Private Law* (Antwerp-Oxford-New York: Intersentia, 2002), 74–84.

18. In order to find a solution for a problem, a judge will first look into the legislative texts, which he will interpret by trying to find the will of the legislator. The judge is thought of as being 'the mouth of the legislator'. However, Belgium's complicated set of institutions led the country to have six different legislators (*see* No. 9 *supra*). The Belgian federalist system does not have 'supremacy' principles where the law of the federal state has priority in case of conflicts between the two norms. Decrees and ordinances enacted by the various parliaments have the same legal standing as the national law. Conflicts are settled by the Constitutional Court (*Grondwettelijk Hof/Cour Constitutionelle*) (*see* No. 10 *supra*).

19. It should also be said that the Council of State (*Raad van State/Conseil d'Etat*) is charged with the responsibility of preventing conflicts of authority. The Legislation Section of the Council of State gives its reasoned recommendation on the wording of all draft or proposed bills and decrees, or on amendments thereto, which are referred to it by the President of the Senate or the House of Representatives or a community or a regional council. Apart from specific urgent cases, ministers of the national government and members of the community or regional executives, each for his own part, shall submit for the reasoned opinion of the Legislation Section of the Council of State, the text of all preliminary drafts of laws, decrees or statutory edicts. This opinion is appended to the Statement of Reasons accompanying proposed laws or decrees, and to reports forwarded to the King and to the Executive.

§4. The Position of the Judiciary

20. As stated here above, Belgian law does not recognise the authority of binding precedent.[15] A judgment is only binding between the parties. It has no precedent value for later judgments or for judgments of lower courts. However, in practice, lower courts often follow their own judgments and those of the higher courts in the interest of legal certainty.

21. The highest court in Belgium is the *Court of Cassation* (*Hof van Cassatie/ Cour de Cassation*). This Court does not, however, have the power to rule on the constitutionality of acts passed by the legislators. There are 5 courts of appeal (*hof van beroep/cour d'appel*); 12 judicial departments (*gerechtelijk arrondissement/ arrondissement judiciaire*), which are each divided in a tribunal of first instance (*rechtbank van eerste aanleg/tribunal de première instance*); a labour tribunal (*arbeidsrechtbank/tribunal du travail*), a commercial tribunal (*ondernemingsrechtbank/tribunal de l'entreprise*) and a arrondissement tribunal (*arrondissementrechtbank/tribunal d'arrondissement*); and 162 judicial cantons, each of which has its own justice of the peace (*vrederechter/juge de paix*), who is a professional judge (contrary to the justice of the peace in the UK).

15. This paragraph was largely inspired by the previous contribution to the IEL Contracts: Belgium by Prof. Dr J. Herbots.

22. The Council of State is the supreme administrative court, competent to rule on the legality of the actions of the government and the administration. As indicated earlier, the Constitutional Court will judge whether the different legislators, when enacting laws or decrees, stay within the material and/or territorial competence which they enjoy under the Constitution. The Court has the power to annul laws of Parliament or Decrees of Regional Councils partly or totally. In cases within its jurisdiction, the Constitutional Court may decide to nullify a law or a decree which is 'ultra vires'. The Constitutional Court may also be seized by another court in the form of a prejudicial question. As stated before, the Court also acts as a Constitutional Court for infringements of the Constitution (*see* No. 10 *supra*). The Court can be seized by a person or company which can prove that it has a sufficient interest.

§5. Distinction Between Public and Private Law ('Administrative Contracts')

23. The present monograph deals with the law of contracts between private persons. Contracts between public authorities are governed by specific rules. What if a private person concludes a contract with a public authority? A distinction must be made between three situations, although one should note that the distinction is often difficult to make in practice.[16] First, the public authority may act as a private person (*gewone overeenkomst met de overheid/contrat de l'administration*), in which case its contract with a particular person will be governed by the rules of private contract law. Second, it may act as an authority, i.e., from a position of superiority and for the protection of the public interest. In that case, the contract is an administrative contract (*administratieve overeenkomst/contrat administratif*) and specific rules apply, e.g., the Law on the Public Services.[17] Contract law is only subsidiary to these specific rules, which grant the public authority special prerogatives and competences, e.g., the possibility to adapt or end the contract unilaterally.[18] Examples of such contracts are public concessions and the contracts regarding public works, supplies and services, e.g., contracts regarding the distribution of water or gas or public transports. A third situation occurs when the public authority makes a policy choice from its superior position and wants to coordinate or execute that policy in cooperation with a private person. The ensuing contract is a policy contract (*beleidsovereenkomst/contrat de gestion politique*). Such contracts are considered temporary, and it is unclear whether or not and to what extent they are binding or must be regarded as (non-binding) political agreements.[19]

16. S. Stijns, *Leerboek Verbintenissenrecht 1* (Brugge: die Keure, 2016), 19.
17. Law of 15 Jun. 2006, *Belgian Official Gazette* 15 Feb. 2007 (*Wet op de overheidsopdrachten/Loi concernant les marchés publics*).
18. A. Mast, J. Dujardin, M. van Damme & J. Vandelanotte, *Overzicht van het Belgisch administratief recht* (Mechelen: Kluwer, 2002), No. 130; W. van Gerven & M. Wyckaert, 'Overeenkomsten met de overheid', *T.P.R.* 1987, 1709.
19. S. Stijns, *Leerboek Verbintenissenrecht 1* (Brugge: die Keure, 2016), 21.

§6. Distinction Between Civil Law and Commercial Law ('Commercial Contracts')

24. See further No. 74 *infra.*

Introduction to the Law of Contracts

§1. Introductory Concept: Definition of Patrimonial Obligation

I. Definition

25. In order to be able to define a contract according to Belgian Law, it is necessary to specify the broader concept of patrimonial obligations. The core of patrimonial obligations is governed by book III of the Belgian Civil Code (CC), under title III. '*Contracten of verbintenissen uit overeenkomst in het algemeen/Des contrats ou des obligations conventionnelles en général*' (regarding contracts or contracted obligations in general), *IV.* '*Verbintenissen buiten overeenkomst/Des engagements qui se forment sans convention*' (obligations without contract) and *V.* '*Vergoeding van de schade door abnormalen veroorzaakt/De la réparation des dommages causes par les anormaux*' (compensation of damages caused by mentally handicapped persons). As indicated by the title of book III, '*Wijze van eigendomsverkrijging/Manières dont on acquiert la propriété*', which can be translated as 'the ways property is obtained', patrimonial obligations are a legal means to handle property, or, stated otherwise, to influence one's patrimony.

26. 'Patrimony' is the totality of assets and rights, capable of valuation in money terms, belonging to a specific person.[20] Rights which are not regarded as appreciable in terms of money, such as political, conjugal or parental rights, are not included. A patrimonial obligation is a legal bond – a *vinculum iuris* – between two or more persons, originating under the law as a consequence of a unilateral or multilateral juridical act or as a consequence of another human behaviour, by virtue of which the one(s) – the creditor(s) – can lay legally enforceable claims appreciable in terms of money against the other(s) – the debtor(s).[21] As a consequence of the obligation, the creditor has the right to demand a performance, while the debtor is obliged to deliver this performance.

20. E. Dirix, B. Tilleman & S. Lierman (eds), *De Valks Juridisch woordenboek* (Antwerp-Oxford: Intersentia, 2018), 478.
21. S. Stijns, *Leerboek Verbintenissenrecht 1* (Brugge: die Keure, 2016), 3; P. Van Ommeslaghe, *Les obligations vol. 1* in *Traité de droit civil, tome II* (Brussels: Bruylant, 2013), 35; T. Vansweevelt & B. Weyts, « Het begrip verbintenis » in T. Vansweevelt & B. Weyts, *Handboek Verbintenissenrecht* (Antwerpen: Intersentia, 2019), 12 et seq.; P. Wéry, *Droit des obligations, I, Théorie générale du contrat* (Brussels: Larcier, 2011), 15.

II. Characteristics

A. A Legal Bond Between Persons: Rights in Personam and Rights in Rem

27. Belgian civil law makes a distinction between rights in personam – i.e., obligations (*vorderingsrecht/droit de créance*) – and rights in rem (*zakelijk recht/droit réel*).[22] Both types of rights are patrimonial rights, and both grant their holder a direct control over a thing or a behaviour.[23] However, there are differences both on an internal and on an external level:[24]

- *Internally*, a right in personam is a bond between at least two persons, resulting in the right for one to lay a claim against the other. As a consequence of this right, one person can claim a certain behaviour (to give, to do something or to abstain from something) from the other. On the other hand, a right in rem creates a bond between one or more persons and a thing. Consequentially, the holder of a right in rem obtains the control (which can strongly vary in intensity) over that good.
- *Externally*, rights in rem are opposable to all persons, or '*erga omnes*'. The situation with rights in personam is far more complex. As a legal fact, the *existence* of the obligation is opposable to third parties, and can be called upon by them (*see* No. 289 *infra*). Hence, when determining their own behaviour, third parties must take both rights '*in personam*' and rights '*in rem*' into account.[25] However, the *claims* derived from rights in personam only affect the involved parties: the performance cannot be enforced against a third party, but only against the debtor.[26] Neither can it be demanded by a third party, as only the creditor is entitled to it.[27] Thus, on the internal level, the consequences of an obligation are relative.[28]

B. Sources of Obligations

28. An obligation is created by a juridical act or another human behaviour to which the law (or the jurisprudence) has tied legal consequences. This means that one can deduce from the law that some types of behaviours result in obligations between persons. Article 1370 Old Civil Code (OCC) lists three sources of obligations: contract, tort and quasi-contracts. In spite of the fact that this legal provision

---

22. Rights *'in rem'* and rights *'in personam'* should not be confused with choses in possession and choses in action. Both type of rights are choses in action, granting their owner a right that can be enforced by legal action (cfr. E.A. Martin & J. Law (eds), *Oxford Dictionary of Law*, 6th ed. (Oxford: University Press, 2006) 94). They are not tangible items, and thus not choses in possession.
23. P. Wéry, *Droit des obligations, I, Théorie générale du contrat* (Brussels: Larcier, 2011), 15.
24. S. Stijns, *Leerboek Verbintenissenrecht 1* (Brugge: die Keure, 2016), 4; W. van Gerven en A. Van Oevelen, *Verbintenissenrecht* (Leuven: Acco, 2015), 32.
25. *See* para. 6 *infra*.
26. P. Wéry, *Droit des obligations, I, Théorie générale du contrat* (Brussels: Larcier, 2011), 16.
27. *Ibid.*
28. S. Stijns, *Leerboek Verbintenissenrecht 1* (Brugge: die Keure, 2016), 4; W. van Gerven en A. Van Oevelen, *Verbintenissenrecht* (Leuven: Acco, 2015), 32.

seems to indicate that these are the only possible sources of obligations, the jurisprudence has granted obligatory consequences to some deeds which are not recognised as a source of obligations by the law, e.g., obligations created by unilateral juridical acts.[29]

29. Juridical acts are human acts with the intention to produce legal consequences.[30] The involved person(s) express their will regarding the desired legal consequences. When at least two persons express their will, the juridical act is multilateral. The typical example is a contract. Article 1134 OCC confirms the obligatory consequences of a contract, as it clearly states that lawfully concluded contracts are considered to be law for the parties. In the case of a unilateral juridical act, only one person expresses his or her will. Although this is not mentioned in the law, both the doctrine and the jurisprudence of the *Court of Cassation* have accepted that one person can bind his/herself with an unilateral expression of will or promise,[31] regardless of its acceptance by another party. An example of such a unilateral expression of will is the offer.[32]

30. The law also recognises the obligatory power of some human behaviours that are not juridical acts (because they do not intend to create legal consequences). This is the case for torts. Articles 1382 and 1383 OCC establish a legal consequence, being an obligation to make compensation, in the case of an illegitimate action or negligence, when it causes damage to third parties. Tortious liability does' apply not only to the damage caused by one's own unlawful behaviour but also to that caused by persons for whom one is responsible (minors, pupils, employees) or by things one has under his or her keeping (e.g., domestic animals).[33] Exceptionally, obligatory consequences are given to damaging acts which are not considered illegitimate (e.g., the obligations due to neighbourhood).

31. Article 1370 OCC also grants obligatory power to quasi-contracts. According to Article 1371, these are 'purely voluntary acts of man, from which any kind of agreement may result towards another, and sometimes a reciprocal engagement

---

29. L. Cornelis, *Algemene theorie van de verbintenis* (Antwerp: Intersentia, 2000), 15; R. Dekkers & A. Verbeke, *Handboek Burgerlijk Recht*, III (Antwerp: Intersentia: 2007), 7; S. Stijns, *Leerboek Verbintenissenrecht 1* (Brugge: die Keure, 2016), 5; T. Vansweevelt & B. Weyts, « Het begrip verbintenis » in T. Vansweevelt and B. Weyts, *Handboek Verbintenissenrecht* (Antwerpen: Intersentia, 2019), 13; P. Wéry, *Droit des obligations, I, Théorie générale du contrat* (Brussels: Larcier, 2011), 37.
30. L. Cornelis, *Algemene theorie van de verbintenis* (Antwerp: Intersentia, 2000), 31; S. Stijns, *Leerboek Verbintenissenrecht 1* (Brugge: die Keure, 2016), 5; W. van Gerven en A. Van Oevelen, *Verbintenissenrecht* (Leuven: Acco, 2015), 32–33; P. Wéry, *Droit des obligations, I, Théorie générale du contrat* (Brussels: Larcier, 2011), 38.
31. Cass. 9 May 1980, *Arr.Cass.* 1970-80, 1132 & *Pas.* 1980, 1120; Cass. 16 Mar. 1989, *Arr.Cass.* 1988-89, 823 & *Pas.* 1989, 737; Cass. 27 May 2002, *Arr.Cass.* 2002, 1355; *Pas.* 2002, 1216; *RW* 2005-06, 383; *T.Aann.* 2007, 67, note A. Delvaux.
32. *See* C. Caufmann, 'De verbindende eenzijdige belofte: een bron van gebondenheid in het Europese privaatrecht', *R.G.D.C.* (2006): 3 et seq.
33. Article 1384, 1385 & 1386 OCC.

of both parties'. The resulting obligations are quite similar to the obligations originated in contracts, which explains their name. Belgian law recognises three types of quasi-contracts: *negotiorum gestio*, money paid but not due and unjust enrichment. These will be described *infra*, Nos 87 ff.

32. Finally, in 1988, the *Court of Cassation* possibly recognised another source of obligations with the doctrine of appearance (*vertrouwensleer/théorie de l'apparence*). According to this doctrine, an apparent situation can have legal consequences towards third parties if they could reasonably believe that the apparent situation corresponded to reality.[34] Although jurisprudence has not specified whether this doctrine can be applied against whoever creates an apparent situation, it is steadily accepted in case of apparent mandate (*leer van het schijnmandaat/ théorie de l'apparence*).[35] This doctrine protects the third party who has acted with an apparently authorised agent. According to the doctrine, a person can be bound by an apparent mandate, when the appearance is imputable to him, i.e., when he contributed to the existence or continuation of this appearance out of free will, by his behaviour, which does not even have to be tortious.[36] Yet, in 2018 the *Cour of Cassation* held that under Belgian law no general principle of the apparent mandate exists.[37] Furthermore, the reform project for the law of obligations states in its preparatory works that the doctrine of appearance is not a recognised source of obligations.[38]

C. *Object of the Patrimonial Obligation*

33. From the position of the creditor, the object of a patrimonial obligation is always one or several claims appreciable in terms of money. From that of the debtor, it is the performance to which he commits himself.

1. Obligations to Do Something, to Abstain from Something or to Give Something

34. It should be noted that the terms 'debtor' and 'creditor' are not confined to money debts. The object of an obligation may be any act or forbearance, or, as stated

34. E. Dirix, B. Tilleman & S. Lierman (eds), *De Valks Juridisch woordenboek* (Antwerp-Oxford: Intersentia, 2018), 481.
35. Cass. 20 Jun. 1988, *Arr.Cass.* 1987-88, 1365 & *Pas.* 1988, 1258; Cass. 25 Jun. 2004, *Pas.* 2004, 1162, *R.W.* 2006-07, 959; Cass. 2 Sep. 2010, C.10.0014.F, *Arr.Cass.* 2010, 2085, *TBBR* 2011, 300, note F. George.
36. Cass. 2 Sep. 2010, C.10.0014.F, *Arr.Cass.* 2010, 2085, *TBBR* 2011, 300, note F. George; 30 Jun. 2016, C.16.0061.N, *TBBR* 2017, 508, note B. Verheye; 26 Sep. 2016, C.16.0107, *TBBR* 2017, 507, note B. Verheye. For more on the subject, *see* I. Samoy, 'Unauthorised Agency in Belgian law', in *The Unauthorised Agent*, ed. D. Busch & L.J. Macgregor (Cambridge: University Press, 2009), 3 et seq.
37. Cass. 22 Feb. 2018, *Arr. Cass.* 2018, 430, *Pas.* 2018, 396.
38. S. Stijns & P. Wéry e.a., *De hervorming van het verbintenissenrecht* in *De hervorming van het Burgerlijk Wetboek – La réforme du Code civil* (Brugge: die Keure, 2019), 92.

by Belgian doctrine, it binds the debtor to do (e.g., to build a house, to repair damages), not to do (e.g., to refrain from competition towards another), or to give (e.g., to pay money).[39] Within the category of the obligations to give, the object of the gift can be either a generic good or a specific one. In the case of a generic good, the first obligation is one to do, as the generic good must be separated from the others before being able to transfer its possession (to give). Usually, both the separation and the transfer will happen at the same time and take place simultaneously with the delivery of these goods, especially in the case of a commercial trade.[40] In the case of a specific good, the transfer of property generally occurs at the same time as the meeting of minds (Article 1138 OCC), after which only an obligation to do, i.e., the obligation to deliver, remains. The distinction between generic goods and specific ones is also important to determine when the transfer of the property occurs, as well as the resulting transfer of the risks. Barring clauses stating otherwise, property and risk of loss due to an extraneous cause are transferred at the same time. For specific goods, this is the time of the meeting of minds, while for generic goods, it is the moment of the individualisation or separation, which usually is the moment of the physical transfer of the good.[41]

2. Duty of Best Efforts Versus Duty to Achieve a Specific Result

35. A more modern classification by the jurisprudence and the doctrine focuses on the difference between duties of best efforts (*inspanningsverbintenissen/obligations de moyens*) and duties to achieve a specific result (*resultaatsverbintenissen/obligations de résultat*). The most important aspect of this distinction lies in the burden of proof in case of non-performance (*see* No. 165 *infra*).

36. A duty to achieve is an obligation which obligates the debtor to achieve a certain result.[42] When the debtor fails to produce the promised result, the faulty behaviour of the debtor is assumed as soon as the creditor can prove both the existence of the obligation and the lack of result. The debtor can only escape liability by proving that his failure has an extraneous cause.[43] Examples of a duty to achieve are the obligation of a lawyer to respect procedural deadlines or that of a mechanic to repair or clean a car. In the case of a duty of best efforts, the debtor only binds

---

39. S. Stijns, *Leerboek Verbintenissenrecht 1* (Brugge: die Keure, 2016), 7; W. van Gerven en A. Van Oevelen, *Verbintenissenrecht* (Leuven: Acco, 2015), 33–34; T. Vansweevelt & B. Weyts, « De verschillende soorten verbintenissen » in T. Vansweevelt and B. Weyts, *Handboek Verbintenissenrecht* (Antwerpen: Intersentia, 2019), 23; P. Wéry, *Droit des obligations, I, Théorie générale du contrat* (Brussels: Larcier, 2011), 27.
40. H. De Page & A. Meinertzhagen-Limpens, *Traité élémentaire de droit civil belge, Title IV/1, La Vente* (Brussels: Bruylant, 1997), No. 23.
41. S. Stijns, *Leerboek Verbintenissenrecht 1* (Brugge: die Keure, 2016), 7–8; V. Sagaert, B. Tilleman & A. Verbeke, *Vermogensrecht in kort bestek* (Antwerp: Intersentia, 2016), 94.
42. E. Dirix, B. Tilleman & S. Lierman (eds), *De Valks Juridisch woordenboek* (Antwerp-Oxford: Intersentia, 2018), 396; T. Vansweevelt & B. Weyts, « De verschillende soorten verbintenissen » in T. Vansweevelt and B. Weyts, *Handboek Verbintenissenrecht* (Antwerpen: Intersentia, 2019), 25.
43. *See* Nos 401 ff. *infra*.

himself to take the measures a reasonable person would take to achieve the purpose of the contract, without promising he will actually achieve it.[44] For the debtor to be liable, the creditor must prove not only the existence of the obligation and the lack of result but also the fact that the debtor has not taken the measures that could be expected from a reasonable person – i.e., a normally careful and well-advised person in the same circumstances. In other terms, unlike in the case of a duty to achieve a certain result, the fault of the debtor is not assumed, but must be proven by the creditor.[45] Examples are: the duty of a doctor to cure his patient or that of a lawyer to advise, negotiate or plead a case.

D. *Enforcement of the Obligation*

37. When a debtor does not willingly fulfil his obligations, the creditor can judicially enforce its execution. The way the execution is enforced depends mostly on the object of the obligation. When the object of the obligation is to give a specific good, the execution can be enforced by a simple revendication, as the creditor has become the owner of the good.[46] With obligations to do or not to do, performance in kind (*see* Nos 415 ff. *infra*) is the preferred way of execution. Although the creditor is not allowed to physically coerce the debtor to do so, there are two ways to enforce performance. First, the creditor can ask the judge the authorisation to let a third party perform (or, in the case of an obligation not to do, to destroy what was done in spite of the obligation) at the expense of the debtor (*see* Nos 418 *infra*). Second, the creditor can ask the judge to attach to a judgment for performance in kind an order that the debtor shall pay a specified sum to the creditor for each day (or other fixed period) that they remain in fault, or for each infraction they commit. This order is called an astreinte (*see* No. 430 *infra*). When the performance in kind has become impossible or when its enforcement would be an abuse of rights by the creditor, he can ask for the performance by equivalent or damages. These remedies are only subsidiary to performance in kind (*see* No. 416 *infra*).[47]

38. Enforceability should be the characteristic which distinguishes legal obligations from other kinds of commitments, promises, agreements and duties, such as purely moral, natural, social, friendly, mundane, religious or familial obligations.[48] In practice, it is often hard to draw the line between 'legal' and 'non-legal' or strictly moral obligations. Parties can decide whether they want to make their agreements enforceable or not, and it is possible for them to exclude enforceability (e.g., gentlemen's agreements). Enforceability may vary in the case of letters of intent and letters of comfort, depending on the intention of the parties. The contents and formulation of these documents, as well as the behaviour of parties, will be helpful

44. E. Dirix, B. Tilleman & S. Lierman (eds), *De Valks Juridisch woordenboek* (Antwerp-Oxford: Intersentia, 2018), 233.
45. S. Stijns, *Leerboek Verbintenissenrecht 1* (Brugge: die Keure, 2016), 8.
46. *Ibid.*, 10.
47. *Ibid.*, 11.
48. T. Vansweevelt & B. Weyts, « Het begrip verbintenis » in T. Vansweevelt and B. Weyts, *Handboek Verbintenissenrecht* (Antwerpen: Intersentia, 2019), 14.

in determining this intention.[49] Natural obligations (*natuurlijke verbintenis/ obligation naturelle*), e.g., the duty of maintenance between siblings,[50] are situated somewhere between legal and strictly moral obligations. They are considered moral duties which cannot be enforced judicially, but if performed voluntarily, the payment of performance cannot be reclaimed as undue (Article 1235 OCC).[51] Because of its voluntary execution, the natural obligation becomes a legal obligation. This is generally explained by the binding unilateral expression of will of the voluntarily performing debtor.[52]

§2. Definition of Contract

I. Definition

39. In Belgian law, a contract is a juridical act where one or several parties obligate themselves towards one or several other parties to give something, do something or not do something.[53] It is founded on a meeting of minds, where one or more persons legally obligate themselves towards one or more other parties. Thus, it requires two coinciding expressions of will. Following this meeting of minds, either one party can obligate him- or herself (unilateral contract,[54] Article 1103 OCC) or the parties can both take obligations upon themselves towards the other party (synallagmatic contract,[55] Article 1102 OCC).[56]

This contribution will only focus on patrimonial contracts, which are contracts which aim to create patrimonial obligations or to establish, transfer, alter or annul rights in rem.[57]

II. Characteristics of a Patrimonial Contract

A. The Meeting of Minds

40. A contract presupposes a meeting of minds, which is the agreement of the wills of all the parties involved (consensus). Generally, consensus is reached after an offer made by one party is accepted by the other party, and the offering party gets

49. S. Stijns, *Leerboek Verbintenissenrecht 1* (Brugge: die Keure, 2016), 11–12.
50. P. Wéry, *Droit des obligations, I, Théorie générale du contrat* (Brussels: Larcier, 2011), 23.
51. E. Dirix, B. Tilleman & S. Lierman (eds), *De Valks Juridisch woordenboek* (Antwerp-Oxford: Intersentia, 2018), 302; P. Wéry, *Droit des obligations, I, Théorie générale du contrat* (Brussels: Larcier, 2011), 22.
52. S. Stijns, *Leerboek Verbintenissenrecht 1* (Brugge: die Keure, 2016), 12.
53. E. Dirix, B. Tilleman & S. Lierman (eds), *De Valks Juridisch woordenboek* (Antwerp-Oxford: Intersentia, 2018), 105.
54. For a definition *see infra* No. 59.
55. *Ibid.*
56. S. Stijns, *Leerboek Verbintenissenrecht 1* (Brugge: die Keure, 2016), 15; T. Vansweevelt & B. Weyts, « De overeenkomst: definitie en soorten » in T. Vansweevelt and B. Weyts, *Handboek Verbintenissenrecht* (Antwerpen: Intersentia, 2019), 109.
57. For a definition of rights in rem, *see supra* No. 29.

knowledge or could reasonably get knowledge of this acceptance. This is also the case for synallagmatic contracts, where all parties involved have to agree with each other. In such case, every party will only give his or her consent provided that the other parties obligate themselves as well. The meeting of minds will be treated in Part 1, Chapter 2, on the conditions of substantive validity.

B. Between Two or More Parties

41. A contract requires at least two contracting parties. In a broader sense, a 'two-party' contract can be concluded between more than two persons, which however can be categorised into two 'groups of parties', which each have the same or a similar interest.[58] It is also possible for a contract to have more than two parties with different interests, in which case it becomes a contract with as many parties as there are different interests.[59]

C. A Juridical Act

42. As a contract is a juridical act, it requires the will of the parties to create legal consequences.[60] More specifically, the intended legal consequences are the creation, transfer, change or undoing of patrimonial obligations or of rights in rem. A valid contract creates obligations. This means that the parties must respect and execute the contract, and will be able to enforce this execution. Even the judge must respect the binding power of a contract. However, the will of the parties to bind themselves is not presumed. It must be proven. Indeed, it is perfectly possible for the parties not to wish to make legally binding agreements (*see* No. 38 *supra*).

§3. Historical Background and Basic Principles of the Law of Contracts

I. Autonomy of Will and Its Restrictions

A. Autonomy of Will

43. The Napoleonic Code which, although partially modernised, is still the base of the CC was written in 1804. At that time, the outlook on society was one of extreme individualism and economic liberalism.[61] There was a strong belief in the rational and free will of each individual, which translated in a law where individual

58. S. Stijns, *Leerboek Verbintenissenrecht 1* (Brugge: die Keure, 2016), 16; P. Wéry, *Droit des obligations, I, Théorie générale du contrat* (Brussels: Larcier, 2011), 61.
59. *See* E. Dirix, 'De meerpartijenovereenkomst', *T.P.R.* (1983): 757–794.
60. *Ibid.* 16.
61. More about this in J. Ghestin, *Traité de droit civil, Les obligations: la formation du contrat* (Paris: L.G.D.J., 1993), No. 36.

freedom was (over) emphasised, and where state interference was restricted to a minimum. In contract law, this resulted in the principle of the autonomy of will. The autonomy of will has the following three aspects: freedom of contracting, the binding power of contracts, and consensualism.

44. The principle of the autonomy of will has been the object of a lot of criticism since the end of the nineteenth century, as the fiction of an absolute freedom and equality, and the principle of economic liberalism came under fire. A person was no longer perceived as an individual independent from society of context, but as a social creature who acted within certain groups and contexts. Contracts could no longer be approached as instruments only used by free and equal individuals but also as social facts necessitating adjustments whenever weaker parties had to contract with stronger ones. In contract law, this resulted in an interaction between the principle of the autonomy of will and the requirements of good faith and the doctrine of appearance. The concept of good faith expects each contracting party not only to respect his or her obligations but also to conclude and execute them loyally and cooperatively.[62] The doctrine of appearance implies that, regardless of the reality, reasonable belief might have consequences (*see* No. 32 *supra*). While the autonomy of will is about what the parties have wanted, good faith and appearance are about what society thinks that a party should have wanted. This evolution radically affected the law of contracts.

45. Another evolution with a great impact on the freedom of the parties is the increased role of the courts in civil procedures, specifically in the interpretation of contracts. This aspect is treated *infra*, Nos 101 ff.

B. Principle of Contractual Freedom

46. Contractual freedom means that each individual is free to contract. Specifically, contractual freedom has three elements: the freedom of whether to contract, the freedom to choose the other contract party, and the freedom to determine the contents of the contract.[63]

However, even in 1804, contractual freedom was not absolute. Article 2 OCC always stipulated that contract parties are not allowed to violate laws of public order (*openbare orde/ordre public*) or public decency (*goede zeden/bonnes moeurs*). A

---

62. E. Dirix, B. Tilleman & S. Lierman (eds), *De Valks Juridisch woordenboek* (Antwerp-Oxford: Intersentia, 2018), 202.
63. For more on the subject of contractual freedom, *see*: A. De Boeck, 'Doorwerking van het gelijkheidsbeginsel in het contractenrecht. De contractsvrijheid in het nauw gedreven?' in *Vrijheid en gelijkheid: de horizontale werking van het gelijkheidsbeginsel en de nieuwe antidiscriminatiewet* (Antwerp: Maklu, 2003), 413–444; I. Samoy (ed.), *Evolutie van de basisbeginselen van het contractenrecht* (Antwerp: Intersentia, 2010), 269; S. Stijns, 'Abus, mais de quel(s) droit(s) ? Réflexions sur l'exécution de bonne foi des contrats et l'abus de droits contractuels', *J.T.* (1990): 33–44; S. Stijns, 'Het verbod op misbruik van contractuele rechten: lees de bijsluiter voor gebruik !' in S. Stijns & P. Wéry (eds) *De rol van de rechter in het contract* (Brugge: die Keure, 2014), 87 et seq.; I. Verougstrate, 'Wil en vertrouwen bij het totstandkomen van overeenkomsten', *T.P.R.* (1990): 1163–1196.

law is of public order when it determines the rules on which the economic or moral order of the society is based. *Goede zeden,* which can be translated as 'public decency', is included in this definition. Rules of public order intend to protect the public interest. The sanction for a breach of public order is absolute nullity.[64] It must be taken into account that the concept of public order has evolved between 1804 and now as social values have evolved. For example, in 1804, unmarried cohabitation was considered against public order. Consequentially, a gift between people who cohabited without being married could be declared null. Nowadays, Belgian society accepts unmarried cohabitation, and gifts between such people are perfectly valid. The only exception is gifts done as '*pretium stupri*' (to pay for sexual relations): this is still against public order; thus a gift done to this effect is null.[65]

47. Besides the laws of public order, there are imperative laws (*dwingende wetten/lois imperatives*), which protect the interests of individuals. These laws, which have first been defined by a judgment of the *Court of Cassation* in 1956, impose additional restrictions on contractual freedom.[66] Their breach is sanctioned with a relative nullity (*see* No. 236 *infra*). As opposed to imperative laws, suppletive laws (*aanvullende wetten/lois supplétives*), which constitute the main body of the (Old) Civil Code, only apply when the contract does not stipulate otherwise. In other words, contract parties are free to deviate from them.

C. Restrictions on Contractual Freedom

48. Due to economic inequalities (and some enterprises in monopoly positions), it is possible for strong parties to force weaker ones to accept disadvantageous adherence contracts and standard clauses, or to refuse to contract altogether. The freedom to contract in these circumstances has been restricted by statute (e.g., compulsory third-party insurance of motorists, compulsory 'minimum service' for providers of water, electricity and banking services).[67]

49. The freedom to determine the contents of a contract has been restricted by new rules of public order or new imperative rules. Doctrine and jurisprudence developed some new legal concepts, such as the prohibition of penalty clauses including a private punishment (*see* Nos 256–261 *infra*), the prohibition on the exemption clauses for one's own intentional fault (*see* Nos 246 ff. *infra*), or the concept of gross disparity (*see* Nos 219 ff. *infra*).

---

64. S. Stijns, *Leerboek Verbintenissenrecht 1* (Brugge: die Keure, 2016), 39.
65. *See also infra* No. 228 on this subject.
66. Cass. 6 Dec. 1956, *Pas.* 1957, 361.
67. S. Stijns, *Leerboek Verbintenissenrecht 1* (Brugge: die Keure, 2016), 48; P. Wéry, *Droit des obligations, I, Théorie générale du contrat* (Brussels: Larcier, 2011), 125.

50. According to the doctrine of the unlawful refusal to contract, the refusal to contract can be an abuse of rights.[68] Also, a refusal to contract possibly can be a fault which causes damages, resulting in tortuous (precontractual) liability according to Article 1382 OCC (*see* Nos 76 ff. *infra*). The principle of equality and non-discrimination, stipulated by the Anti-discrimination Laws of 25 February 2003,[69] 20 January 2003[70] and 10 May 2007,[71] forbids both authorities and citizens to discriminate, when contracting within the 'public sphere'.[72] Discrimination is forbidden in both the precontractual and the contractual phase. This restriction applies to both the offer of goods and the adherence and participation in economic, social, cultural or political activities open to the public. Breaches of this rule are sanctioned by the nullity of the forbidden clause.

II. Binding Power of Contracts

51. Another aspect of autonomy of will is the obligatory or binding power of contracts. Legal certainty is often cited as the ground for this rule,[73] although some recent authors claim that a contract is only obligatory because it is useful and on the condition that it is just.[74] It has consequences for the parties to the contract, the judge and third parties. For parties to the contract, this principle is stated in Article 1134 OCC. This article's first paragraph stipulates that lawfully concluded contracts are considered to be law for the parties. This means that each party must respect his or her obligations. The second paragraph states that one party cannot unilaterally alter or end the contract. Consequentially, contracts can only be altered by mutual consent. Exceptions to this rule must be established by law (e.g., agency). In addition, it is possible for parties to include a renegotiation or abrogation clause in their contract.[75] The judge must observe the contract as well, as he has to grant it the consequences the parties have wanted. He is not allowed to alter its contents, even if they are unfair. The respect of this principle is controlled by the *Court of Cassation*. The most important exception to this rule is worded by Article 1244, paragraph 2 OCC. Regardless of the contractual deadlines, the judge may grant the debtor a

---

68. Cass. 27 Apr. 2020, C.19.0435.N, *TBBR* 2021, 155, note S. Jansen and S. Stijns, *RW* 2021, to be published, T. Hick and F. Van den Abeele; Cass. 7 Oct. 2011, *Arr. Cass.* 2011, 2032, *RW* 2012-13, 1181, note S. Jansen and S. Stijns; *TBBR* 2012, 489, note A. De Boeck. *See also* S. Stijns, 'Het verbod op misbruik van contractuele rechten: lees de bijsluiter voor gebruik !' in S. Stijns & P. Wéry (eds) *De rol van de rechter in het contract* (Brugge: die Keure, 2014), 87 et seq.
69. Wet van 25 februari 2003 ter bestrijding van discriminatie en tot wijziging van de Wet van 15 februari 1993 tot oprichting van een Centrum voor gelijkheid van kansen en voor racismebestrijding, *Belgian Official Gazette* 17 Mar. 2003.
70. Wet van 20 januari 2003 tot versterking van de wetgeving tegen racisme, *Belgian Official Gazette* 12 Feb. 2003.
71. Wet van 10 mai 2007 ter bestrijding van bepaalde vormen van discriminatie, *Belgian Official Gazette* 30 May 2007.
72. The law excludes private matters from its scope of application.
73. S. Stijns, *Leerboek Verbintenissenrecht 1* (Brugge: die Keure, 2016), 42.
74. For example, M. Coipel, *Eléments de théorie générale des contrats* (Diegem: Story-Scientia, 1999), 28.
75. S. Stijns, *Leerboek Verbintenissenrecht 1* (Brugge: die Keure, 2016), 42.

moderate respite for the payment of his debt.[76] As for third parties, the principle of the relativity of contracts applies. It is a logical consequence of the autonomy of will that a contract can only bind the contracting parties. However, at the beginning of the twentieth century, the principle of the opposability of contracts was recognised. According to this principle, contracts are social facts which third parties both base themselves upon and which they have to take into account.[77] For more about relativity and opposability of contracts, *see* No. 287 *infra*.

52. While the traditional vision on the autonomy of will dictates that parties can only be bound by their actual intentions, it is a fact that one's actual inner will can differ from his or her expressed outer will. According to the principle of the autonomy of will, the will to be taken into consideration is the inner will. However, due to the theory of appearance, when a party could reasonably believe in the expressed will of the other, both will be bound according to the outer will.

53. While autonomy of will remains the base of a contract, the judge also has a role in determining its binding power through the application of the principle of good faith. This will be described *infra*, Nos 101 ff.

III. Consensualism

54. In principle, the contract is concluded '*solo consensu*'; this is as soon as there is a consent from all parties.[78] There are no other formal requirements for the validity of the contract. A contract may be concluded by verbal agreement. In this case, written instruments will only be established for proof purposes (*see* Nos 149 ff. *infra*). Real and solemn contracts[79] are exceptions to this rule. Real contracts require for the good to be handed over. In the case of solemn contracts, some formalities are required in addition to the parties' consent.[80]

55. However, under the principle of the autonomy of will, parties have the right to deviate from the principle of consensualism and agree that certain formalities will be necessary to the validity of their contract, e.g., they can stipulate that they will only be bound after a written document is signed.

56. In some cases, in addition to the consensus of parties, parties will need to respect some formal requirements in order for the contract to be valid. For example, making a written document mandatory will protect the weaker party by helping him

---

76. *Ibid.*, 43.
77. *Ibid.*
78. S. Stijns, *Leerboek Verbintenissenrecht 1* (Brugge: die Keure, 2016), 43; T. Vansweevelt & B. Weyts, « Grondbeginselen van het contractenrecht » in T. Vansweevelt and B. Weyts, *Handboek Verbintenissenrecht* (Antwerpen: Intersentia, 2019), 131; P. Wéry, *Droit des obligations, I, Théorie générale du contrat* (Brussels: Larcier, 2011), 129.
79. For definitions, *see infra* Nos 60–61.
80. For more about solemn contracts, *see* No 58 *infra*.

or her to realise which obligations he or she takes upon him or herself, ponder things more slowly, and have a document to review his or her rights.

The amount of rules involving such protecting measures has gradually increased, especially in matters where consumers are involved. For example, a sale to a consumer which has to be paid for in several instalments has to be laid down in writing, with the inclusion of several mandatory clauses. The contract will not be valid unless these clauses are included in a signed written contract and an advance payment has been made.[81]

§4. Classification of Contracts

57. Following classification of contracts only includes patrimonial contracts. For a definition of 'patrimonial', *see* No. 25 *supra*.

I. Consensual, Real and Solemn Contracts

58. At the level of the conclusion of contracts, a distinction is made between consensual, real and solemn contracts. Consensual contracts (*consensueel contract/contrat consensuel*) are validly concluded as soon as there is a consent from all contracting parties, without any formal requirements (*see* No. 54 *supra*). In Belgian law, consensual contracts are the rule, while real and solemn contracts are the exception. Real contracts (*zakelijk contract/contrat réel*) come into existence by the delivery of the object of the contract (a thing or (a part of) a price).[82] Examples are a loan of money intended for consumption, a loan for use, a pledge or a deposit. Solemn contracts (*plechtig contract/contrat solennel*) are only valid when certain formal requirements are met,[83] in addition to the consent of all parties. An example is a notarised act, i.e., a document drawn up by a notary (*see infra*) for a gift (Article 931 OCC) or a mortgage (Article 76 of the Law on Mortgages). As discussed in No. 56 *supra*, the recent years have seen a 'revival' of solemn contracts, as formal requirements are often used as a means to protect weaker parties.[84]

II. Unilateral and Synallagmatic Contracts

59. A contract is unilateral (*éénzijdig contract/contrat unilatéral*) when it only creates obligations for one party (Article 1103 OCC). This is the case for gratuitous custody, pledge, and loan for use, as all are obligations in rem resulting in the sole

81. Article VII. 78 CEL.
82. E. Dirix, B. Tilleman & S. Lierman (eds), *De Valks Juridisch woordenboek* (Antwerp-Oxford: Intersentia, 2018), 107.
83. *Ibid.*
84. P. Wéry, *Droit des obligations, I, Théorie générale du contrat* (Brussels: Larcier, 2011), 130.

obligation to give back the thing that was handed over at the conclusion of the contract. A contract is synallagmatic or reciprocal (*wederkerig contract/contrat synallagmatique*) when the contracting parties bind themselves mutually (Article 1102 OCC). Not only does it create reciprocal obligations, but, as emphasised by the doctrine, these obligations are also connected, in that one obligation is concluded *because* of the other.[85]

60. This distinction has several consequences. First, in the case of non-performance due to an extraneous cause, the risk allocation differs. In the case of a unilateral contract, the debtor is freed of his obligations while the creditor bears the risk. In the case of a synallagmatic contract, the debtor is also freed, but the creditor does not have to perform either. Consequentially the risk lies with the debtor (*see* No. 404 *infra*). Second, in the case of a breach of a synallagmatic contract, the aggrieved creditor has the right to terminate the contract or to call upon the *exceptio non adimpleti contractus*. These possibilities do not exist in the case of a unilateral contract (*see* Nos 431 ff. *infra*). Third, with synallagmatic contracts, the objective cause of the obligation of one party lies in the obligation of the other party (quid pro quo). If one of these obligations lacks a (licit) cause, the whole contract becomes null because it has no (licit) cause (*see* No. 224 *infra*). Finally, different rules apply when it comes to the proof of unilateral or synallagmatic contracts (*see* Nos 149 ff. *infra*).

61. Contracts which start out as unilateral contracts may become synallagmatic later on when obligations towards the other party come into being during their execution. These contracts are called imperfect synallagmatic contracts (*onvolmaakt wederkerige overeenkomst/contract synallagmatique imparfait*). A typical example is (gratuitous) agency, which is unilateral – only the agent binds himself (*see* Articles 1984 et seq. OCC). However, if the agent must incur expenses in order to execute his mandate, the principal has to refund those expenses (Article 1999 OCC), and the unilateral contract becomes synallagmatic. The question of whether and to which extent these contracts must be treated as unilateral or reciprocal is disputed.[86] As a final remark, we should point out that the distinction between unilateral and synallagmatic contracts is not the same as that between unilateral and bilateral juridical acts. All contracts are necessarily bilateral juridical acts (*see* No. 42 *supra*).

85. S. Stijns, *Leerboek Verbintenissenrecht 1* (Brugge: die Keure, 2016), 24; W. van Gerven en A. Van Oevelen, *Verbintenissenrecht* (Leuven: Acco, 2015), 61; P. Wéry, *Droit des obligations, I, Théorie générale du contrat* (Brussels: Larcier, 2011), 74.
86. S. Stijns, *Leerboek Verbintenissenrecht 1* (Brugge: die Keure, 2016), 25; W. van Gerven en A. Van Oevelen, *Verbintenissenrecht* (Leuven: Acco, 2015), 61; P. Wéry, *Droit des obligations, I, Théorie générale du contrat* (Brussels: Larcier, 2011), 74.

III. Onerous and Gratuitous Contracts

62. A contract is onerous (*onder bezwarende title/à titre onéreux*) when both parties obligate themselves to give, do, or not do something, one obligation as compensation for the other (e.g., sale of goods).[87] It is gratuitous (*om niet/à titre gratuit*) when one obliged party confers an economical advantage to the other party but gains no such advantage in return (e.g., a gift).[88] In this case, the cause is '*animus donandi*', or the will to give something to someone.[89]

IV. Commutative and Aleatory Contracts

63. Commutative and aleatory contracts are distinctions within the category of onerous contracts. Commutative contracts (*vergeldend contract/contrat commutatif*) are contracts where each party obligates himself to give, or to do something, which he considers equivalent to what is given to or done for him.[90] Consequentially, one knows from the beginning which mutually equivalent performances are due. A contract is aleatory (*kanscontract/contrat aléatoire*) when the equivalence of the performances cannot be determined in advance and these performances depend on some future uncertain event (e.g., an insurance).[91]

64. The most important practical consequence of this distinction is that the remedy of rescission for *laesio* (i.e., gross disparity, *see* Nos 219 ff. *infra*) is not available in the case of aleatory contracts, as parties accept at the formation of the contract that performances might turn out to be disproportionate. An exception is made when the contract is only aleatory in appearance, e.g., a contract where a party sells land to another and receives a life annuity as the price when the seller is already extremely old or ill.[92]

V. *Intuitu Personae* and *Intuitu Pecuniae* Contracts

65. A contract is called *intuitu personae* when the identity or qualities of one party was determining for the other party's will to contract (e.g., a lawyer or an

87. E. Dirix, B. Tilleman & S. Lierman (eds), *De Valks Juridisch woordenboek* (Antwerp-Oxford: Intersentia, 2018), 107.
88. *Ibid.*
89. S. Stijns, *Leerboek Verbintenissenrecht 1* (Brugge: die Keure, 2016), 26.
90. E. Dirix, B. Tilleman & S. Lierman (eds), *De Valks Juridisch woordenboek* (Antwerp-Oxford: Intersentia, 2018), 107.
91. E. Dirix, B. Tilleman & S. Lierman (eds), *De Valks Juridisch woordenboek* (Antwerp-Oxford: Intersentia, 2018), 105; S. Stijns, *Leerboek Verbintenissenrecht 1* (Brugge: die Keure, 2016), 26.
92. S. Stijns, *Leerboek Verbintenissenrecht 1* (Brugge: die Keure, 2016), 26.

architect).[93] It is called *intuitu pecuniae* when the economic advantage was determining for a party's will to contract, and the other party's identity was less important.[94]

VI. Nominate, Innominate and 'Mixed' Contracts

66. Contracts regulated explicitly in the Civil Code or other statutes are called nominate (*benoemd/nommé*) contracts (e.g., sale of goods).[95] Contracts which are not explicitly regulated in these statutes are called innominate (*onbenoemd/innommé*) (e.g., leasing, factoring, franchising).[96] Such agreements are regulated by their clauses as drafted by the contracting parties, by the general rules of contract law, and, by analogy, by the rules governing similar nominate contracts. Contracts containing elements of different nominate contracts are called 'mixed' contracts. If by the combination of such different elements a new kind of contract comes into being, it is treated as an innominate contract (sui generis theory). If it is possible to distinguish between the different elements, then one applies the specific rules to each specific element, unless there is a clause to the contrary (combination theory). If one element is accessory, then the specific rules of the main contract are applied to the whole contract (absorption theory).[97]

VII. Contracts with an Instantaneous Execution, Fixed-Term Contracts, Open-Ended Contracts and Long-Term Contracts

67. A contract with an instantaneous execution (*contract met onmiddellijke uitvoering/contrat à execution instantanée*) is a contract which is executed by a one-time performance from both parties,[98] e.g., a sale of goods. In the case of a contract with a continuous execution (*duurcontract/contrat à exécution continue*), the execution of the performance(s) is spread in time (e.g., a hire).

68. Contracts with a continuous execution are concluded for a definite (fixed-term) (*bepaalde duur/durée déterminée*) or an indefinite (open-ended) (*onbepaalde duur/durée indeterminée*) duration. While a fixed-term contract cannot be terminated unilaterally (unless it contains a rescission clause or statute to that effect), an open-ended contract can be terminated unilaterally at all times. The principle of the

---

93. E. Dirix, B. Tilleman & S. Lierman (eds), *De Valks Juridisch woordenboek* (Antwerp-Oxford: Intersentia, 2018), 106; W. van Gerven en A. Van Oevelen, *Verbintenissenrecht* (Leuven: Acco, 2015), 62–63.
94. E. Dirix, B. Tilleman & S. Lierman (eds), *De Valks Juridisch woordenboek* (Antwerp-Oxford: Intersentia, 2018), 106.
95. *Ibid.*
96. E. Dirix, B. Tilleman & S. Lierman (eds), *De Valks Juridisch woordenboek* (Antwerp-Oxford: Intersentia, 2018), 106. Innominate contracts according to Belgian law should not be confused with innominate terms (also called intermediate terms) in English law.
97. W. van Gerven en A. Van Oevelen, *Verbintenissenrecht* (Leuven: Acco, 2015), 63–64.
98. E. Dirix, B. Tilleman & S. Lierman (eds), *De Valks Juridisch woordenboek* (Antwerp-Oxford: Intersentia, 2018), 106.

autonomy of will implies that one cannot obligate himself indefinitely without the possibility to free himself from his obligations.

69. Long-term contracts (*contracten van lange duur/contrats à long terme*), such as a cooperation agreement or a joint venture, have become increasingly important. In their regard, the doctrine advises a supple application of certain rules of general contract law, such as the completive and the moderative functions of good faith (*see infra* Nos 104 et seq.). Contracts often contain clauses allowing a party decision or a binding third-party decision (*see infra*, No. 234), or clauses governing the post-contractual phase, thus surviving after the end of the contract, such as competition and confidentiality clauses.[99]

VIII. Main Contracts and Accessory Contracts

70. An accessory contract (*bijkomende contract/contrat accessoire*) is a contract the existence of which is linked to the existence of another contract,[100] the main or principal contract (*hoofdcontract/contrat principal*). If, for instance, the main contract is void, the accessory contract vanishes (*accessorium sequitur principale*). Examples of accessory contracts are pledge, mortgage and suretyship.[101]

IX. Frame-Contracts and Preliminary Contracts

71. A frame-contract (*raamcontract/contrat cadre*) is a contract which creates a frame in which later contracts will be entered into, e.g., a sale distributor's agreement. A preliminary contract (*voorovereenkomst/avant-contrat*) is a contract which prepares (usually) one later contract and has a direct link with this contract, e.g., a promise to contract (*see* Nos 115 ff. *infra*).[102]

X. Negotiated and Adhesion Contracts and the Use of Standard Terms

72. Negotiated contracts (*onderhandeld contract/contrat négocié*) are contracts where both parties have a say about the contents of the contract. Adhesion contracts (*toetredingscontract/contrat d'adhésion*) are contracts between two parties where one (economically weaker) party has no say about the contents of the contract which is fixed in a unilateral way by the other (economically stronger) party. The weaker party only has the freedom to choose whether they adhere to this contract or not. Adhesion contracts often contain standard terms.

---

99. S. Stijns, *Leerboek Verbintenissenrecht 1* (Brugge: die Keure, 2016), 29.
100. E. Dirix, B. Tilleman & S. Lierman (eds), *De Valks Juridisch woordenboek* (Antwerp-Oxford: Intersentia, 2018), 106.
101. W. van Gerven en A. Van Oevelen, *Verbintenissenrecht* (Leuven: Acco, 2015), 63.
102. S. Stijns, *Leerboek Verbintenissenrecht 1* (Brugge: die Keure, 2016), 30–31.

73. Although, as a rule, lack of negotiations and great inequalities between parties do not affect the validity or obligatory power of a contract, both legislation and jurisprudence attempt to protect the weaker party against abuses. Several contracts are regulated by statute (e.g., contract of employment, contractual tenancy when the object of the hire is one's main residence), and some terms are mandatory for certain types of contracts (e.g., the model contract for third-party insurance of motorists). Jurisprudence uses such figures as good faith and information duties to protect the weaker party. Book VI of the Code of Economic Law (hereinafter CEL), especially Articles VI. 82–87, grants wide powers to the courts to annul certain terms for being *unfair*.[103]

XI. Commercial Contracts and Contracts with Consumers

74. Commercial contracts (*handelscontracten/contrats commerciaux*) are contracts concluded between enterprises only. Enterprises (*ondernemingen/entreprises*) are each of the following organisations: (a) natural person who exercises independently a profession; (b) legal person (except public legal persons which do not offer goods or services on the market and public entities); (c) other organisation without legal personality whose purpose is the payment of dividends, in fact pays dividends to his members or staff which influence the working of the entity.[104] Although the general rules of contract law apply to commercial contracts, commercial law knows some specific laws regarding contracts, e.g., the Law of 2 August 2002 on combating late payment in commercial transactions, *Belgian Official Gazette* 7 August 2002.

As of 1 of December 2020, the CEL contains several provisions that are aimed to mitigate reasonable practices between enterprises by providing that certain clauses are either per se unlawful (Article VI.91/4 CEL) or presumed to be unlawful (Article VI.91/5 CEL); prohibit abuse of economic dependency (Article IV.2/1 CEL) and dishonest practices between enterprises (Article VI.104/1 CEL).[105] The prohibited clauses seem to have been largely influenced by the prohibited clauses in consumer contracts, which leaves scholars somewhat puzzled, given that the new provisions apply to contracts between all types of enterprises. In general, the reception of the law has been rather negative. It remains to be seen how smoothly the new provisions will be in practice.[106]

75. Consumer contracts are contracts between an enterprise and a consumer. In this regard, a consumer is 'any natural person who acts for purposes outside of his

103. Code of Economic Law, *Belgian Official Gazette* 28 Feb. 2013.
104. Article I.1, 1° CEL; H. Vanhees, E. Dirix & R. Steennot, *Ondernemingsrecht in hoofdlijnen* (Mortsel: Intersentia, 2019), 5, nr. 7.
105. Introduced by the law of 4 Apr. 2019 (*Wet houdende wijziging van het Wetboek van Economisch Recht met betrekking tot misbruiken van economische afhankelijkheid, onrechtmatige bedingen en oneerlijke marktpraktijken tussen ondernemingen*) *BS* 24 Mai 2019.
106. On the subject *see* W. Devroe, E. Terryn & B. Keirsblick (eds), *Nieuw economisch recht in b2b-relaties* (Antwerp: Intersentia, 2020) 242; E. De Duve, T. Duriau & P.A. Foriers, e.a. (eds), *Les clauses abusives B2B après la loi du 4 avril 2019* (Limal: Anthemis, 2020), 591.

commercial or professional activity'.[107] Several European directives, to which the European countries had to adapt their laws, improved the situation of consumers.[108] At present, those directives have been implemented and grouped in books VI and XIV of the CEL of 28 February 2013. The protection of consumers is realised through the use of several techniques.[109] Examples are the general duty of sellers to inform the consumer (Article VI.2 CEL), consumer-friendly interpretation rules (Article VI. 83 CEL), and a 'black list' of forbidden terms (Article VI. 83 CEL).

§5. Contract and Torts

I. Tort Law and Contract Law

A. The Difference Between Tortious, Contractual and Criminal Liability

76. As seen in Nos 30–32 *supra*, juridical acts (including contracts) and torts are both sources of obligations. Contractual liability (*contractuele aansprakelijkheid/ responsabilité contractuelle*) can be incurred when a contracting party does not perform a contractual obligation in a way that is accountable to him (*see* Nos 391 ff. *infra*).[110] The source of the obligation to perform is a juridical act. On the other hand, extracontractual or tortious liability (*buitencontractuele* or *aquiliaanse* or *delictuele aansprakelijkheid/responsabilité extracontractuelle* or *aquillienne* or *délictuelle*) can be incurred when an illegitimate action or negligence causes damage to third parties. In that case, the obligation is not caused by a juridical act, but by the law, which attaches a legal consequence, being an obligation to make compensation, to human behaviours that are not juridical acts.

77. The principles regarding tortious liability are laid down in Articles 1382–1386 OCC. According to Article 1382 OCC, any act of man which causes damage to another obliges the person by whose fault it occurred to compensate that damage. Article 1383 OCC states that one is liable not only for damage caused by his own act but also for damage caused by his negligence or imprudence. In addition, according to Article 1384 OCC, some categories of persons are liable for the

107. Article I.1, 2° CEL.
108. The most important ones are Council Directive 93/13/EEC of 5 Apr. 1993 on unfair terms in consumer contracts, Directive 97/7/EC of the European Parliament and of the Council of 20 May 1997 on the protection of consumers in respect of distance contracts, Directive 1999/44/EC of the European Parliament and of the Council of 25 May 1999 on certain aspects of the sale of consumer goods and associated guarantees; Directive 2011/83/EU of 25 Oct. 2011 on consumer rights, amending Council Directive 93/13/EEC and Directive 1999/44/EC of the European Parliament and of the Council and repealing Council Directive 85/577/EEC and Directive 97/7/EC on the European Parliament and of the Council.
109. S. Stijns, *Leerboek Verbintenissenrecht 1* (Brugge: die Keure, 2016), 35; T. Vansweevelt & B. Weyts, « De overeenkomst: definitie en soorten » in T. Vansweevelt and B. Weyts, *Handboek Verbintenissenrecht* (Antwerpen: Intersentia, 2019), 128.
110. E. Dirix, B. Tilleman & S. Lierman (eds), *De Valks Juridisch woordenboek* (Antwerp-Oxford: Intersentia, 2018), 7.

damage caused by persons for whom they are responsible (minors, pupils, employees). Furthermore, one may be held responsible for things one has in his or her keeping (Article 1384 OCC), domestic animals in particular (Article 1385 OCC), or buildings one owns (Article 1386 OCC).

78. Contractual and tortious liability are similar in the fact that both require a fault, damages, and a causal link between both. However, there are many differences as well. The most important ones originate in laws which apply to specific types of contracts (e.g., because they stipulate a shorter prescription period – *see* No. 384 *infra*) or in contractual clauses (e.g., exemption clauses). In that case, it is in the interest of a plaintiff to ground his claim on tortious liability rather than contractual liability.[111] Furthermore, the victim of tort can demand the integral compensation of the loss he suffered as a consequence of the fault,[112] whereas the compensation in case of breach of contract is limited by Articles 1150–1151 OCC (*see* No. 422 *infra*).

79. Contractual and tortious liability, which together are called civil liability (*civielrechtelijke aansprakelijkheid/responsabilité civile*), must be distinguished from criminal liability (*strafrechtelijke aansprakelijkheid/responsabilité pénale*). Criminal liability is the duty to undergo penal sanctions as the consequences for committing a crime for which one has been called to account and for which one has been found guilty.[113] In contrary to civil duties to compensate, penal sanctions may be inflicted regardless of whether or not damage was caused. Nevertheless, civil and criminal responsibility may both be caused by a single behaviour if this behaviour caused damages and is a criminal offence. A typical example is the criminal offence of 'unintentional battery' or 'unintentional manslaughter'. One who commits this crime will be criminally liable according to Article 418 of the Penal Code,[114] but he will also be liable for tort according to Article 1382 OCC, and be obligated to compensate for the damages suffered by the victim.[115] The possibility for concurrence between civil and penal liability is important to resolve some issues of concurrence between tortious and contractual liability (*see* Nos 83–84 *infra*).

B. The Concepts of Concurrence and Coexistence

80. In order to describe the interactions between tortious and contractual liability, one has to make a distinction between the concept of concurrence and the concept of coexistence. Concurrence (*samenloop/cumul*) happens when several claims can be made due to a single behaviour by the same person, and these claims belong

111. W. van Gerven en A. Van Oevelen, *Verbintenissenrecht* (Leuven: Acco, 2015), 310.
112. *Ibid.*, 462.
113. E. Dirix, B. Tilleman & S. Lierman (eds), *De Valks Juridisch woordenboek* (Antwerp-Oxford: Intersentia, 2018), 7.
114. *Strafwetboek/Code Pénal* of 8 Jun. 1867, *Belgian Official Gazette* 9 Jun. 1867.
115. S. Stijns & I. Samoy, *Leerboek Verbintenissenrecht 1bis* (Brugge: die Keure, 2020), 163, nr. 128.

to different systems of liability (e.g., contractual and tortious, or civil and penal).[116] Coexistence (*coëxistentie/coexistence*), on the other hand, requires a relation between at least three persons. Active coexistence is the possibility to call two or more persons into account regarding a behaviour that caused damage, while passive coexistence is the possibility to be called into account by two or more persons, by virtue of the same or a different system of liability.

II. Concurrence of Contractual and Tortious Liability

A. Concurrence of Civil and Criminal Liability

81. Civil and criminal liability may concur in cases where criminal and civil law apply the same concept of fault.[117] The *Court of Cassation* judged that this is the case for Articles 418 and 420 of the Penal Code ('unintentional battery' or 'unintentional manslaughter', *see* No. 79 *supra*), which require the same lack of prudence or diligence as Articles 1382–1383 OCC.[118] Consequentially, the victim of the crime will be able to claim damages from the offender according to Articles 1382–1383 OCC.

Also, as every breach of criminal law is considered a fault according to Articles 1382–1383 OCC, if the offender has caused damages to someone due to his offence, he may be condemned to pay damages to this person. It is also possible for a breach of contract to be a criminal offence, which may result in concurrence of contractual, tortious and criminal liability, e.g., if an employer fails to pay wages to his employee, or if a doctor commits a medical fault due to which harm is done to a patient he had a contract with.[119]

82. Concurrence of criminal and civil liability has some important procedural implications. First, the decision of the criminal judge on the criminal judge is res judicata for the civil judge on the question of the civil wrong. Second, the civil claim in compensation can, according to Article 4 of the Preliminary Title to the Criminal Code, be brought in front of the same judge and at the same time as the criminal claim. In that case, the adage '*le criminel tient le civil en état*' is applied. That means that the civil claim will be suspended (ex officio) until the criminal judge has come to a definitive verdict on the criminal claim. Thereby, no risk of contradicting decisions arises and the criminal res judicata is not put at risk. In order to shorten the time litigation takes in cases of complex damage cases, the foregoing rule takes an exception in cases of faultless liability – except where the determination of the fault also requires the determination of fault by a third party. Third, the civil claims caused by a criminal offence cannot become extinct due to prescription (*see* Nos 382 ff. *infra*) before the criminal claim is prescribed as well. These procedural implications, however, may not breach the fundamental right of fair trial,

116. *Ibid.*
117. *Ibid.*, 129.
118. Cass. 26 Oct. 1990, *Arr.Cass.* 1990-91, 244.
119. S. Stijns & I. Samoy, *Leerboek Verbintenissenrecht 1bis* (Brugge: die Keure, 2020), 164, nr. 130.

described in Article 6.1 of the European Convention on Human Rights of 4 November 1950. In application of this principle, the *Court of Cassation* stated that a party in a later civil dispute must have the chance to contest the data derived from the criminal dispute if he was no party to the criminal dispute or could not assert his interests at the criminal dispute.[120] For example, in a case where the insurer of the offender, who was not a party in the criminal dispute where the criminal court had acquitted the owner of a dancing from the charge of arson, the Court judged that the insurer was entitled to contest the acquittal.[121]

B. Concurrence of Contractual and Tortious Liability

83. The topic of discussion is whether or not it is possible for a contracting party, who is already liable contractually, to be liable for tort as well. This would, of course, not allow a double recovery, on the ground that the defendant's behaviour was wrongful in two respects. However, it may, in certain cases, be advantageous for a contracting party to be able to claim for tort rather than for breach of contract (*see* No. 78 *supra*).

84. Concurrence of contractual and tortious liability is, in principle, forbidden.[122] There are, however, two exceptions to this principle. First, concurrence of contractual and tortious liability is allowed when the accountable non-performance is also a criminal offence (*see* No. 81 *supra*).[123] If this is the case, the contracting party will be able to demand damages for tort. Second, according to the most recent judgment on the matter of the *Court of Cassation*,[124] a contracting party may be liable for tort 'if the fault of which he is accused is not only a shortcoming towards his contractual obligations, but also a breach of the general duty of care, and if this fault has caused other damages than those due to the faulty performance of the contract'.

---

120. Cass. 19 Jun. 2014, *Arr. Cass.* 2014, 1612, *Pas.* 2014, 1605; Cass. 7 Mar. 2008, *NJW* 2008, 492; Cass 24 Apr. 2006, *P&B* 2007, 343; Cass. 5 Jan. 2004 *De Verz.* 2004, 477; Cass. 24 Jun. 2002, *NJW* 2002, 353; Cass. 3 Dec. 1998, *Pas.* 1998, 1175; Cass. 2 Oct. 1997, *R.W.* 1997-98, 814; Cass. 14 Jun. 1996, *Arr. Cass.* 1996, 589; Cass. 14 Apr. 1994, *Arr. Cass.* 1994, 372; Cass. 15 Feb. 1991, *Arr. Cass.* 1991-92, 32.
121. Cass. 24 Jun. 2002, *NJW* 2002, 353. With its decision from 14 Feb. 2019 (nr. 24/2019, §B.11), the Constitutional Court contributed to the further evolution of the issue. *See* S. Stijns & I. Samoy, *Leerboek Verbintenissenrecht 1bis* (Brugge: die Keure, 2020), 167, nr. 134.
122. Cass. 4 Jun. 1971, *Arr.Cass.* 1971, 989; Cass. 7 Dec. 1973, *Arr.Cass.* 1974, 395.
123. Cass. 26 Oct. 1990, *Arr.Cass.* 1990-91, 244.
124. Cass. 12 Mar. 2020, C.19.0408.N, *TBBR* 2020, 438; Cass. 17 Mar. 2017, *RW* 2018-19, 382, *TBH* 2017, 952, note P. Gillaerts; Cass. 29 Sep. 2006, *NJW* 2006, 946 & *R.W.* 2006-07, 1717.

III. Coexistence of Claims in Contract and Tort

A. *Active Coexistence: The Contractual Auxiliary Performer*

85. Active coexistence concerns the situation where a person who suffered damages draws the right to demand compensation from two or more persons from a single incident. This may, e.g., occur when a contracting party (main contractor) calls in an auxiliary (employee or independent contractor, *see* No. 332 *infra*) to perform his contractual obligations. This is normally permitted. If there is an accountable non-performance, caused by the auxiliary, the main contractor remains liable contractually. Is it possible to demand damages from the auxiliary as well? As he is not a party to the contract, no contractual claims can be laid. But can he be held liable tortiously? This question is discussed in No. 332 *infra.*

B. *Passive Coexistence*

86. Passive coexistence concerns the possibility to be called into account by two or more persons, by virtue of the same or different kinds of liability, e.g., when a contracting party shows faulty behaviour due to which both his contracting partner and a third party suffer damages. For example, when an elevator crashes due to the negligence of the lift maintenance firm, both the owner of the lift and third parties who were in the lift when it crashed may sue the maintenance firm, the owner contractually and the third parties for tort.[125] Coexistence of contractual and tortious liability is possible on the condition that the breach of contract is also a breach of the general duty of care.[126] The question of whether the aggrieved third party may invoke the contents of the contract to demonstrate the breach of due care (e.g., clauses about the type and the frequency of the maintenance of the lift) is answered affirmatively in the doctrine.[127]

§6. Contract and Quasi-Contracts

87. Quasi-contracts are described by Article 1371 OCC as 'purely voluntary acts of man, from which any kind of engagement may result toward a third party, and sometimes a reciprocal obligation for both parties'. The Civil Code mentions two types of quasi-contracts: *negotiorum gestio* (*zaakwaarneming/gestion pour autrui*) (Articles 1371–1375 OCC) and restitution of payments not due (*onverschuldigde betaling/paiement indu*) (Articles 1376–1381 OCC). The jurisprudence developed a third type of quasi-contract: unjustified enrichment (*ongerechtvaardigde verrijking/ enrichissement injustifié*).

---

125. S. Stijns & I. Samoy, *Leerboek Verbintenissenrecht 1bis* (Brugge: die Keure, 2020), 189, nr. 158.
126. Cass. 26 Mar. 1992, *Arr.Cass.* 1991-92, 722 & *Pas.* 1992, 675; Cass 20 Jun. 1997, *Arr.Cass.* 1997, 673 & *Pas.* 1997, 708.
127. S. Stijns & I. Samoy, *Leerboek Verbintenissenrecht 1bis* (Brugge: die Keure, 2020), 189, nr. 158.

I. *Negotiorum Gestio*

88. Negotiorum gestio (*zaakwaarneming/gestion pour autrui*) is the voluntary management of the interests of another, which cannot be done out of generosity or only out of self-interest, outside any specific legal or contractual obligation, with or without knowledge of that other, whereby one can reasonably assume that the manager's actions would have been performed by the other (the so-called 'master of the matter') for the benefit of its own interests if he had had the occasion for it.[128] A typical example is the rescuing of the furniture out of a burning building by a passer-by.

89. Following requirements must be met in order for a situation to be regarded as *negotiorum gestio*.[129] First, the management must have occurred for the benefit of the master of the matter, and may not be based only on self-interest on the part of the manager. Second, it must have been useful. The jurisprudence sometimes even requires necessity instead of usefulness. Third, the manager must not have had the intention to donate. Fourth, the management may not have occurred in execution of the manager's legal or contractual duty. Finally, it must be reasonably assumed that the master of the matter would also have performed the manager's actions if he had been able to.

90. If these requirements are met, several obligations on the part of the manager and of the master of the matter come into existence. Once the manager has started to manage the interests of another, he must continue to do so until the master of the thing or his heirs are able to do it themselves (Articles 1372 and 1373 OCC). He must perform in the same manner an agent would (Article 1372 OCC) and act like a *bonus pater familias* (Article 1374 OCC). The master of the matter, on the other hand, must perform the obligations which were contracted in his name by the manager, compensate for all personal obligations he took upon him, and reimburse all useful and necessary expenses (Article 1375 OCC). However, the courts may moderate the damages the manager suffered due to his fault or negligence (Article 1374 OCC). Most of the doctrine and jurisprudence consider that the manager cannot demand wages, unless he is a professional.

II. Restitution of Undue Payments

91. Article 1235 OCC provides that 'each payment supposes a debt: that what has been payed without being due can be claimed in restitution'. This action requires the fulfilment of the following three conditions. First, there must be a payment meant to pay a pre-existing debt. Second, the payment may not be due; this

---

128. S. Stijns & I. Samoy, *Leerboek Verbintenissenrecht 1bis* (Brugge: die Keure, 2020), 5, nr. 3; E. Dirix, B. Tilleman & S. Lierman (eds), *De Valks Juridisch woordenboek* (Antwerp-Oxford: Intersentia, 2018), 523. For more on this subject, *see*: E. Beysen, *Zaakwaarneming*, in *APR* (Mechelen: Kluwer, 2006), 181; T. Vansweevelt & B. Weyts, « De rechtsfeiten » in T. Vansweevelt and B. Weyts, *Handboek Verbintenissenrecht* (Antwerpen: Intersentia, 2019), 676.
129. W. van Gerven en A. Van Oevelen, *Verbintenissenrecht* (Leuven: Acco, 2015), 280.

means that it has no legal cause.[130] This condition may take two forms. Either the debt did not exist objectively, e.g., because it never existed, because one paid more than what was due or because one debt was paid twice,[131] or the debt did exist, but the debtor paid it to another than the actual creditor (Article 1376 OCC), or the debt was paid by someone who was not the actual debtor and who did not have the intention to pay someone else's debt, nor considered himself held to pay it (Article 1377 OCC).

92. If these three conditions are fulfilled, according to Article 1376 OCC, the person who received what was undue to him must make restitution to him from whom he has unduly received. The extent of this restitution duty depends on whether or not the receiver was bona fide.[132] In both cases, the receiver must restitute the sum of money he received, and he is entitled to reimbursement of all the necessary and useful expenses he made to preserve the thing (Article 1381 OCC).

A bona fide receiver may also keep interests and profits. If he received an immovable or a material thing, he has to restitute it in kind if it still exists (Article 1379 OCC). If it was sold, he will only have to restitute the selling price, even if the thing was sold for a lesser price than its worth (Article 1380 OCC). If the thing was destroyed or damaged, the receiver must only restitute what is left of it, although there is subrogation to the benefit of the one who paid, for the rights and claims the receiver might have obtained regarding the destroyed thing.

If, on the other hand, the receiver is not bona fide, he will have to restitute capital, interests and profits from the day of the payment (Article 1378 OCC). If he sold the thing, he will have to restitute its selling price, except where the value exceeds the selling price; in that case the value needs to be restituted (Article 1380 OCC). If the thing was destroyed or damaged, whether due to his fault or not, he will have to compensate for the damages, even in case of an extraneous cause (Article 1379 OCC). If the damages suffered by the person who paid are not covered by the restitution, the receiver may be condemned to pay additional damages.

III. Unjustified Enrichment

93. Enrichment without cause (*ongerechtvaardigde verrijking/enrichissement injustifié*) is a source of obligations in case of a shift in the patrimony of one person (the impoverished person) towards the patrimony of another person (the enriched person) without legal cause for this shift.[133] Although there are some applications

130. Cass. 26 Jun. 1998, *Arr.Cass.* 1998, 765; Cass. 22 Feb. 1999, *R.W.* 1999-2000, 538; Cass. 16 May 2002, *R.W.* 2002-03, 659; Cass. 19 Mar. 2020, F.16.0110.N, www.juportal.be.
131. W. van Gerven en A. Van Oevelen, *Verbintenissenrecht* (Leuven: Acco, 2015), 286.
132. S. Stijns & I. Samoy, *Leerboek Verbintenissenrecht 1bis* (Brugge: die Keure, 2020), 22, nr. 24.
133. E. Dirix, B. Tilleman & S. Lierman (eds), *De Valks Juridisch woordenboek* (Antwerp-Oxford: Intersentia, 2018), 479.

of this concept in the law,[134] the Civil Code holds no general provisions on this subject. However, it has been recognised as a general principle of law and a source of obligations by the *Court of Cassation*.[135]

94. Following requirements must be met. First, there must be an impoverishment of the claimant. Second, there must be an enrichment of the defendant. Belgian law allows an enrichment claim where the benefit for the defendant is merely indirect, i.e., where it comes to him only after passing through the assets of a third party. The enrichment may also take the form of the saving of a loss, e.g., the extinction of a debt. Third, there must be a causal link between the impoverishment and the enrichment. Fourthly, there may not be a cause for the shift in the patrimonies. This means that it may not be done due to a legal or judicial obligation, nor because of a contract, a natural obligation, tort or the will of the impoverished person.[136] Finally, the impoverished person may not hold any other claim against the enriched person. In other words, enrichment without cause is subsidiary to any other claim.[137] However, a claim against a third party does not hinder the claim for enrichment without cause.

95. If these conditions are fulfilled, the impoverished person obtains the right to claim compensation (*actio de in rem verso*), which amounts to the sum of the impoverishment, yet may never be more than the enrichment.

§7. Contract and the Law of Property

96. The law of obligations, and thus the law of contracts, which are a type of obligation, concerns rights in personam. The law of property, on the other hand, concerns rights in rem. The definition of these types of rights and the differences between them are treated in No. 27 *supra*.

97. However, it should also be stated that, although there are considerable differences between both types of rights, there are also some points of connection.[138] For instance, the transfer of some rights in rem may be achieved through a contract; e.g., a sale transfers the ownership of a good from the patrimony of the vendor to the patrimony of the buyer. Also, some rights in rem, e.g., mortgage, are used to enforce the execution of contracts, and are accessory to these contracts.

---

134. For example, Art. 555 OCC regarding the reimbursement of plants, buildings and works done by a person with his own materials on another person's ground.
135. Cass. 17 Nov. 1983, *Arr.Cass.* 1983-84, 315. Recently confirmed Cass. 4 Jun. 2020, C.19.0371.N, *JT* 2020, nr. 6823, 558, note Y LELEU, *T.Fam* 2020, 247 note M. AERTS.
136. Cass. 4 Jun. 2020, C.19.0371.N, *JT* 2020, nr. 6823, 558, note Y LELEU, *T.Fam* 2020, 247 note M. AERTS; Cass. 9 juni 2017, C.16.0382.N, *TBBR* 2017, 503, note F. DEGUEL and *RW* 2017-18, 1104, noot M. AERTS; Cass. 23 Oktober 2014, C.140207.F, concl. T. WERQUIN, *TBBR* 2015, 560, note J. LAMBRECHTS; Cass. 19 Jan. 2009, *Arr.Cass.* 2009, 176, concl. Mortier, *Pas.* 2009, 153, *RCJB* 2012, 69, note J.-F. ROMAIN, *RW* 2009-10, 1084, note E. Nordin.
137. Cass. 25 Mar. 1994, *R.W.* 1996-97, 45, note; W. van Gerven en A. Van Oevelen, *Verbintenissenrecht* (Leuven: Acco, 2015), 294.
138. P. Wéry, *Droit des obligations, I, Théorie générale du contrat* (Brussels: Larcier, 2011), 18.

§8. Contract and Trust

98. A trust is a legal relationship created by a party (the settlor) by a juridical act during his life or by testament, whereby goods are transferred to another party (the trustee) with the duty to administer these goods to the benefit of a third party (the beneficiary) or a specific goal.[139] Trust creates a division of property between the trustee (*legal title*) and the beneficiary (*equitable title*). Consequently, the beneficiary obtains a proprietary right. Belgian law does not include trust in its domestic law. There are two objections to the introduction of this figure in Belgian law: the *numerus clausus* principle of rights in rem, due to which the list of existing rights in rem is limitative, and the principle of the indivisibility of patrimony.

99. So-called fiduciary relationships or fiduciary transfer exists besides the actual trust. There is a fiduciary relationship when a person (the fiduciant) transfers the full ownership of a good to another person (the fiduciary), who obligates himself to manage the transferred rights not on his own behalf but to the benefit of another person (the beneficiary) and to transfer these rights to the beneficiary after having accomplished his mission. The beneficiary can be the original owner or a third party. A fiduciary relationship allows to achieve a threefold purpose: a gift, a management or a surety. The recent reform of the Civil Code vainly had tried to introduce fiduciary ownership in Belgian law.[140]

100. Doctrine suggests using the concept of indirect representation to obtain the result which is achieved through trust in common law jurisdictions.[141]

§9. Good Faith and Fair Dealing

101. The principle of the performance of contracts in good faith is laid down in Article 1134, 3rd section OCC. A distinction is made between its complementing function and its moderating function.

I. Complementing the Contract

102. Complementing a contract is a legal technique whereby a judge can complete an incomplete contract. In other words, when there is a gap in a contract, the

139. *See*: Hague Trust Convention of 1 Jul. 1985. Belgian did not yet adhere to his convention. On this subject, *see*: J.H. Herbots, 'Pleidooi voor de invoering in België van het fiduciecontract naar het trustnabootsende Franse model', *R.W.* 1993-94, 313; V. Sagaert, *Zakelijke subrogatie* (Antwerp: Intersentia, 2003), 227 et seq.; I. Samoy, *Middelijke Vertegenwoordiging* (Antwerp: Intersentia, 2005), 501 et seq.; H. Swennen, 'Trustachtige figuren in België?', *T.P.R.* 1992, 1100; W. van Gerven, *Algemeen deel* in *Beginselen van Belgisch privaatrecht, I* (Antwerp: Story-Scientia, 1987), 250; W. van Gerven, *Bewindsbevoegdheid* (Brussels: Bruylant, 1962), 29.

140. P. Lecocq & R. Popa, 'Dispositions générales' in *Le nouveau droit des biens*, N. Bernard & I. Durant, e.a. (eds) (Bruxelles: Larcier, 2020), 24.

141. I. Samoy, *Middelijke Vertegenwoordiging* (Antwerp: Intersentia, 2005), 501 et seq.

judge can fill it in and lay supplementary obligations upon the parties. This possibility is founded on the complementing function of good faith.[142] Article 1134, 3rd section OCC, lays down the principle of the performance of contracts in good faith. In general, this means that the parties have a duty of loyalty towards each other. In addition to their own interests, the parties also have to take the other party's legal interests into consideration. The duties imposed by good faith are the duties which a reasonable contract party placed in the same circumstances would have taken upon themselves.[143] This general principle has been refined by the doctrine and the jurisprudence, which have derived some specific duties from it. Examples of such duties are: the duty of information, according to which parties are obliged to inform each other about elements which may have implications for the other party during the performance of the contract (parties are hereby entitled to take the other parties' expertise into account[144]), the duty for the aggrieved party to reasonably limit the damages,[145] and the duty to renegotiate in the case of a long-term contract.

II. Moderation of the Exercise of Contractual Rights

103. Article 1134, 3rd section OCC is also the base for the moderation of contracts, i.e., a legal technique whereby a judge moderates the exercise of contractual rights. However, this technique is founded both on Article 1134, 3rd section OCC *and* on the doctrine of the prohibition of abuse of rights. Article 1134, 3rd section OOCC lays down the principle that contracts must be performed in good faith. In 1983, the *Court of Cassation* recognised the moderating function of good faith and based the prohibition of the abuse of rights on this article, arguing that the principle of good faith forbids a contracting party to abuse the rights deriving from the contract.[146] This jurisprudence has been followed ever since. The exact link between (lack of) good faith and abuse of rights remained unclear, until the Court declared in a judgment of 17 May 1990 that a breach of Article 1134, 3rd section OCC was only possible if there was an abuse of rights.[147] In other words, in Belgian law, Article 1134, 3rd section on itself is not enough to found a moderation. There must also be an abuse of rights.

104. The general criterion for abuse of rights is 'the exercise of a right in such a manner that it *evidently* crosses the boundaries of the normal pursuit of that right

---

142. S. Stijns, *Leerboek Verbintenissenrecht 1* (Brugge: die Keure, 2016), 65; P. Van Ommeslaghe, *Les obligations vol. 1* in *Traité de droit civil, tome II* (Brussels: Bruylant, 2013), 193; W. Buelens, « Uitvoering te goeder trouw » in T. Vansweevelt and B. Weyts, *Handboek Verbintenissenrecht* (Antwerpen: Intersentia, 2019), 305; P. Wéry, *Droit des obligations, I, Théorie générale du contrat* (Brussels: Larcier, 2011), 136 and 378.
143. S. Stijns, *Leerboek Verbintenissenrecht 1* (Brugge: die Keure, 2016), 66.
144. Cass. 9 Mar. 1989, *Arr.Cass.* 1988-89, 790 & *Pas.* 1989, 707.
145. Cass. 14 May 1992, *Arr.Cass.* 1991-92, 855 & *Pas.* 1992, 798; Cass. 17 May 2001, *Pas.* 2001, 889.
146. Cass. 19 Sep. 1983, *Arr.Cass.* 1983-84, 52 & *Pas.* 1984, 55.
147. Cass. 17 May 1990, *Arr.Cass.* 1989-90, 1188 & *Pas.* 1990, 1061.

by a prudent and careful person'.[148] 'Evidently' means that the breach must be clear and obvious, which limits the judge's control to what the doctrine calls a marginal review competence ('*marginale toetsing/contrôle marginal*', literal translation: '*marginal screening*').[149] The judge must exercise restraint and can only moderate the rights of a contracting party in case of clear and obvious abuse. The jurisprudence has also developed some specific criteria for the abuse of rights, among which: the exercise of a right with the exclusive intention to cause damage;[150] taking actions without reasonable or sufficient interest while causing damage;[151] choosing the most harmful way of exercising a right when there are several ways to exercise this right to the same effect;[152] the proportionality criterion: when there is a disproportion between the advantage for the party exercising their right and the disadvantage they cause to the other party;[153] the exercise of a right in betrayal of the legitimate trust of another.[154]

105. Abuse of rights is sanctioned with the reduction of the abusive exercise of a right to the normal exercise of this right.[155] This can be achieved either by imposing the normal exercise of the right (performance in kind) or by the compensation of the damage caused by the abuse (performance by equivalent).[156] The *Court of Cassation* even judged that if an abuse of rights concerns the application of a clause (in this case a penalty clause), the compensation of the damages inflicted by the abuse of rights may be the denial for the creditor to invoke that clause.[157] The right itself remains valid and continues to exist, but its exercise is moderated or even forbidden.[158]

---

148. Cass. 10 Sep. 1971, *Arr.Cass.* 1972, 31 & *Pas.* 1972, 28.
149. *See* among others R. Kruithof et al., 'Overzicht', *T.P.R.* 1994, No. 125; W. Buelens, « Uitvoering te goeder trouw » in T. Vansweevelt and B. Weyts, *Handboek Verbintenissenrecht* (Antwerpen: Intersentia, 2019), 321; P. Wéry, *Droit des obligations, I, Théorie générale du contrat* (Brussels: Larcier, 2011), 137.
150. Gent 27 Jan. 1854, *Pas.* 1854, II, 233; Colmar 2 May 1855, *D.* 1856, 9.
151. Cass. 30 Jan. 2003, *T.B.B.R.* 2004, 405; Cass. 17 May 2002, *Rev. not.b.* 2003, 86; Cass. 15 Mar. 2002, *R.W.* 2003-04, 1261.
152. Cass. 12 Jul. 1917, *Pas.* 1918, 65.
153. Cass. 10 Sep. 1971, *Arr.Cass.* 1972, 31 & *Pas.* 1972, 28, Cass. 17 May 2002, *Rev. not.b.* 2003, 86; Cass. 15 Mar. 2002, *R.W.* 2003-04, 1261.
154. Cass. 1 Oct. 2010, *Arr. Cass* 2010, 2385; *Pas.* 2010, 2470; *RW* 2011-12, 142, note S. Jansen and S. Stijns; *TBBR* 2012, 387, note P. Bazier; *TBH* 2011, 77. *See* further S. Stijns & I. Samoy, 'La confiance légitime en droit privé des contrats' in *The Belgian reports at the Congress of Utrecht of the International Academy of Comparative Law*, ed. D. Dirix & Y.-H. Leleu (Brussels: Bruylant, 2006), 275; W. van Gerven en A. Van Oevelen, *Verbintenissenrecht* (Leuven: Acco, 2015), 101–102.
155. S. Stijns, 'Abus, mais de quel(s) droit(s)? Réflexions sur l'exécution de bonne foi des contrats et l'abus des droits contractuels', *J.T.* 1990, 33–44; S. Stijns, W. van Gerven & P. Wéry, 'Chronique', *J.T.* 1996, No. 46; S. Stijns, 'Het verbod op misbruik van contractuele rechten: lees de bijsluiter voor gebruik !' in S. Stijns & P. Wéry (eds.) *De rol van de rechter in het contract* (Brugge: die Keure, 2014), 111.
156. Cass. 16 Dec. 1982, *Arr.Cass.* 1982-83, 518 & *Pas.* 1983, 472.
157. Cass. 8 Feb. 2001, *Arr.Cass.* 2001, 245 & *Pas.* 2001, 244.
158. S. Stijns, *Leerboek Verbintenissenrecht 1* (Brugge: die Keure, 2016), 77.

§10. Drafting Style

106. Belgian contracts are rather short and simple when compared to Anglo-American ones. The existence of a broad legislation means that it is usually sufficient for contracting parties to state only the essentials and let the law fill in the gaps. For most types of contracts, a detailed and systematic framework of legislation exists, provided by the Civil Code (e.g., hire, sale), completed by other laws (e.g., consumer loans). As such, the draftsman proceeds from the knowledge that the main incidents of the contract are provided for, and concentrates only on those points where the contracting parties wish to swerve from the (suppletive) laws. When contracting parties have a contract in mind which is not yet detailed in the law, a more extensive drafting will be necessary, including those points which are of particular concern to the parties.

107. Another factor which allows for Belgian contracts to be more concise than contracts in common law jurisdictions is the influence of the principle of good faith. As stated in No. 26 *supra*, the principle of good faith allows the courts to complete contracts according to the standards of reasonableness and fairness, and to moderate the exercise of contractual rights through the prohibition of abuse of rights. As the principle of good faith is automatically applicable to all contracts, the inclusion of provisions regarding its application in the contract is often regarded as unnecessary. For instance, good faith imposes a duty of information upon parties. This duty is applicable regardless of the terms of the contract, unless, of course, parties would include specific terms which deviate from it, e.g., to limit or increase this duty by providing a verbatim list of the information that must be shared. However, even these contract terms will be subjected to the control on the prohibition of abuse of rights.

§11. Sources of the Law of Contracts

I. Legislation

108. As stated earlier (*see* No. 25 *supra*), the main body of rules concerning the law of contracts is to be found in the Civil Code and, in ever-increasing measure, in legislation supplementary to the Code. Legislation and treaties are published in an official daily publication, the *Belgian Official Gazette* (*Belgisch Staatsblad/Moniteur Belge*). They are cited as follows: law of day-month-year (the date of the signature) with regard to (subject), *B.S./M.B.* day-month-year (day of the publication), p. xxx. The *Belgian Official Gazette* is online since 1997 in Dutch, French and German (http://www.just.fgov.be/). The same internet site provides a search engine for laws since 1945. For older laws and decisions, or original versions of laws that have been modified afterwards, one may consult the *Omnilegie* (bilingual, from 1950 to 1998), or the *Pasinomie* (only French, from 1788 until present). One can also consult collections of legislation in the concerned branch of the law, called codes and edited by private editors, as, for instance, the bilingual (French-Dutch) codes of *Story*, *Larcier* or *die Keure*. Juportal (https://juportal.be/home/welkom)

(free) and Jura (http://www.jura.be/) (Kluwer, not free) also grant access to a great part of the consolidated body of legislation. All these codifications are unofficial: the only valid text is the text in the *Belgian Official Gazette*. Documents of the Chamber and the Senate since the creation of Belgium in 1830 can be found on the following sites: www.fed-parl.be, www.dekamer.be or www.senaat.be. Documents of the Flemish Council can be consulted on www.vlaamsparlement.be, documents of the French Community and Parliament on www.pcf.be and parlement.wallonie.be, documents of the Brussels-Capital Region on www.bruparl.irisnet.be, and documents of the German Community on www.dgparlament.be.

II. Jurisprudence

109. Although decisions of the courts and the tribunals are public, not all these decisions are published or even available as a copy for everyone.[159] The easiest way to find jurisprudence is to use one of the many online databanks, for instance, www.jura.be, www.juportal.be, www.stradalex.com or www.jurisquare.be. The three highest courts have their own websites: www.grondwettelijkhof.be for the *Constitutional Court*, www.cass.be for the *Court of Cassation* (summaries since 1965, full text since 1990) and www.raadvanstate.be for the *Council of State*. Another tool to find jurisprudence is provided by the overviews of jurisprudence published by several journals (*see* Selected Bibliography). One may also try to find jurisprudence in one of the many available journals (more than two hundred). An overview of these journals can be found on the site www.rechtsaf.be.

III. Doctrine

110. Doctrine may be published in the form of books or journal articles. Aforementioned online databanks allow searching for doctrine on a specific subject. Other useful instruments are the online catalogues of the university libraries.[160] https://www.law.kuleuven.be/apps/rechtgenoot/ provides a basic bibliography of the most important Belgian doctrine. Www.rechtsreeks.be provides digitalised scans of journal articles and classics of Belgian legal literature in open access.

159. G. Martyn & R. Devloo, *Een kennismaking met recht en rechtspraktijk* (Brugge: die Keure, 2008), 105.
160. *Ibid.*, 109.

Part I. General Principles of the Law of Contract

Chapter 1. Formation

§1. Phases in the Formation Process

I. The Negotiation Phase

A. General Principles

111. In principle, a contract is considered concluded when a party, who made a binding offer to another party, is informed that his offer was accepted by the other party (*see* Nos 207 ff. *infra*).[161] As long as parties are negotiating and no binding offer has been made, there is no obligatory bond between negotiators.[162] In principle, they are free to break off negotiations. However, in practice, the plurality of parties and the intricacy of the obligations often require long negotiations. Sometimes, several documents precede the actual multiparty agreement. Thus, determining when and to what extent obligations start to exist can be a complex matter.[163]

112. First, the freedom to negotiate does not release the parties from their duty to exercise due caution (some authors mention good faith as well).[164] Whoever

161. For more on this subject, *see*: A. De Boeck, *Informatierechten en – plichten bij de totstandkoming en uitvoering van overeenkomsten* (Antwerp: Intersentia, 2000); A. De Boeck, 'De tussenkomst van de rechter in de precontractuele fase: mogelijkheden en grenzen' in S. Stijns & P. Wéry (eds) *De rol van de rechter in het contract* (Brugge: die Keure, 2014); E. Dirix, 'Gentlemen's agreements en andere afspraken met onzekere rechtsgevolgen', *R.W.* (1985-86): 2119–2146; M. Fontaine (ed.), *Le processus de formation du contrat* (Brussels-Paris: Bruylant-L.G.D.J., 2002); F. Peeraer, T. Hick & F. Auvray, 'Nieuw verbintenissenrecht: de totstandkoming van het contract (dynamisch en statisch bekeken)' in S. Stijns (ed.) *Themis 108 – Verbintenissenrecht* (Brugge: die Keure, 2019).

162. S. Stijns, *Leerboek Verbintenissenrecht 1* (Brugge: die Keure, 2016), 123; W. van Gerven en A. Van Oevelen, *Verbintenissenrecht* (Leuven: Acco, 2015), 152.

163. On this evolution, *see*: S. Stijns, *Leerboek Verbintenissenrecht 1* (Brugge: die Keure, 2016), 124 and references in footnote 213; W. van Gerven en A. Van Oevelen, *Verbintenissenrecht* (Leuven: Acco, 2015), 152 et seq.

164. R. Dekkers & A. Verbeke, *Handboek Burgerlijk Recht, III* (Antwerp: Intersentia: 2007), 53; S. Stijns, *Leerboek Verbintenissenrecht 1* (Brugge: die Keure, 2016), 124; W. van Gerven en A. Van Oevelen, *Verbintenissenrecht* (Leuven: Acco, 2015), 152–153; P. Wéry, *Droit des obligations, I, Théorie générale du contrat* (Brussels: Larcier, 2011), 149.

breaks off negotiations in a faulty way or acts without due care during negotiations and thereby causes loss to the other party is liable for precontractual fault (*see* Nos 129 ff. *infra*).

113. Second, it may be unclear when the realm of negotiations is left and the area of contractual obligations is entered. This transition may occur implicitly, without explicit mention or even intention by the parties.[165] Sometimes, parties put the state of negotiations in writing. The contents and formulation of these documents, as well as the behaviour of parties, are helpful in determining whether or not these were intended to be obligatory (*see* No. 207 *infra*).[166]

114. It is also important to be aware of the fact that preliminary documents can be taken into account when interpreting the later agreement. Indeed, according to Article 1156 OCC, when a contract or one of its clauses is unclear and a dispute arises, courts must determine the common intent of the contracting parties (*see* Nos 264 *infra*). If the contract is not laid down in a written document (yet), or if the written document is unclear, courts may take external elements into account, i.e., elements which are not in the written contract, such as documents that were exchanged during negotiations.[167]

The next section delves deeper into the different types of preliminary documents.

B. Preliminary Documents

115. Written documents drawn up during the negotiation phase may be enforceable or not, depending on the intention of the (future) contracting parties. They may choose to exclude enforceability. In that case, their agreements will be non-legal or strictly moral, and there will be no legal obligations sanctioned with contractual liability. Faulty behaviour may only be sanctioned if the requirements for *precontractual* liability are met (*see* Nos 129 ff. *infra*). A typical example of a strictly moral agreement is a gentlemen's agreement. Enforceability varies in the case of letters of intent and letters of comfort.[168] Also, if a letter of intent pertains and leads to the conclusion of a later contract, it may be considered binding. Thus, parties should draft these documents to be perfectly clear regarding their intentions.

116. It is possible for parties to conclude one or several preparatory contracts during the negotiations, before concluding the final contract. This practice is

---

165. R. Dekkers & A. Verbeke, *Handboek Burgerlijk Recht, III* (Antwerp: Intersentia: 2007), 53; S. Stijns, *Leerboek Verbintenissenrecht 1* (Brugge: die Keure, 2016), 125; W. van Gerven en A. Van Oevelen, *Verbintenissenrecht* (Leuven: Acco, 2015), 159–160.
166. S. Stijns, *Leerboek Verbintenissenrecht 1* (Brugge: die Keure, 2016), 126.
167. Cass. 24 Sep. 1987, *A.C.* 1987-88, 116, *Pas.* 1988, 112 and *RW* 1987-88, 813; Cass. 5 Jun. 1986, *A.C.* 1985-86, 1360 and *Pas.* 1986, 1221; S. Stijns, *Leerboek Verbintenissenrecht 1* (Brugge: die Keure, 2016), 59–60; W. van Gerven en A. Van Oevelen, *Verbintenissenrecht* (Leuven: Acco, 2015), 159–160.
168. P. Wéry, *Droit des obligations, I, Théorie générale du contrat* (Brussels: Larcier, 2011), 202.

referred to as progressive contracting.[169] These contracts have a direct link to the final contract but do not coincide with it. Preparatory contracts (*voorbereidende overeenkomsten/contrats préparatoires*) are independent contracts which prepare later contracts, although their obligations do not correspond with the obligations of the later contract(s) and they do not automatically contain an obligation to effectively conclude later contract(s). When a preparatory contract only prepares a single contract and obliges at least one party to conclude the later contract according to certain modalities, it is called a 'preliminary contract' (*voorovereenkomst/contrat préliminaire* or *précontrat*).[170] Examples of preliminary contracts are option contracts, priority contracts, and promises to contract.

117. Preparatory contracts usually contain one or more provisions according to which parties obligate themselves to continue the negotiations in good faith and to attempt to succeed in concluding the final agreement. These obligations may be obligations to achieve or obligations of best efforts (*see* Nos 35–36 *supra*). In the case of an obligation to achieve, parties to the preparatory contract are liable if the final contract is not concluded. In the case of a duty of best efforts, they are only liable if they did not take all the measures that could be expected from a reasonable person in the same circumstances in order to conclude the final contract.[171]

118. However, even when the preparatory contract does not obligate the parties to conclude the final contract, their behaviour is submitted to the criterion of the contractual duty to perform according to (contractual) good faith (Article 1134,3 OCC), in addition to the more lenient precontractual duty to act like a normal and reasonable person (*see* Nos 133–136 *infra*). In addition, in case of a dispute about a negotiator's withdrawal from the negotiations, the contents of the preparatory contract may be useful to determine whether or not he had a valid reason to withdraw. This can be regulated explicitly in the preparatory contract, e.g., by a clause allowing parties to withdraw without justification, as long as they give prior notice to the other parties, or, on the contrary, by a clause obliging parties to provide an adequate written justification in case of withdrawal. Parties may also stipulate a withdrawal fee. The possibility to withdraw may also be influenced indirectly; e.g., when the preparatory contract contains a clause stating that 'the contract will contain the

---

169. S. Stijns, *Leerboek Verbintenissenrecht 1* (Brugge: die Keure, 2016), 126; W. van Gerven en A. Van Oevelen, *Verbintenissenrecht* (Leuven: Acco, 2015), 159–160.
170. Traditionally, doctrine divides preparatory and preliminary contracts into two separate categories, whereby preparatory contracts do not contain the obligation to conclude the later contract, while preliminary contracts do (see: E. Dirix, B. Tilleman & S. Lierman (eds), *De Valks Juridisch woordenboek* (Antwerp-Oxford: Intersentia, 2018), 498; S. Stijns, *Leerboek Verbintenissenrecht 1* (Brugge: die Keure, 2016), 127). However, some doctrine also states that preparatory contracts may contain obligations to achieve the conclusion of the later contract (I. Samoy, 'Pijnpunten bij het opstellen van consortium- en andere overeenkomsten met meer dan twee partijen', in *Themis-cahier Verbintenissenrecht*, ed. S. Stijns (Brugge: die Keure, 2006–2007), 60). Consequentially, it is more consistent to assume that preparatory contracts may (or may not) contain such obligations, and that preliminary contracts are to be regarded as a subcategory of preparatory contracts.
171. I. Samoy, 'Pijnpunten bij het opstellen van consortium- en andere overeenkomsten met meer dan twee partijen', in *Themis-cahier Verbintenissenrecht*, ed. S. Stijns (Brugge: die Keure, 2006–2007), 60.

usual clauses for this type of contract', the negotiators will not be allowed to break off negotiations because of dispute about the inclusion of such a clause in the final contract.

119. Preparatory contracts may also contain terms which do not immediately pertain to the conclusion of the main contract itself, such as confidentiality clauses, exclusivity clauses, clauses on duration and survival, clauses on the costs of the negotiations, resolution of issues, or even exemption (*see* No. 246 *infra*) of penalty clauses (*see* No. 254 *infra*).

II. Offer and Acceptance

A. *Offer*

120. In principle, the conclusion of a contract is reached when an offer made by one party is accepted by the other party, and the offering party gets knowledge or could reasonably get knowledge of this acceptance.

An offer is a definite and clear proposal to contract by one of the parties, which includes all the essential and substantial elements necessary to the formation of the intended contract, such that the other party must only accept it for the contract to be concluded.[172] In order to be binding, an offer requires a material element (the precise description of the essential elements of the contract) and an intentional element (the intention of the offering party to be bound in case of acceptance).[173] If both elements are present, the offer binds the offerer.[174] If either element is lacking, it will not be considered an offer, but a non-binding proposal. As obligations can be created by unilateral intent (*see* No. 29 *supra*), the offer binds the offerer.[175] The binding power of the offer means that when an offer has been communicated to the offeree, the offerer can no longer alter or withdraw it. He is bound to keep the offer open for a given period. When no period is specified by the offerer, the offer binds him for a reasonable time for reflexion,[176] whose duration depends on the circumstances, such as customs, type of contract, offered goods or services and the way the offer was made (fax, email, letter). If the offeree refuses the offer, even before the time period is over, the offer expires. If the offer is withdrawn before the time

---

172. Cass. 23 Sep. 1969, *Arr.Cass.* 1970, 84 & *Pas.* 1970, 73. Elements of a contract are 'essential' when they are decisive for the acceptance of the contract (e.g., price and object in the case of sale of goods). 'Substantial' elements are secondary elements which, objectively, may not seem of essential importance, but which were elevated to be decisive parts of their contract by the parties (or, in other terms 'essentialised' – P. Wéry, *Droit des obligations, I, Théorie générale du contrat* (Brussels: Larcier, 2011), 156). Hereinafter the term 'essential element' will refer to both types of elements unless stated otherwise.
173. A. De Boeck, *Informatierechten en – plichten bij de totstandkoming en uitvoering van overeenkomsten* (Antwerp: Intersentia, 2000), 109; T. Vansweevelt & B. Weyts, « De totstandkoming van de overeenkomst » in T. Vansweevelt and B. Weyts, *Handboek Verbintenissenrecht* (Antwerpen: Intersentia, 2019), 162.
174. S. Stijns, *Leerboek Verbintenissenrecht 1* (Brugge: die Keure, 2016), 128.
175. *Ibid.*, 128.
176. P. Wéry, *Droit des obligations, I, Théorie générale du contrat* (Brussels: Larcier, 2011), 159.

limit has expired, the contract will still come into existence if the offeree accepts the offer within aforementioned time period (and can prove this). However, in practice, judges will rather grant pecuniary damages to the offeree who loses the chance to contract.[177]

B. Acceptance

121. Acceptance requires the unconditional assent to an offer. The contract is concluded upon the acceptance of the offer. If a reservation is made about an essential or substantial part of the contract, this answer is considered a counter-offer towards the initial offerer, who, in turn, is free to accept it or not. Acceptance can be explicit or silent, although only the 'circumstantial silence' can create a contract, i.e., a silence which, considering the circumstances, cannot be interpreted in any other way than as an acceptance.

122. When parties contract by correspondence, the contract is considered to start when and where the offerer has gotten knowledge (or reasonably could get knowledge) of the acceptance by the other party. The acceptance must be timely: it must have reached the offerer within the period specified in the offer, or, if none has been specified, within a reasonable period.

123. In certain specific cases, a right of withdrawal may be granted to the party who accepted an offer. For instance, in order to protect consumers against aggressive sale methods, Article VI.109/3 CEL stipulates that when a consumer receives a product he did not order, he is not obligated to pay for it nor send it back. As for the consumer who did order a product, Article VI.47 CEL grants him a reflection period of at least seven days during which he can renounce the sale. He can use this renunciation right without payment of a fine and without motivation.

III. Consideration

A. Does this Requirement Exist in Your Legal System?

124. Consideration is not a requirement of the Belgian law of contracts. In the continental tradition, a contract consists of an agreement.[178] In English law, it can be said to be a promise given in return for good consideration. Where the consideration is itself a promise, there is no practical difference between the two approaches. The difference between the two systems lies in the requirement of consideration. What, if anything, takes its place in the legal systems of the French family? It has been usual to give this role to the cause, but, though cause sometimes

177. S. Stijns, *Leerboek Verbintenissenrecht 1* (Brugge: die Keure, 2016), 129.
178. This paragraph was borrowed from the previous contribution to the IEL Contracts: Belgium by Prof. Dr J. Herbots.

coincides with consideration, the only functions which it can be said to perform do not include that of determining which agreements should be enforceable, which is the main function of consideration.

125. Let us take the case of *Stilk v. Myrick* (1809) to make this point clear.[179] A shipowner hired a crew in London for a voyage to Petersburg under contracts of employment which obliged the sailors to perform their services to the best of their strength notwithstanding the dangers of the journey. Some of the sailors jumped ship in Kronstadt and no replacements could be found for them. So in order to keep the remaining members of the crew in good spirits, the captain promised to pay them extra if they did the work of the runaways. The men agreed and on their return asked for the additional pay they had been promised. The shipowner refused to pay and the sailors brought an action. The Court dismissed the claim on the ground that the captain's promise was invalid and not actionable since the sailors, as promisees, had given him no consideration for it. They were already obliged by the original contract to take on any extra duties which might arise during the voyage, including the work of those who had jumped ship. In Belgian law, and on the Continent in general, the plaintiff should have succeeded in obtaining the promised extra payment. There was indeed an agreement – there was a cause for it, and the promise has to be kept. No 'consideration' is required in Belgian law.

126. Let us take another case, *Herrington v. Taylor* (1945). A saved B's life, but in doing so was himself so severely injured that he was crippled for life. In gratitude, B promised A to pay him a certain sum per month, but when B died, his heirs refused to continue the payments. In the Common law, technically, B's promise to pay should be invalid since the act of rescue was already over and done with when the promise was made, and therefore could not constitute good consideration. In Belgian law the contract is valid. The contract has a cause. If the proper construction of a transaction shows that the promisor wished to make a gift out of his estate for the benefit of the recipient, Article 931 OCC requires the promise to be notarised. But a contract made in gratitude for rendered services is taken out of the law of gift and away from the formal requirement of Article 931 OCC. A baron promised in writing to make an annuity to a servant as '*une preuve de I'amitie que nous lui portons.*' After the baron's death, his heirs refused to continue the payments. The courts did not consider the contract as a gift, and '*les services que Justine avail rendus au baron*' were considered to be a sufficient cause. See what is written below further on 'cause'. The doctrine of the cause is not a version of the common law doctrine of consideration.

179. This example is chosen by K. Zweigert & H. Kotz in their classical *An Introduction to Comparative Law* (translated by T. Weir) (North-Holland Publishing Company, 1977), II, p. 63.

B. Gratuitous Promise

127. Given the absence of the requirement of consideration in Belgian law, the figure of the gratuitous promise (i.e., a promise without consideration) is not known in the Belgian system. It should, however, not be confused with gratuitous contracts (*see* No. 62 *supra*).

C. 'Natural Obligations' (Do They Exist in Your Legal System?)

128. *See* No. 38 *supra*.

§2. LIABILITY AND NEGOTIATIONS: PRECONTRACTUAL LIABILITY

129. Problems regarding the start of a contract can be sanctioned in two different ways. First, when one of the conditions of substantive validity has not been met (*see* Chapter 2, *infra*), it is sanctioned with nullity. Second, when there is a case of precontractual liability, it is sanctioned with damages (Nos 137–138 *supra*). However, certain cases of precontractual liability may result in nullity, when the fault causing the liability results in the breach of a condition of substantive validity.

I. Definitions

130. As stated before, if the negotiators concluded a binding contract regarding the negotiations, faulty behaviour is sanctioned according to the rules applicable to contractual liability (*see* Nos 421 ff. *infra*). If no binding agreements were made, faulty behaviour during the negotiations is sanctioned as precontractual liability, which is submitted to the rules regarding extracontractual liability (Articles 1382–1383 OCC).

131. Belgian law makes a distinction between two types of precontractual liability.[180] Precontractual liability *sensu stricto* occurs when the contract is not concluded, although a party had raised the legitimate expectation that the contract would be concluded towards the other party (intentionally or out of negligence). A typical example is the sudden interruption of negotiations. Precontractual liability *sensu stricto* is sanctioned by reparation or by damages (*see* Nos 137–138 *infra*). Precontractual liability *sensu lato* occurs when the contract is concluded, despite the existence of precontractual faults. A typical example is a breach of the precontractual duty of information.[181] Precontractual liability *sensu lato* can result in the nullity of the contract (*see* Chapter 2 *infra*), or cause damage without affecting validity.

180. S. Stijns, *Leerboek Verbintenissenrecht 1* (Brugge: die Keure, 2016), 124; P. Wéry, *Droit des obligations, I, Théorie générale du contrat* (Brussels: Larcier, 2011), 352.

181. For more on this subject, *see*: A. De Boeck, *Informatierechten en – plichten bij de totstandkoming en uitvoering van overeenkomsten* (Antwerp: Intersentia, 2000), 572.

132. Like any other type of extracontractual liability, precontractual liability requires the existence of a fault, of a loss, and of a causal link between both (Articles 1382–1383 OCC).[182]

II. Precontractual Fault

133. Behaviour is considered faulty when it either: (1) infringes on legal rules or (2) is not the behaviour of a normal and careful person (the abstract criterion of the '*bonus pater familias*') placed in the same concrete circumstances.[183] A distinction is made between external (e.g., time and place but also social status, professional knowledge and education) and internal circumstances (e.g., age, gender, intelligence and personality). Only external circumstances are taken into account.

134. Given the freedom of negotiations, their rupture is only considered faulty if one party elicits legitimate expectations that the contract will be concluded towards the other party, yet lets him down wilfully or out of negligence.[184] Several elements can be taken into consideration when it comes to determining whether or not the rupture is faulty, among which the state, intensity and progression of negotiations, whether documents were drawn up, and whether the motive for rupture was valid or not.

135. Another frequent precontractual fault is a breach of the duty of information. Although negotiators do not have to share every bit of information they possess, they have the general duty to share the information that they derive from qualities (e.g., professional expertise) which were taken into account by the other party, and that they know to be necessary or deemed important by the other party in order to evaluate his or her contracting position.[185] In addition, certain laws impose additional information duties to specific contracts, e.g., Articles X.26–X.34 of the CEL imposing information duties in the context of commercial cooperation-agreements or Articles VI. 1/1–VI.2 CEL impose information duties on enterprises

182. R. Dekkers & A. Verbeke, *Handboek Burgerlijk Recht, III* (Antwerp: Intersentia: 2007), 53; S. Stijns, *Leerboek Verbintenissenrecht 1* (Brugge: die Keure, 2016), 124; P. Wéry, *Droit des obligations, I, Théorie générale du contrat* (Brussels: Larcier, 2011), 353.
183. W. van Gerven en A. Van Oevelen, *Verbintenissenrecht* (Leuven: Acco, 2015), 371; P. Wéry, *Droit des obligations, I, Théorie générale du contrat* (Brussels: Larcier, 2011), 353.
184. A. De Boeck, 'De precontractuele aansprakelijkheid: een vergelijking tussen het Belgische recht en de Principles of European Contract Law' in *Totstandkoming van de overeenkomst naar Belgisch en Nederlands recht*, eds. S. Stijns en J. M. Smits (Antwerp: Intersentia, 2002), 87; F. Peeraer, T. Hick & F. Auvray, 'Nieuw verbintenissenrecht: de totstandkoming van het contract (dynamisch en statisch bekeken)' in S. Stijns (ed.) *Themis 108 – Verbintenissenrecht* (die Keure, Brugge, 2019), 50; T. Vansweevelt & B. Weyts, « De totstandkoming van de overeenkomst » in T. Vansweevelt and B. Weyts, *Handboek Verbintenissenrecht* (Antwerpen: Intersentia, 2019), 144; S. Stijns, *Leerboek Verbintenissenrecht 1* (Brugge: die Keure, 2016), 124.
185. A. De Boeck, 'De precontractuele aansprakelijkheid: een vergelijking tussen het Belgische recht en de Principles of European Contract Law' in *Totstandkoming van de overeenkomst naar Belgisch en Nederlands recht*, eds. S. Stijns en J. M. Smits (Antwerp: Intersentia, 2002), 115.

selling to consumers. However, the receiver of the information must also behave as a normally careful person, and must, consequentially, gather and share information as such a person would.[186]

III. Causal Link

136. Only loss which has been *caused* by the precontractual fault must be compensated by the person responsible. In order to obtain compensation, the victim must prove that the damage would not have happened in the same way without the fault.[187]

IV. Loss and Compensation

137. Precontractual liability is sanctioned according to the rules applicable to tort. The aggrieved party is entitled to the integral compensation of the loss he suffered as a consequence of the fault.[188] The loss is determined by the comparison of two positions: the actual situation of the aggrieved party, as it was caused by the fault, and the hypothetical situation wherein he would have been if the fault had not occurred.[189] It is independent of the gravity of the fault.[190] Like contractual damages, extracontractual damages include both the loss which the aggrieved party incurred (*damnum emergens*) and the gain of which he was deprived (*lucrum cessans*).[191] Examples of *damnum emergens* are the loss of time, credibility or opportunities to conclude an agreement with other persons. An example of *lucrum cessans* is the loss of a chance to conclude the contract itself.[192]

138. The compensation of the loss may take two forms: reparation in nature (*herstel in natura/reparation en nature*), i.e., bringing back the victim as close as possible in the situation where he would have been if the faulty behaviour had not taken place, or, if reparation in nature is not possible, reparation by equivalent or damages (*vergoeding/compensation pécuniaire*), i.e., an equivalent payment in

---

186. A. De Boeck, *Informatierechten en – plichten bij de totstandkoming en uitvoering van overeenkomsten* (Antwerp: Intersentia, 2000), Nos 460–467.
187. W. van Gerven en A. Van Oevelen, *Verbintenissenrecht* (Leuven: Acco, 2015), 436; T. Vansweevelt & B. Weyts 'De totstandkoming van de overeenkomst' in T. Vansweevelt and B. Weyts *Handboek Verbintenissenrecht* (Antwerpen: Intersentia, 2019), 147; P. Wéry, *Droit des obligations, I, Théorie générale du contrat* (Brussels: Larcier, 2011), 354.
188. W. van Gerven en A. Van Oevelen, *Verbintenissenrecht* (Leuven: Acco, 2015), 462.
189. E. Dirix, *Het begrip schade* in *Aansprakelijkheidrecht* (Antwerp: Maklu, 1988), 16.
190. Cass. 10 Oct. 1949, *RW* 1949-50, 745.
191. W. van Gerven en A. Van Oevelen, *Verbintenissenrecht* (Leuven: Acco, 2015), 460.
192. M. Vanwijck-Alexandre, 'La réparation du dommage dans la négociation et la formation des contrats', *Ann. Dr. Liège*, 1980, 28, 32 and 77–85; F. Peeraer, T. Hick & F. Auvray, 'Nieuw verbintenissenrecht: de totstandkoming van het contract (dynamisch en statisch bekeken)' in S. Stijns (ed.) *Themis 108 – Verbintenissenrecht* (die Keure, Brugge, 2019) 56 et. seq.; P. Wéry, *Droit des obligations, I, Théorie générale du contrat* (Brussels: Larcier, 2011), 355.

money.[193] Although reparation in nature is the favoured form of compensation, pre-contractual liability is usually compensated by (monetary) damages.[194] However, there is an evolution from the compensation of the negative contracting interests (i.e., bringing back the victim in the situation where he would have been if no negotiations had taken place) towards the compensation of the positive contracting interests (i.e., granting the financial equivalent of what a party would have received if the contract had been concluded, with inclusion of the benefits this contract would have generated). The doctrine is rather hesitant on this approach, due to their resistance to what they regard as a breach of the autonomy of will. However, some jurisprudence granted compensations for positive contracting interests in cases where the negotiators had reached a 'point of no return' before one of them broke off negotiations.[195] This evolution must be regarded in the context of the recognition of the doctrine of appearance as an autonomous source of obligations (*see* Nos 32 *supra*). When one party could legitimately believe that the contract would be concluded due to appearances created by the other party, that other party loses its freedom to break off negotiations.[196]

§3. Formal and Evidential Requirements

I. Formal Requirements

A. *Contracts Under Seal: Does This Term of Art Exist in Your Legal System?*

139. There are no contracts under seal in Belgian law. The formalities of the deed according to English law are totally different from the formalities of the '*actes authentiques*' of the French legal family, and have different consequences.

B. *'Solemn' Contracts: Do They Exist in Your Legal System?*

140. As seen in No. 58 *supra*, solemn contracts are only valid when certain formal requirements are met *in addition* to the consent of all parties. Examples of solemn contracts are a donation, a mortgage, a marriage settlement, or a credit contract between a bank and a consumer. The first three require an authentic act (*see* No. 143 *infra*), while the latter requires certain handwritten mentions by the borrower.[197] In the case of solemn contracts, the formalities are conditions of substantial validity. If

193. W. van Gerven en A. Van Oevelen, *Verbintenissenrecht* (Leuven: Acco, 2015), 462.
194. T. Vansweevelt & B. Weyts 'De totstandkoming van de overeenkomst' in T. Vansweevelt and B. Weyts *Handboek Verbintenissenrecht* (Antwerpen: Intersentia, 2019), 148.
195. *See* A. De Boeck, *Informatierechten en – plichten bij de totstandkoming en uitvoering van overeenkomsten* (Antwerp: Intersentia, 2000), 88–91; F. Peeraer, T. Hick & F. Auvray, 'Nieuw verbintenissenrecht: de totstandkoming van het contract (dynamisch en statisch bekeken)' in S. Stijns (ed.) *Themis 108 – Verbintenissenrecht* (die Keure, Brugge, 2019) 56 et. seq.
196. S. Stijns, *Leerboek Verbintenissenrecht 1* (Brugge: die Keure, 2016), 124 and 150.
197. Articles VII.70, §1 CEL.

the formal requirements are not met, the resulting contract will be invalid. This type of formal requirements is what distinguishes solemn contracts from consensual contracts.

141. Formal requirements for the validity of contracts should not be confused with types of formal requirements which do not affect validity, but only affect proof (*see* Nos 149 ff. *infra*) or opposability (*see* Nos 289–290 *infra*). The sale of immovables illustrates this distinction. The sale itself is valid between parties as soon as a consensus has been reached (it is a consensual contract). However, as soon as the price is superior to EUR 3.500, a written document is required to prove it (*see* No. 183 *infra*). For the sale to be opposable to third parties, a notarial act must be drawn and copied into the registry at the mortgage office.[198]

II. Evidential Requirements

A. The Parol Evidence Rule

142. The parol evidence rule from the common law jurisdictions that prevents a party to a written contract from presenting extrinsic evidence that contradicts or adds to the written terms of the contract that appears to be whole is not applicable as such in Belgian law. Although there is a preference for written evidence (*see* No. 149 *infra*), these rules are quite dissimilar from the parol evidence rule.

B. Function of the Notary: Does the 'Notaire' Exist in Your Legal System? If Not, Which Legal Profession Assumes This Role?

143. In Belgium, the notary (*notaris/notaire*) is a public officer responsible for drawing up of authentic acts (*see infra* 172), the keeping of the originals of these acts, and the delivery of certified copies with a formulary of execution.[199] The main law in regard to this profession is the Law of 16 March 1803 on the function of the notary.[200]

144. The duties of the Belgian notary (*notaris/notaire*) are far more extensive than those of an Anglo-American notary public, whose profession consists of certificating deeds or other documents and notes or protests dishonoured bills of exchange.[201] The main function of the Belgian notary is the drawing of legal instruments. Belgian law does not grant the notary or any profession a monopoly for the drawing of ordinary contracts. However, in some cases, transactions, in order to be

198. Articles 1 & 2 *Loi des hypothèques* (Mortgage Law).
199. This paragraph was largely inspired by the previous contribution to the IEL Contracts: Belgium by Prof. Dr J. Herbots.
200. Wet van 25 ventôse jaar XI op het notarisambt/Loi du 25 ventôse an XI contenant organisation du notariat.
201. cfr. E.A. Martin & J. Law (eds), *Oxford Dictionary of Law*, 6th ed. (Oxford: University Press, 2006), 358.

valid, must be incorporated in notarial acts (e.g., antenuptial agreements and donations). Other transactions, including all instruments concerning the transfer of real property (e.g., sale of immovables, *see* No. 142 *supra*), require this in order to be opposable to third parties.

145. The requirement for certain documents to be prepared by a notary in the special form prescribed for notarial acts aims to protect both the parties and the public in general. Next to the protection offered by the fact the contract will be drafted by a competent person, the use of the notary prevents fraud and, perhaps even more importantly, claims of fraud. Before preparing any instrument, the notary is under a strict obligation to ascertain the correct identity of the parties and to make sure that they have the legal capacity to act. Furthermore, the notary does not give the original instrument (called '*minuut/minute*') prepared by him to the parties; it is kept permanently in his office and thus protected against alterations. Certified copies of notarial documents may be issued to interested parties. Since the notary is a quasi-public officer, a notarial document offers the additional advantages regarding their probative force (*see* No. 172 *infra*). A notary may also act as a depository of documents not drawn by him. In that case, however, he may not prepare copies.

146. Notaries may also draw all other instruments, unless exclusive power to do so has been granted to another public officer, e.g., a *gerechtsdeurwaarder/huissier de justice*, another public officer designated by the King with the exclusive capacity to draw up and signify writs and to execute titles.[202] Notaries and *gerechtsdeurwaarders/huissiers* share the power to protest negotiable instruments and the power to conduct public sales of movable property.

147. Often, notaries, especially notaries having a long-continuing relationship with a client, also act as general advisers and representatives, and take care of purchases and sales (especially of real property), and also of loans, investments, and similar transactions. In addition to his work on behalf of private clients, the notary may be delegated by the court to perform certain quasi-judicial functions, especially in partition proceedings or in connection with the division of community property after a divorce.

148. The duties of the notary are prescribed by law. A notary must make his services available to any person requesting them for a lawful purpose; he may not refuse to act in a matter in which he is competent.[203] On the other hand, no notary may perform any of his functions outside the district for which he has been appointed.[204] The notary is under a strict duty to observe all formal requirements for the preparation of notarial acts. He must ascertain the identity of the parties as well as their capacity to act[205] and is personally responsible for the validity of the

202. E. Dirix, B. Tilleman & S. Lierman (eds), *De Valks Juridisch woordenboek* (Antwerp-Oxford: Intersentia, 2018), 194.
203. Article 3 of the Law of 16 Mar. 1803.
204. Article 5 of the Law of 16 Mar. 1803.
205. Article 11 of the Law of 16 Mar. 1803.

instruments he prepares. He has to inform all parties about the duties and rights ensuing from the juridical acts for which he is involved, and to counsel them in an impartial manner.[206] No notary may engage in commercial activities. He may not have personal interest in any transaction in which he participates, nor may he become a surety for a loan negotiated by him.[207] Each notary must carry liability insurance as protection for his clients.

III. Proof

A. *Introductory Concepts*

149. Belgian civil patrimonial law, including contract law, is characterised by a strongly regulated system of proof (Articles 8.1–8.39 CC)[208] and by a preference for written instruments above non-written ones (Article 8.9 CC, *see* No. 183 *infra*). This creates a stark contrast between, on one side, the principle of consensualism for the validity of juridical acts and, on the other, the principle of formalism for their proof.[209]

150. An exception is made in commercial matters. Proof between *or against* enterprises grants the parties as well as the court more freedom.[210] There is no preference for written instruments, and proof can be delivered by all legal means, testimonies and presumptions included. Furthermore, two additional means of proof are accepted: accepted invoices and accountancy. The reasons for this flexibility are the greater alertness which is expected from enterprises (as opposed to non-professionals) and the necessity for more fluency. The system of proof in criminal matters is more flexible than that in civil matters as well, as it allows the court to actively search for the objective truth. On the other hand, proof in family matters is regulated even more rigidly than in patrimonial ones, as it often concerns matters of public order (for a definition of public order, *see* No. 46 *supra*).

151. The rules of proof in civil, patrimonial matters are not of public order, nor mandatory laws (*see* No. 46 *supra*).[211] Consequentially, in principle, contracts and

---

206. Article 9 of the Law of 16 Mar. 1803.
207. Article 6 of the Law of 16 Mar. 1803.
208. S. Stijns, *Leerboek Verbintenissenrecht 2* (Brugge: die Keure, 2020), 156; I. Samoy & W. Vandenbussche, 'Het nieuwe bewijsrecht', in S. Stijns (ed.) *Verbintenissenrecht*, Themis-cahier 108 (Brugge: die Keure 2019), 118; W. van Gerven en A. Van Oevelen, *Verbintenissenrecht* (Leuven: Acco, 2015), 663.
209. For more on proof, *see*: I. Samoy & W. Vandenbussche, 'Het nieuwe bewijsrecht', in S. Stijns (ed.) *Verbintenissenrecht*, Themis-cahier 108 (Brugge: die Keure 2019); T. Vansweevelt & B. Weyts, *Het nieuwe bewijsrecht* (Mortsel: Intersentia, 2020); B. Vanlerberghe, *Het nieuwe burgerlijke bewijsrecht* (Mortsel: Intersentia, 2019) 54.
210. Article 25 of the Code of Commerce (*Wetboek van Koophandel/Code de Commerce, Belgian Official Gazette* 10 Sep. 1807).
211. Cass. 20 Jun. 1957, *Arr.Cass.* 1957, 885 & *Pas.* 1957, 1256; Cass. 27 Jun. 1963, *Pas.* 1963, 1131; Cass. 20 Apr. 1978, *Arr.Cass.* 1977-78, 958.

clauses about proof (e.g., clauses where parties regulate the repartition of the burden of proof, broaden or restrict the probative instruments and/or their probative power, etc.) are valid. However, the general exceptions to the freedom to contract remain applicable (*see supra*, No. 46). Clauses about proof may not breach rules of public order, such as the right of access to a court. There are also limitations where contracts between professional and consumers are involved (*see* No. 75 *supra*); e.g., clauses which limit the probative instruments the consumer may use are forbidden.[212]

152. The Belgian law of proof has been modernised in 2019 (applicable since 1 October 2020) through the introduction of a book 3 into the reformed Belgian Civil Code.

B. Basic Principles in the Context of Court Proceedings

153. Initially, proof in civil patrimonial law was governed by the principle of passivity of the court,[213] which derived from the principle of the autonomy of will (*see* No. 43–45 *supra*). Parties were the only ones responsible for carrying their claim or defence: the demander had the burden to state a demand with a determinate object (outside which's boundaries the court was not competent to judge), while the defender carried the burden to defend himself against the claim.

154. However, the principle of passivity of the court has been nuanced since the introduction of the new Judicial Code in 1967,[214] which imposes a duty to cooperate upon parties. Article 871 of the Judicial Code grants the court the possibility to order parties to produce any evidence they possess. Article 877 of the Judicial Code further concretises this by stipulating that 'When there are important, specific and consistent presumptions that a party or third party possesses an item which is proof of a relevant fact, the court can order for this item or a certified copy to be added to the file of the judicial procedure.' The court may even issue this order without having been demanded to do so by parties.[215] Consequentially, the court can both take the initiative when parties neglect to do so and force parties to cooperate loyally. Article 8.4 al. 3 CC codifies this duty to cooperate in the new law of proof.

155. The right of initiative of the court is still limited by the prohibition for the court to judge *ultra petita*, i.e., to pronounce judgment on things that were not demanded by parties, or to grant more than was demanded (*beschikkingsbeginsel/principe dispositive*). It is also limited by the '*beginsel van tegenspraak/principe du contradictoire*', according to which the rights of the defence must be respected, and the court can only allow evidence which has been the object of a debate in which

212. Article VI.83, 21° CEL.
213. H. De Page, *Traité élémentaire de droit civil belge,* III (Brussels: Bruylant, 1967), No. 716.
214. *Gerechtelijk wetboek/Code judiciaire* of 10 Oct. 1967, *Belgian Official Gazette* 10 Oct. 1967.
215. Cass. 2 Jun. 1977, *Arr.Cass.* 1977, 1019 & *Pas.* 1977, 1012; Cass. 14 Dec. 1995, *Arr.Cass.* 1995, 1128 & *Pas.* 1995, 1165.

both parties had the opportunity to explain their point of view and refute that of the other party in equal and fair circumstances.[216] Consequentially, a court is not allowed to pronounce judgment grounded on facts or proof of which one party was unaware, or about which a party could not pronounce himself.[217]

156. Furthermore, the principle of lawful proof (*beginsel van geoorloofd bewijs/ principe de la régularité de la preuve*) implies that the court can exclude unlawful proof, i.e., not take it into account. There are three kinds of unlawful proof: proof whose credibility is questionable due to an unlawfulness; proof that, if admitted, would violate the right to a fair trial of one of the parties or if the norm violated imposes nullity for that unlawfulness.[218]

C. *Object of Proof*

157. Not everything must be proven. A party must only prove the facts to which a rule of law binds the legal consequence(s) aimed at by this party, but not the rule of law itself. Furthermore, facts must only be proven if they are contested by the other party. Consequentially, legal rules, generally known facts and non-contested facts must not be proven. Only facts which are both relevant and contested must be (Article 8.3 CC).[219]

158. Rules of law, general principles of law, customs (*gewoonten/coutumes*)[220] and even foreign law must not be proven.[221] Usages (*gebruiken/usages*), which are not considered an independent source of law, must be proven if disputed, unless they are generally known.[222] The existence of a certain usage is a fact which can be proven with all legal means.

216. S. Stijns, *Leerboek Verbintenissenrecht,* vol. 2 (Brugge: die Keure, 2020), 162.
217. Cass. 13 Nov. 1989, *Arr.Cass.* 1989-90, 351.
218. Cass. 10 Mar. 2008, *Arr.Cass.* 2008, 678; *JLMB* 2009, 580, note R. De Baerdemaeker; *NJW* 2010, 195, note K. Van Kildonck; *Pas.* 2008, 652; *RCJB* 2009, 325, note F. Kefer. *See also* J. Van Doninck, *Het lot van onrechtmatig bewijs* (Antwerpen: Intersentia, 2020), 380; S. Stijns, *Leerboek Verbintenissenrecht,* vol. 2 (Brugge: die Keure, 2020), 163; B. Allemeersch, I. Samoy & W. Vandenbussche, 'Het burgerlijk bewijsrecht', *TPR* 2015, 669 ff.
219. *Ibid.* 164; P. Van Ommeslaghe, *Les obligations vol. 3* in *Traité de droit civil, tome II* (Brussels: Bruylant, 2013), 2318 et seq.
220. The meaning of the term 'customary law' (*gewoonterecht/droit coutumier*) in Belgium somewhat differs from the meaning of this term in common law countries. In Belgium, it is defined as 'written or unwritten rules of law which came into being out of general, continuous, durable and public customs without intervention from the government, about which's mandatory character a permanent, uncontested conviction exists within a society' (E. Dirix, B. Tilleman & S. Lierman (eds), *De Valks Juridisch woordenboek* (Antwerp-Oxford: Intersentia, 2018), 198).
221. R. Dekkers & A. Verbeke, *Handboek Burgerlijk Recht*, III (Antwerp: Intersentia: 2007), 379; W. van Gerven en A. Van Oevelen, *Verbintenissenrecht* (Leuven: Acco, 2015), 666.
222. Usage should not be confused with custom. Usage is defined as 'a conduct which is generally common in social life or in certain professional environments, which is not legally enforceable, but which sometimes is used by the court to fill in certain standards' (E. Dirix, B. Tilleman & S. Lierman (eds), *De Valks Juridisch woordenboek* (Antwerp-Oxford: Intersentia, 2018), 182).

159. Generally known facts must not be proven either. Examples of facts that have been accepted to be generally known are the fact that two Belgian municipalities were located at a certain distance from each other,[223] and that no credit institution would renounce to a security unless a new and better security is obtained at the same time, or the debt is paid.[224] However, it is important to state that the court may not base itself upon a judge's personal knowledge of the facts, e.g., when he takes the initiative to visit relevant places or do some research on the internet. This prohibition is grounded on the rights of the defence (*see* No. 155 *supra*).[225]

160. In sum, only relevant and contested facts must be proven.[226] Facts are considered relevant when they contribute to the formation of the court's judgment. Facts are *contested* when they are disputed by the other party. However, it should be noted that lack of contestation does not imply a recognition or admission of the statements of the other party.[227]

161. Furthermore, a distinction must be made between facts to which an open system of proof applies, and facts which are submitted to the regulated system of proof of the CC (*see* No. 149 *supra*). Strictly material facts, events, and human behaviours to which the law has granted obligatory power, but which are not juridical acts (*see* No. 42 *supra*), may be proven by any legal means. The regulated system of proof of the Civil Code only applies to juridical acts (for a definition of 'juridical act' *see* No. 42 *supra*).

D. *Burden of Proof*

1. Rule and Role of the Parties and the Judge

162. Article 8.4 CC allocates the burden of proof as follows: whoever demands the execution of an obligation must prove its existence ('*actori incumbit probatio*') and whoever states to be freed from an obligation must prove the legal act or fact that supports his claim ('*reus in excipiendo fit actor*'). Article 870 of the Judicial Code stipulates that 'each party must prove the facts it invokes', thus broadening the aforementioned rule to more than obligations only.[228]

223. Cass. 21 Oct. 1988, *Arr.Cass.* 1988-89, 217.
224. Cass. 7 Feb. 2006, A.R. nr. P.05-1375.N, *Arr.Cass.* 2006, 321.
225. S. Stijns, *Leerboek Verbintenissenrecht,* vol. 2 (Brugge: die Keure, 2020), 165; 127.
226. Cass. 18 Apr. 2008, AR C.07.0409.F, *Arr.Cass.* 2008, 957.
227. Cass. 10 May 2001, *Arr.Cass.* 2001, 841 and *Pas.* 2001, 807.
228. Gerechtelijk wetboek/Code judiciaire of 10 Oct. 1967, *Belgian Official Gazette* 10 Oct. 1967.

2. Exceptions

163. There are three types of exceptions to aforementioned allocation of the burden of proof: exceptions by law, jurisprudential exceptions, and contractual exceptions.

164. First, Article 8.4 CC foresees a general exception to the aforementioned attribution of the burden of proof. A judge can deviate from these rules in exceptional circumstances if upholding them would lead to a manifestly unjust outcome, provided he gives a special motivation. The judge can only do so if he has ordered all useful investigation measures and assured that parties have lived up to their duty of cooperation. That such a reversal of the burden of proof is an *ultimum remedium*, is clear from the very demanding conditions of application. Such an exceptional case could, for instance, be that where a customer of a bank intends to withdraw cash from a cash dispenser but receives no money whereas the money is deducted. If the bank then does not collaborate in discharging the proof, the burden of proof may be imposed upon her.

Additionally to this general exception, the legislator has, in certain cases, reversed the burden of proof in order to protect weaker parties. When this is the case, the weaker party still has to make a statement, but he is relieved from his burden of proof. It is up to the other, stronger party to prove the opposite. Article VII.2, §4 *in fine* CEL provides an example. It places the burden to prove that the credit provider has fulfilled the creditworthiness assessment of the consumer and if appropriate of the proposer of a personal security on the credit provider himself.

In some cases, the protection of the weaker party is achieved through the use of legal presumptions (*see* No. 179 *infra*). The beneficiary of such a legal presumption is exempted from proof (Article 8.7 CC). When a presumption is irrefutable, no proof to the contrary is allowed, and the beneficiary does not have to carry any burden of proof. When it is refutable, proof to the contrary is possible, and the presumption only results in a reversal of the burden of proof.[229] An example of a refutable legal presumption is the presumption of tortuous liability against the parents of an underage child in case of damage caused by the fault of this child laid down in Article 1384 CC. An example of an irrefutable legal presumption, in the same Article, is the tortuous liability of the employer in case of damage caused by his employees.

165. Second, the jurisprudential distinction between a duty to achieve and a duty of best efforts also has implications for the burden of proof (for definitions, *see* No. 163 *supra*). In case of a duty to achieve, if the debtor fails to produce the promised result, his faulty behaviour is assumed as soon as the creditor can prove both the existence of the obligation and the lack of result. The debtor can only escape liability by proving that his failure has an extraneous cause (*see* Nos 391 ff. *infra*). Conversely, in case of a duty of best efforts, the creditor must prove not only the

229. Cass. 11 maart 2010, *Arr. Cass.* 2010, 729, *Pas.* 2010, 784, *RW* 2012-2013, 422, note; Cass. 23 Sep. 1996, *Arr.Cass.* 1996, 790 & *Pas.* 1996, 846; Cass. 7 Oct. 1996, *Arr.Cass.* 1996, 880 & *Pas.* 1996, 941.

existence of the obligation and the lack of result but also the fact that the debtor has not taken the measures that could be expected from a reasonable person. In other terms, unlike in the case of a duty to achieve a certain result, the fault of the debtor is not assumed, but must be proven by the creditor.[230]

166. Third, as the rules of proof are suppletive (*see* No. 153 *supra*), parties can deviate from the legal rules and validly regulate the repartition of the burden of proof in their contract.

E. Standard of Proof

167. The standard of proof indicates with which intensity a fact needs to be proven. Generally, a reasonable degree of certainty suffices (Article 8.5 CC). That means that a judge needs to be convinced by the invoked probative instruments (*see* Nos 170 ff. *infra*) without being required to prove the allegated facts with scientific certainty. This standard of proof is determinant in a free system of proof. In a regulated system of proof, the law defines which elements ought to convince the judge.

The standard of proof is lowered to probability when a negative fact needs to be proven (Article 8.6 CC). Proving a negative fact consists of proving that something did not happen; e.g., the fact that someone was not at a certain place at a certain time, or did not show a certain behaviour, must be proven. Some positive facts can also be subject to this lowered standard of proof. That is the case if it would be impossible or unreasonable to bring the proof of the positive fact in question (Article 8.6 CC).[231]

F. Probative Instruments

168. The probative instruments are divided into five categories: written proof, testimony, presumption, admission and party-oath.[232] Although other probative instruments are recognised in the Civil Code, the Judicial Code and other law, this contribution will limit itself to the aforementioned five.

1. Written Proof

a. Acts in General

169. Acts are written documents intended to serve as proof of a juridical act, which are signed by the parties and/or a public officer.[233] The two main functions of

230. S. Stijns, *Leerboek Verbintenissenrecht 1* (Brugge: die Keure, 2016), 8–10.
231. S. Stijns, *Leerboek Verbintenissenrecht 2* (Brugge: die Keure, 2020), 172–173.
232. *Ibid.*, 174.
233. *Ibid.*, 174–175.

the requirement of a signature are the *identification* of the author of the act and *confirmation* of the consent of the author with its contents.[234] Initially, the only form of signature which was considered valid by the *Court of Cassation* was the self-applied, complete written name, applied directly on the document.[235] Due to the rise of modern technology, this principle came under fire. With Article 8.1, 2° CC, the legislator has provided for a definition of the signature which includes the electronical signature (Article 8.1, 3° CC).

170. Like the concept of signature, that of 'written document' got a more functional definition in Article 8.1, 1° CC.[236]

171. Within the category of acts, a distinction is made between authentic acts, i.e., acts drawn up by a public officer, and acts under private signature. Written documents, which were not specifically drawn up as proof, such as bills, correspondence and accountancy, are not considered acts.

b. Authentic Acts

172. According to Article 8.1, 5° CC, an authentic act (*authentieke akte/acte authentique*) is an act drawn up in a legal form in the presence of a public officer competent in the area where it was drawn up. The most common example of such acts is notarial acts (drawn up by a notary). Article 8.15, first sentence CC, states that an authentic act can be stored on any type of support, provided it is stored according to the legal requirements. Thereby the validity of electronic authentic acts is explicitly recognised. Within authentic acts, a distinction is made between authentic and non-authentic statements.[237] Authentic statements are statements which the public officer was able and obliged to verify (e.g., the date, the presence and identity of the parties). These statements can only be contested through an accusation of falsification (Article 8.17 CC), which requires a special procedure. Non-authentic statements are statements which the public officer could not verify (e.g., the mental health of parties) and only have value of proof unless proven otherwise, which can be done according to the general rules of proof.

---

234. *See*. P. Van Eecke, *De handtekening in het recht. Van pennentrek tot elektronische handtekening* (Gent: Larcier, 2004), 191–197.
235. *See* Cass. 28 Jun/ 1982, *Arr.Cass.* 1981-82, 1367 & *Pas.* 1982, 1286.
236. B. Vanlerberghe, 'De krachtlijnen van het nieuwe burgerlijke bewijsrecht' in T. Vansweevelt and B. Weyts, *Het nieuwe bewijsrecht* (Mortsel: Intersentia, 2020), 15.
237. S. Stijns, *Leerboek Verbintenissenrecht 2* (Brugge: die Keure, 2020), 176; R. Dekkers & A. Verbeke, *Handboek Burgerlijk Recht*, III (Antwerp: Intersentia: 2007), 692; H. De Page, *Traité élémentaire de droit civil belge,* III (Brussels: Bruylant, 1967), No. 758; W. van Gerven en A. Van Oevelen, *Verbintenissenrecht* (Leuven: Acco, 2015), 682.

c. Acts under Private Signature

i General Rules

173. A signed instrument (*onderhandse akte/acte sous seeing privé*) is an act which intends to create legal consequences, which has been signed by the parties with the intention to agree with the content of it and is no authentic act (Article 8.1, 4° CC). Its form is free, and its signature is the sole requirement for its validity.[238] According to Article 8.18 CC, signed instruments have the same probative effect as authentic acts between parties. They also have the same probative effect towards third parties, except for their date. According to Article 8.22 CC, the date is only considered proven towards third parties if this date is 'fixed', i.e., when it has been settled by one of the limitative cases mentioned in Article 8.22 CC. These are the registration of the act, at least one of the parties can no longer amend the act or its date, *inter alia*, due to the death of one of them, or the day when its contents have been established in acts drawn up by public officers.

174. Transcripts (*afschriften/copies*) are copies which are literal and identical in contents, but generally do not contain an original signature, e.g., a fax, copy, or microfilm. Transcripts of written documents can be used as proof and have the same probative effect as the original, on the condition that they are not contested. However, according to Article 8.25 CC, if a statutory norm stipulates differently, the transcript merely is a factual presumption or, when applicable, a beginning of written proof. If the original still exists, its production can always be demanded. In practice, transcripts are generally accepted, and cases where they are contested are rare. If disputed, the transcript can still be regarded as a beginning of written proof (*see* No. 177 *infra*) or as a presumption (*see* No. 179 *infra*).

ii Specific Rules for Certain Signed Instruments

175. Article 8.20 CC requires for synallagmatic contracts (*see* No. 61 *supra*) to be drawn up in as many originals as there are parties with a separate interest, and for the number of originals to figure on each original. The sanction is the relative nullity (*see* Nos 235 ff. et al. *infra*) of the act, i.e., the probative instrument. It does not affect the contractual obligations between parties, although it makes the document proving the existence of these obligations invalid.

176. Article 8.21 CC regulates the specific case of unilateral legal acts of payment. It stipulates that, irrespective of the value at stake, a written instrument only serves as proof if it contains a mention of the amount to be payed or the quantity of goods to be delivered written by the person obliging herself and her signature. The requirements of Article 8.21 are subject to a strict interpretation by courts.[239]

---

238. S. Stijns, *Leerboek Verbintenissenrecht 2* (Brugge: die Keure, 2020), 176; H. De Page, *Traité élémentaire de droit civil belge,* III (Brussels: Bruylant, 1967), No. 777.
239. S. Stijns, *Leerboek Verbintenissenrecht,* vol. 2 (Brugge: die Keure, 2020), 179.

d. Beginning of Written Proof

177. If a written document does not fulfil the requirements to qualify as an authentic act or an act under private signature, it can still count as a beginning of written proof. A beginning of written proof is any written document which can be attributed to the party contesting the allegated juridical act and which makes the allegated legal act likely (Article 8.1, 7° CC).

2. Testimony

178. Testimony (*getuigenbewijs/preuve testimoniale*) is a probative instrument consisting of the declaration, made in front of the court, by a witness, i.e., a person who has experienced the matter to be proven with his own senses (direct witness) or who has been told about it by a person who has experienced it (indirect witness) (Article 8.1, 8° CC). The procedure for testimonies is described in Articles 915–961 of the Judicial Code. A testimony can take the form of an oral declaration in honour before a judge or of a written submission to the judge (Article 961/1 Judicial Code). Testimony can only prove the existence of material or legal facts, not legal qualifications as only the court is competent to give legal qualifications and bind legal consequences to them.[240] When a party wishes to call upon a testimony, he must demand an authorisation to the court beforehand. The court determines if the facts this party wishes to prove are relevant and precise and if testimony can be useful.[241] It remains free to judge the probative effect of both direct and indirect testimonies (Article 8.28, second sentence CC).[242] It is also possible for the court to take the initiative to order a testimony (Article 916 of the Judicial Code).

3. Presumptions

179. Presumptions (*vermoedens/présomptions*) are deductions made by law (legal presumptions) or the court (factual presumptions) where an unknown fact is deduced from a certain one. Quasi-legal presumptions are those that are not established by law, but which are granted the same probative effect as legal presumptions.[243] The probative effect of a factual presumption is free and thus left to the discretion of the judge (Article 8.29 CC). Legal presumptions, to the contrary, have a fixed probative effect: if the certain fact is proven, the judge must conclude that the unknown fact is proven, too (Article 8.7 CC).

Presumptions can be refutable or irrefutable (*see* No. 164 *supra*). If they are refutable, they merely reverse the burden of proof. That is the case for factual presumptions and some legal presumptions. An irrefutable presumption discharges a party

240. *Ibid.*, 181.
241. Cass. 17 Feb. 1995, *Pas.* 1995, 190; L. Cornelis, *Algemene theorie van de verbintenis* (Antwerp: Intersentia, 2000), No. 189.
242. Cass. 25 Feb. 1980, *Pas.* 1980, 768 & *Arr.Cass.* 1979-80, 769.
243. S. Stijns, *Leerboek Verbintenissenrecht*, vol. 2 (Brugge: die Keure, 2020), 182.

from its burden of proof. Whoever calls upon a presumption must prove that the requirements for that presumption to be applicable are met.[244]

4. Admissions

180. An admission (*bekentenis/aveu*) is a recognition by a person, or his representative to this end, of a fact that can have legal consequences against itself (Article 8.1, 10° CC). With an admission a person recognises a material fact, a juridical fact or a juridical act whose recognition is not in its own interest.[245] Article 8.30 CC makes a distinction between judicial admissions, i.e., admissions made during a judicial procedure, and extrajudicial ones, i.e., admissions made outside such procedure. None of them is subject to any formal requirements; it can be written or oral, explicit or implicit without necessarily having been issued with the intention to proof the alleged facts or acts (Article 8.30 CC).

Both have the same legal probative effect (Article 8.31, third alinea CC). A judge is free to decide whether or not he finds the admission is made honestly (*oprecht/sincère*). If he finds the admission to be made honestly, he must consider the admitted facts or acts to be proven (Article 8.32, alinea 2 CC). By making an admission, a party often disposes of a contested right. Consequentially, he must be capable of disposing of that right, and no admission may be made about things of which the law does not allow to dispose, or things about which out of court settlements cannot be made.[246] Admissions are always allowed, except in matters of public order.

181. Article 8.32, third alina CC stipulates that admissions are indivisible, except where the admission is internally contradictory. Consequentially, anyone who calls upon the admission of the other party must take the admission as a whole. Even the court is not allowed to take some parts of an admission into account and to ignore other ones.[247] Furthermore, Article 8.32, alinea 2 CC stipulates that admissions are irrevocable, except when the person who made the admission can prove a mistake about the facts. In case of mistake about the law, i.e., about the legal consequences of the admission, it cannot be revoked.[248]

5. Party-Oath

182. A judicial party-oath (*gerechtelijke eed/serment judiciaire*) is a formal declaration by a party where he confirms the truthfulness of his own statements (Article 8.1, 12° CC).[249] While the Civil Code (Article 8.33 CC) recognises two kinds of

244. Cass. 23 Sep. 1996, *Arr.Cass.* 1996, 790 & *Pas.* 1996, 846.
245. S. Stijns, *Leerboek Verbintenissenrecht,* vol. 2 (Brugge: die Keure, 2020), 183.
246. Cass. 13 Nov. 2000, *Arr.Cass.* 2000, 1774 & *Pas.* 2000, 1737; Cass. 24 Apr. 2006, *R.W.* 2006-07, 1002.
247. Cass. 13 Jan. 1994, *Arr.Cass.* 1994, 33 & *Pas.* 1994, 33.
248. S. Stijns, *Leerboek Verbintenissenrecht,* vol. 2 (Brugge: die Keure, 2020), 185; W. van Gerven en A. Van Oevelen, *Verbintenissenrecht* (Leuven: Acco, 2015), 700.
249. S. Stijns, *Leerboek Verbintenissenrecht,* vol. 2 (Brugge: die Keure, 2020), 185.

party-oaths, i.e., the decisive oath (*beslissende eed/serment décisoire*) (Articles 8.34–8.37 CC) and the judicially imposed oath (Articles 8.38–8.39 CC); they are hardly ever used. A decisive oath is assigned by one party to the other party to determine how the procedure will be solved. The initiative must thus be taken by a process party. The court then decides whether to allow the oath or not. If the oath is allowed and taken by the other party, this point of the dispute is solved in his advantage. Its scope is the same as that of admissions. The judicially imposed oath is imposed on one party at the initiative of the judge, who remains free to determine the probative effect of the oath (Article 8.38 CC).

G. Hierarchy of Probative Instruments

1. Article 8.9 of the Civil Code: Priority of Written Proof

183. According to Article 8.9 CC, to prove a juridical act worth more than EUR 3.500, an act is required, while testimonies and presumptions are not allowed. Furthermore, even for juridical acts worth less than EUR 3.500, proof against acts can only be given with other acts, admissions or party-oaths and thus never with testimonies and presumptions.

184. It is important to take the limited scope of Article 8.9 CC into account. The aforementioned rules are only applicable for the proof of bilateral juridical acts (other facts may be proven with testimonies and presumptions), only for proof between parties, only as far as parties did not contract otherwise and only in case none of the parties can call upon one of the many exceptions to this rule.[250] The exclusion of other probative instruments is also limited to testimonies and presumptions. Consequentially, admissions and party-oaths are not excluded.

2. Legal Exceptions on Article 8.9 of the Civil Code

185. Article 8.10 CC specifies that unilateral legal acts can be proven with all means of proof.

186. Article 8.9 CC must not be taken into account in commercial cases, where proof is open (*see* No. 150 *supra*) (Article 8.11 CC).

187. According to Article 8.13 CC, the rules of Article 8.9 do not apply in case there is a beginning of written proof (*begin van bewijs door geschrift/ commencement de preuve par écrit*), i.e., any written document which can be attributed to the party contesting the allegated juridical act and which makes the allegated legal act likely (Article 8.1, 7° CC). Examples of a beginning of written proof are a signed document which breaches Article 8.20 CC (*see* No. 175 *supra*), a letter, an

250. *Ibid.*, 189–190.

advertisement, or a computer outprint, an SMS, a WhatsApp. As soon as there is a beginning of written proof, it can be completed with testimonies and presumptions, in which case this probative instrument obtains the same probative effect as an act.[251]

188. Article 8.12 CC states an exception to the general rule in every case where it was materially or morally impossible for the creditor to obtain a written proof of the obligation concluded towards him. The court decides whether or not there was a situation of impossibility, which must be proven by the person calling upon this exception (proof by all legal means, seeing how this is a fact). *Material impossibility* is present when the creditor could not think about demanding a written document because of practical circumstances.[252] *Moral impossibility* refers to cases where the nature of the relationship between parties (e.g., spouses) made it impossible to ask for a written document. The existence of the relationship is however not enough to decide upon a moral impossibility. It must elaborately be explained and proven. Finally, *impossibility due to a certain and general usage* concerns situations where the court recognises that a certain and general usage exists not to draw up any written document, e.g., between a doctor and his patient.

Article 8.12, alinea 2 CC extends the exception of this article to cases where a creditor lost the documents which served as written proof because of unforeseen incident caused by irresistible force, e.g., when parties confided a signed instrument to a notary, who then lost it. Irresistible force must be proven by the party calling upon this article.

189. Article 8.14 CC provides that third parties can prove a juridical act by all means of proof. They can also prove above and against an act by all means. Inversely, also parties can prove against third parties by all means, safe for the proof of the date of an act.

3. Hierarchy of Probative Instruments and Their Probative Effect

190. Judicial and extrajudicial admissions and decisive party-oaths top the hierarchy. They have a legal probative effect and are always allowed, even against acts, except for cases of *openbare orde/ordre public*. No proof is possible against them. Yet, the purely oral admission merely is admitted when proof with all legal means of proof is admitted (Article 8.31, al. 1 CC).

191. The following probative instruments with a legal probative effect are next in the hierarchy. Proof against them is allowed in certain cases. Acts (authentic acts and acts under private signature) are equal among each other, except for the authentic mentions in authentic acts. Proof against them is possible according to the rules

251. *Ibid.*, 193.
252. *Ibid.*, 192–193.

of Article 8.9 CC. The legal presumptions come next. Refutable presumptions can be refuted, while irrefutable ones can only be contradicted by party-oaths and judicial admissions.

192. Probative instruments with an open probative effect come lowest in the hierarchy. The court has the full authority to decide whether or not to grant the instrument any probative effect and can evaluate proof against it freely. First, these are all written documents (except for acts) issued by the other party or which the other party appropriated himself. The beginning of written proof is included, although this specific instrument acquires the same probative effect as acts if it can be completed with testimonies and presumptions (Article 8.13 CC). Second, these are testimonies and factual presumptions, whose permissibility is governed by Articles 8.28 and 8.29 CC. According to this first article, when testimonies are allowed, factual presumptions must be as well. Both have the same probative effect. They cannot prove juridical acts between parties, unless the worth of said acts is no more than EUR 3.500. However, they can be used for facts which are not juridical acts, proof by and against third parties, proof in case of one of the exceptions on the rule of Article 8.9 CC and as a completion of a beginning of written proof.

Chapter 2. Conditions of Substantive Validity

193. Article 1108 OCC enumerates the four conditions for a contract to be valid: capacity of the parties (*handelingsbekwaamheid/capacité*), meeting of minds, cause (*oorzaak/cause*) and object (*voorwerp/object*). In principle, these same conditions are applicable to other juridical acts as well.[253] Their presence is generally assessed at the conclusion of the contract, although a judge might take elements of proof anterior to its conclusion into account.[254] However, where object is concerned, the jurisprudence also evaluates its existence during the contract (*see* No. 233 *infra*). This is only exceptionally the case for the cause (*see* No. 223 *infra*). The four conditions of substantive validity will be discussed in this chapter.[255]

§1. Capacity of the Parties

I. Capacity to Hold Rights and Capacity to Participate in Legal Transactions

194. First and foremost, one's legal capacity must not be confused with one's factual capacity. Factual capacity answers the question of whether a person is physically able to commit a certain material (e.g., writing) or juridical act (e.g., are they mentally able to give an informed consent), or whether they are accountable for their faults, i.e., whether they have the actual ability to realise the effects of their actions and to control them.[256] Legal capacity concerns both the capacity to hold rights and owe duties and the capacity to participate in legal transactions, i.e., the legal possibility to exercise these rights and perform these duties themselves.[257] Both are legal categories, as opposed to one's practical capacity (i.e., their being physically able to act in a certain way).

---

253. S. Stijns, *Leerboek Verbintenissenrecht 1* (Brugge: die Keure, 2016), 81.
254. Cass. 11 Apr. 1991, *Arr.Cass.* 1990-91, 822, *Pas.* 1991, 726 & *R.W.* 1993-94, 1064, note; Cass. 11 Oct. 1991, *T.R.V.* 1992, 83, note P. Van Hoogten; Cass. 24 Sep. 2007, *Arr.Cass.* 2007, 1743, *Pas.* 2007, 1609, *RW* 2009-10, 1609, *RW* 2009-10, 1640, note E. Nordin, *TBBR* 2009, 216, note D. Philippe and *JLMB* 2008, 1171 en S. Stijns, *Leerboek Verbintenissenrecht 1* (Brugge: die Keure, 2016), 81.
255. For more on conditions of substantive validity and nullity, *see*: F. Peeraer, T. Hick & F. Auvray, 'Nieuw verbintenissenrecht: de totstandkoming van het contract (dynamisch en statisch bekeken)' in S. Stijns (ed.) *Themis 108 – Verbintenissenrecht* (Brugge: die Keure, 2019); J.M. Smits & S. Stijns (eds) *Totstandkoming van de overeenkomst naar Belgisch en Nederlands recht* (Antwerp: Intersentia, 2002); E. Swaenepoel, *Toetsing van het contractuele evenwicht* (Antwerp: Intersentia, 2011); R. Van Ransbeek (ed.), *Wilsgebreken* (Brugge: die Keure, 2006).
256. F. Swennen, *Het personen- en familierecht* (Mortsel: Intersentia, 2019), 150–151.
257. S. Stijns, *Leerboek Verbintenissenrecht 1* (Brugge: die Keure, 2016), 101–102; P. Wéry, *Droit des obligations, I, Théorie générale du contrat* (Brussels: Larcier, 2011), 260.

II. Categories of People Incapable of Holding Rights

195. In principle, every person, regardless of their age and sex, is equally capable of holding rights, as every person has the possibility to carry both rights and duties. A complete incapacity to hold rights would be impossible, as it would imply the denial of one's very personality. The two exceptions to this rule involve a partial incapacity.

A. *Aliens*

196. Although aliens are capable of holding rights, some rights are solely granted to Belgian citizens. There is a distinction to be made between aliens who are citizens of the European Union (EU), aliens from outside the EU who reside legally in Belgium, and illegal immigrants.

197. The first two categories benefit rights almost equal to those Belgian citizens enjoy. The most important difference is the right to vote, which is limited to municipal elections,[258] plus elections for the European Parliament for EU citizens.[259] However, these aliens will often have to file administrative requests to obtain the rights which are automatically granted to Belgian citizens, e.g., the requirement of a so-called 'labour-card' to be allowed to work in Belgium for non-European aliens.[260]

---

258. *Omzendbrief/Circulaire* of 30 Jan. 2006 *betreffende de inschrijving van vreemdelingen die in België verblijven en die geen onderdanen zijn van een lidstaat van de Europese Unie als kiezers voor de gewone vernieuwing van de gemeenteraden/Circulaire relative à l'inscription des citoyens étrangers qui résident en Belgique et qui ne sont pas ressortissants d'un Etat membre de l'Union européenne comme électeurs en prévision du renouvellement ordinaire des conseils communaux, Belgian Official Gazette* 3 Feb. 2006.

259. Article 39, para. 1 of the Charter of Fundamental Rights of the European Union, *Pub.* C 364, 18 Dec. 2000; Council Directive 93/109/EC of 6 Dec. 1993 laying down detailed arrangements for the exercise of the right to vote and stand as a candidate in elections to the European Parliament for citizens of the Union residing in a Member State of which they are not nationals, in *Official Journal of the European Communities (OJEC).* 30 Dec. 1993, No L 329, pp. 34–38; Law of 11 Apr. 1994 (*Wet tot wijziging van de wet van 23 maart 1989 betreffende de verkiezing van het Europese Parlement en tot uitvoering van richtlijn nr. 93/109/E.G. d.d. 6 december 1993 van de Raad van de Europese Gemeenschappen/Loi modifiant la loi du 23 mars 1989 relative à l'élection du Parlement européen et portant exécution de la directive du Conseil des Communautés européennes No. 93/109/C.E. du 6 décembre 1993*), *Belgian Official Gazette* 16 Apr. 1994; *Omzendbrief/Circulaire* of 24 Dec. 2008 *betreffende de inschrijving van de burgers van de lidstaten van de Europese Unie, die in België verblijven, als kiezers en, in voorkomend geval, als kandidaten voor de verkiezing van het Europees Parlement op zondag 7 juni 2009, Belgian Official Gazette* 12 januari 2009.

260. *Koninklijk besluit* of 9 Jun. 1999 *houdende de uitvoering van de wet van 30 april 1999 betreffende de tewerkstelling van buitenlandse werknemers/Arrêté royal portant exécution de la loi du 30 avril 1999 relative à l'occupation des travailleurs étrangers, Belgian Official Gazette* 26 juni 1999.

198. The rights of illegal immigrants are much more limited. For example, instead of the extremely vast coverage of the national health insurance legal residents enjoy, only urgent medical care must be provided to them,[261] and, some exceptions aside, they are not allowed to work.[262]

B. Certain Categories of Criminally Condemned Persons

199. In case of a criminal condemnation, the sentence may deprive the condemned of some specific rights, either for life or for a shorter period. These are, e.g., the right to exercise public offices, services or functions, the right to be elected, the right to wear honorary signs or have a nobility title, the right to be in a jury or to be a specialist in court, to act as a witness for written acts or to testify in court, to become a guardian or curator, to exercise the office of legal counsel or conservator, the right to make, alter, repair, wear or transport a weapon, the right to serve in the armed forces, and the right to vote.[263]

III. Categories of People Incapable of Participating in Legal Transactions

200. The general rule is that every person is considered capable of participating in legal transactions. However, in order to protect certain categories of people, there are some specific exceptions to this rule, namely for minors and factually incapables. Given the fundamentality of the principle, these exceptions must be stated by law, and be subjected to a limitative interpretation.[264]

A. Minors

201. Although a minor holds every right and duty another person would, he cannot exercise most of his rights.[265] This incapacity is general; i.e., the incapacity to participate in legal transactions applies to all legal transactions. The incapacity is

261. Article 57 of the Organic Law of 8 Jul. 1976 (*Organieke wet betreffende de openbare centra voor maatschappelijk welzijn/Loi organique des centres publics d'aide sociale*), *Belgian Official Gazette* 5 Aug. 1976.
262. Law of 30 Apr. 1999 (*Wet betreffende de tewerkstelling van buitenlandse werknemers/Loi relative à l'occupation des travailleurs étrangers), Belgian Official Gazette* 21 May 1999.
263. Articles 31–34 of the Criminal Code (*Strafwetboek/Code Pénal* of 8 Jun. 1867).
264. S. Stijns, *Leerboek Verbintenissenrecht 1* (Brugge: die Keure, 2016), 101; F. Swennen, *Het personen- en familierecht* (Mortsel: Intersentia, 2019), 151; T. Vansweevelt & B. Weyts, 'Geldigheidsvereisten van de overeenkomst', in T. Vansweevelt and B. Weyts, *Handboek Verbintenissenrecht* (Antwerpen: Intersentia, 2019), 211.
265. S. Stijns, *Leerboek Verbintenissenrecht 1* (Brugge: die Keure, 2016), 102; T. Vansweevelt & B. Weyts, 'Geldigheidsvereisten van de overeenkomst', in T. Vansweevelt and B. Weyts, *Handboek Verbintenissenrecht* (Antwerpen: Intersentia, 2019), 213.

also complete, meaning that the minor cannot act himself but has to be represented.[266] This general and complete incapacity to participate in legal transactions however needs to be nuanced.

202. It is generally accepted that minors can validly conclude casual legal transactions, such as buying a loaf of bread or acts which do not alter their patrimony. It is assumed that minors do not require a specific protection for this type of act.[267] Based on the same assumption, some legal provisions limit the minors' capacity to act. Article 904 OCC provides that a minor older than 16 years can administer 50% of the part of his patrimony he could administer if he was adult by testament. In other cases, an approval of a parent or the guardian will be required for the legal act to be validly concluded. To validly conclude a contract of employment, the minor can do so on his own provided he has been authorised by either his parents or his guardian.[268]

203. As a matter of principle, acts of administration (*daden van beheer/acte de gestion*)[269] taken by a minor are null. Yet, a difference must be made depending on whether or not the minor has reached the age of discretion. If the minor has not yet reached the age of discretion, any legal action he takes is null by virtue of law. If he had reached the age of discretion, nullity depends on whether or not the minor has been a victim of *laesio* (*benadeling/lesion*) (Articles 1305–1306 CC). Only in case of *laesio*, an act of administration will be annullable, be it an intrinsic or extrinsic *laesio*. *Laesio* is intrinsic if there is a disparity between the obligations of the parties. *Laesio* is extrinsic if the quid pro quo as such is acceptable, but not in the specific circumstances of the minor in question. Think about a minor who pays a ski-vacation for himself and three friends for a price of EUR 3.000.[270] An act of disposal (*daad van beschikking/acte de disposition*),[271] however, will in all cases be voidable (Article 410 OCC).

204. The acts taken by a minor that can be voidable are always relatively void. That implies that the minor can confirm the act he has done and the other party cannot invoke the nullity of that act (Article 1225 OCC).[272] As mentioned here above (*see* No. 203 *supra*), the judge must verify whether or not the minor has been prejudiced by the acts of administration the minor has committed if he has reached the

266. *Ibid.*
267. *Ibid.*
268. Article 43 of the Law of 3 Jul. 1978 on Labour Contracts (*Arbeidsovereenkomstenwet/Loi relative aux contrats de travail*), *Belgian Official Gazette* 22 Aug. 1978.
269. E. Dirix, B. Tilleman & S. Lierman (eds), *De Valks Juridisch woordenboek* (Antwerp-Oxford: Intersentia, 2018), 113.
270. F. Swennen, *Het personen- en familierecht* (Mortsel: Intersentia, 2019), 160–161; T. Vansweevelt & B. Weyts, 'Geldigheidsvereisten van de overeenkomst', in T. Vansweevelt and B. Weyts, *Handboek Verbintenissenrecht* (Antwerpen: Intersentia, 2019), 214.
271. E. Dirix, B. Tilleman & S. Lierman (eds), *De Valks Juridisch woordenboek* (Antwerp-Oxford: Intersentia, 2018), 113.
272. S. Stijns, *Leerboek Verbintenissenrecht 1* (Brugge: die Keure, 2016), 103; T. Vansweevelt & B. Weyts, 'Geldigheidsvereisten van de overeenkomst', in T. Vansweevelt and B. Weyts, *Handboek Verbintenissenrecht* (Antwerpen: Intersentia, 2019), 215.

age of discretion. If he has not reached the age of discretion or has committed an act of disposal, the judge must pronounce the nullity asked by the minor.[273]

205. Some minors get the status of emancipated minors (*ontvoogde minderjarigen/mineur émancipé*).[274] This concerns minors who are considered to require lesser protection due to the maturity they have reached. If they get emancipated, they are allowed to take a limited number of acts. A minor can be emancipated if he gets married (Article 476 OCC) or if the family tribunal pronounces his emancipation. The emancipation will always be decided in the best interest of the minor.[275]

B. Certain Categories of Persons with a Mental Disorder

206. Since a legal reform in 2013,[276] Belgian law knows a generalised framework for factually incapables. Given their factual incapability to take legal acts, they have become statutorily protected. Among these factually incapables figure those whose (mental)health does not allow to act according to their best interest and prodigals.[277]

§2. The Meeting of Minds

I. Concept and Scope

207. A valid contract requires the meeting of minds of *all* the parties to this contract.[278] This meeting of minds requires an expression of will by all parties, which may be either explicit or silent.[279] It is explicit when it is expressed by a behaviour intended to be an expression of will. It is silent or implicit when it is not established

---

273. S. Stijns, *Leerboek Verbintenissenrecht 1* (Brugge: die Keure, 2016), 103.
274. E. Dirix, B. Tilleman & S. Lierman (eds), *De Valks Juridisch woordenboek* (Antwerp-Oxford: Intersentia, 2018), 321.
275. S. Stijns, *Leerboek Verbintenissenrecht 1* (Brugge: die Keure, 2016), 102; F. Swennen, *Het personen- en familierecht* (Mortsel: Intersentia, 2019), 182 et seq.; T. Vansweevelt &B. Weyts, 'Geldigheidsvereisten van de overeenkomst', in T. Vansweevelt and B. Weyts, *Handboek Verbintenissenrecht* (Antwerpen: Intersentia, 2019), 215.
276. Law of 17 Mar. 2013 (Wet tot hervorming van de regelingen inzake onbekwaamheid en tot instelling van een nieuwe beschermingsstatus die strookt met de menselijke waardigheid), *Belgian Official Gazette* 14 Jun. 2013.
277. F. Swennen, *Het personen- en familierecht* (Mortsel: Intersentia, 2019), 185 et seq.; T. Vansweevelt & B. Weyts, 'Geldigheidsvereisten van de overeenkomst', in T. Vansweevelt and B. Weyts, *Handboek Verbintenissenrecht* (Antwerpen: Intersentia, 2019), 216.
278. S. Stijns, *Leerboek Verbintenissenrecht 1* (Brugge: die Keure, 2016), 81; W. van Gerven en A. Van Oevelen, *Verbintenissenrecht* (Leuven: Acco, 2015), 73; T. Vansweevelt & B. Weyts, « De totstandkoming van de overeenkomst » in T. Vansweevelt and B. Weyts, *Handboek Verbintenissenrecht* (Antwerpen: Intersentia, 2019), 173–174.
279. R. Dekkers & A. Verbeke, *Handboek Burgerlijk Recht*, III (Antwerp: Intersentia: 2007), 23; S. Stijns, *Leerboek Verbintenissenrecht 1* (Brugge: die Keure, 2016), 81; W. van Gerven en A. Van Oevelen, *Verbintenissenrecht* (Leuven: Acco, 2015), 109; P. Wéry, *Droit des obligations, I, Théorie*

by such behaviour, yet it can be deduced from a behaviour (an action or inaction) which could not be interpreted otherwise and necessarily implies the will to contract.[280] The expression of will must regard all the essential and substantial elements of the contract.[281] Elements of a contract are 'essential' when they are decisive for the acceptance of the contract (e.g., price and object in the case of sale of goods). 'Substantial' elements are secondary elements which, objectively, may not seem of essential importance, but which were elevated to be decisive parts of their contract by the parties.[282] Hereinafter the term 'essential element' will refer to both types of elements unless stated otherwise.

208. What happens in case of discrepancy between a party's actual will (inner will) and his declared will (outer will)? If the discrepancy is unintentional, e.g., because of a slip of the tongue or the pen, the contract is considered null.[283] However, the possibly harsh consequences of this principle are somewhat softened by the doctrine of appearance (*vertrouwensleer/théorie de l'apparence*). According to this doctrine, an apparent situation can have legal consequences towards third parties if they could reasonably believe that the apparent situation corresponded to reality.[284] Although jurisprudence has not specified whether this doctrine can be applied against whoever creates an apparent situation, it is steadily accepted in case of apparent mandate (*see* No. 32 *supra*).[285]

209. Matters differ if the discrepancy is intended by the parties. Simulation (*veinzing/simulation*) aims at the situation where parties willingly pretend that they have a certain contract or other juridical act in public while they secretly contract otherwise. Thus, parties conclude two contracts: the apparent or public contract (*schijnovereenkomst/acte apparent*) and the hidden contract or counter letter (*tegenbrief/contre-lettre*). Article 1321 OCC states that 'counter letters are effective only between the contracting parties; they are not effective against third parties'. Thus, the contracting parties are bound towards each other by the hidden contract.[286] This contract is proven by the counter letter. However, the hidden contract is not opposable to third parties. Third parties may choose to accept the existence of

---

générale du contrat (Brussels: Larcier, 2011), 223; B. Weyts & T. Vansweevelt, 'Geldigheidsvereisten van de overeenkomst', in B. Weyts and T. Vansweevelt, *Handboek Verbintenissenrecht* (Mortsle, Intersentia, 2019), 174.

280. S. Stijns, *Leerboek Verbintenissenrecht 1* (Brugge: die Keure, 2016), 81–82.

281. Cass. 12 Jun. 1980, *A.C.* 1979-80, 1248 and *RW* 1981-82, 937; S. Stijns, *Leerboek Verbintenissenrecht 1* (Brugge: die Keure, 2016), 83.

282. Or, in other terms 'essentialised' – *see* P. Wéry, *Droit des obligations, I, Théorie générale du contrat* (Brussels: Larcier, 2011), 156.

283. S. Stijns, *Leerboek Verbintenissenrecht 1* (Brugge: die Keure, 2016), 86.

284. E. Dirix, B. Tilleman & S. Lierman (eds), *De Valks Juridisch woordenboek* (Antwerp-Oxford: Intersentia, 2018), 481.

285. *See* however Cass. 22 Feb. 2018, *RW* 2018-19, 296; *TBBR* 2019, 38, note B. Weyts and N. Portugaels; *TBH* 2018, 495; *TBO* 2018, 309; *T.Verz.* 2019, 373.

286. L. Cornelis, *Algemene theorie van de verbintenis* (Antwerp: Intersentia, 2000), No. 42; H. De Page, *Traité élémentaire de droit civil belge*, III (Brussels: Bruylant, 1967), No. 626; S. Stijns, *Leerboek Verbintenissenrecht 1* (Brugge: die Keure, 2016), 252; W. van Gerven en A. Van Oevelen, *Verbintenissenrecht* (Leuven: Acco, 2015), 138; P. Wéry, *Droit des obligations, I, Théorie générale du contrat* (Brussels: Larcier, 2011), 225. However, this seems to have been contradicted in a recent

the apparent contract or of the hidden contract.[287] The possibility to call upon the apparent contract is an application of the theory of appearance in the relationship between contracting parties and third parties. This means that the third party may, if he wishes to, consider the apparent situation instead of the actual one, provided that he acted in good faith and believed in the apparent situation at the time of his own actions. However, he may also choose to call upon the actual, hidden contract because this contract corresponds to the will of the parties.[288]

II. Defects of Consents

210. The most common difficulties when it comes to the meeting of minds are the defects of consent (*wilsgebreken/vices du consentement*). According to Article 1109 OCC, the will to contract is invalid in case of mistake (*dwaling/erreur*), deceit (*bedrog/dol*), and violence (*geweld/violence*). Article 1118 adds *laesio* (*benadeling/lesion*) to this list, although it is only considered a defect of consent under certain stringent conditions, or when it can be considered qualified lesion.[289] Without these circumstances, the will would have been different or altogether absent. In case of defects of consent, the contract is affected by relative nullity, which can only be called upon by the party who was victim of the mistake, deceit, violence or *laesio* (*see* Nos 211 et seq. *infra*).

A. *Mistake*

211. Mistake *(dwaling/erreur)* is a defect of consent whereby a party unwillingly has an erroneous perception of reality.[290] Three requirements must be met:[291] (1) the mistake must be present at the time of the conclusion of the contract, (2) it must be essential,[292] and (3) it must be excusable, which means that a reasonable

judgment of the Court of Cassation (Cass. 29 Jan. 2010, C.08.0267.F, *J.T.* 2010, 389) which states that an authentic act or an act under private signature constitutes proof between parties, even if this act is fictive.

287. Cass. 11 Dec. 1987, *Arr.Cass.* 1988, 481 and *Pas.* 1988, 449.
288. S. Stijns, *Leerboek Verbintenissenrecht 1* (Brugge: die Keure, 2015), 253; P. Wéry, *Droit des obligations, I, Théorie générale du contrat* (Brussels: Larcier, 2011), 877.
289. R. Dekkers & A. Verbeke, *Handboek Burgerlijk Recht*, III (Antwerp: Intersentia: 2007), 26.
290. E. Dirix, B. Tilleman & S. Lierman (eds), *De Valks Juridisch woordenboek* (Antwerp-Oxford: Intersentia, 2018), 135; S. Stijns, *Leerboek Verbintenissenrecht 1* (Brugge: die Keure, 2016), 87; T. Vansweevelt & B. Weyts, «Geldigheidsvereisten van de overeenkomst» in T. Vansweevelt and B. Weyts, *Handboek Verbintenissenrecht* (Antwerpen: Intersentia, 2019), 181.
291. S. Stijns, *Leerboek Verbintenissenrecht 1* (Brugge: die Keure, 2016), 87; P. Wéry, *Droit des obligations, I, Théorie générale du contrat* (Brussels: Larcier, 2011), 231. B. Weyts and T. Vansweevelt add a fourth requirement, namely that mistake has not been contractually excluded. B. Weyts & T. Vansweevelt, 'Geldigheidsvereisten van de overeenkomst', in B. Weyts and T. Vansweevelt, *Handboek Verbintenissenrecht* (Mortsle, Intersentia, 2019), 182.
292. Cass. 3 Mar. 1967, *Arr.Cass.* 1967, 829 and *Pas.* 1967, 811; Cass. 27 Oct. 1995, *Arr.Cass.* 1995, 920, *Pas.* 1995, 950, *RW* 1996-97, 298 and *J.T.* 1996, 61; Cass. 24 Sep. 2007, *RW* 2009-10, 1735; Cass. 29 Apr. 2019, C.18.0439.N, www.juportal.be. For a definition of essential elements, *see* No. 207 *supra*.

person in similar circumstances would have made the same mistake.[293] The mistake might as well concern a matter of fact as a matter of law. However, due to the requirement of excusability, and the principle that everyone is considered to know the law, a mistake on a matter of law will generally not be accepted as a defect of consent.[294] The jurisprudence is extremely strict on this matter, considering a mistake inexcusable even if the party who made it had sought advice from legal counsels, who made a mistake in the given advice.[295]

212. The existence of the mistake must be proven by the party who made it. As the proof regards an actual situation (and not a legal one), every legal means of proof may be used. In case the mistake was caused by a precontractual fault by the other party, the party who made the mistake will be entitled to demand complementary damages if the nullity does not suffice to compensate for all suffered damages. It is also possible for him to accept the damages and to decide not to pursue nullity (*see infra* No. 236).

B. Misrepresentation (Deceit)

213. Deceit (*bedrog/dol*) is a deceptive action, declaration or omission by a contract party with the intention to convince the other party to contract.[296] Following requirements must be met. First, Article 1116 OCC requires the use of artifices. This notion is interpreted broadly, and may consist of actions (e.g., falsification of documents), declarations (e.g., lies, exaggerations), or omissions (in case the party had the obligation to speak and willingly remained silent[297]).[298] Second, Article 1116 OCC prescribes that the deceit must be committed by the other party. In other words, deceit committed by a third party will not lead to nullity. However, deceit committed by a representative of a party may be attributed to this party.[299] It is also possible for a party to be an accomplice in the deceit of a third party, in which case

---

293. Cass. 28 Jun. 1996, *A.C.* 1996, 664, *Pas.* 1996, 714 and *J.L.M.B.* 1997, 12; Cass. 20 Apr. 1978, *Arr.Cass.* 1978, 960 and *Pas.* 1978, 950; Cass. 10 Apr. 1975, *Arr.Cass.* 1975, 871, *Pas.* 1975, 785 and *R.C.J.B.* 1978, 198, note by M. Coipel 'L'erreur de droit excusable'; Cass. 6 Jan. 1944, *Arr.Cass.* 1944, 66 & *Pas.* 1944, 133; S. Stijns, *Leerboek Verbintenissenrecht 1* (Brugge: die Keure, 2016), 87.
294. S. Stijns, *Leerboek Verbintenissenrecht 1* (Brugge: die Keure, 2016), 90.
295. Cass. 10 Apr. 1975, *A.C.* 1975, 871, *Pas.* 1975, 785 & *R.C.J.B.* 1978, 198, note by M. Coipel 'L'erreur de droit excusable'.
296. S. Stijns, *Leerboek Verbintenissenrecht 1* (Brugge: die Keure, 2016), 91; T. Vansweevelt & B. Weyts, «Geldigheidsvereisten van de overeenkomst» in T. Vansweevelt and B. Weyts, *Handboek Verbintenissenrecht* (Antwerpen: Intersentia, 2019), 193.
297. Cass. 8 Jun. 1978, *A.C.* 1978, 1189, *Pas.* 1978, 1156, *RW* 1978-79, 1777 and *R.C.J.B.* 1979, 525, note by J.P. Masson 'Les fourberies silencieuses'; Cass. 21 Apr. 1988, *T.B.H.* 1991, 203, note by C. Jassogne; Cass. 16 Sep. 1999, *A.C.* 1999, 1116, *Pas.* 1990, 1160, *RW* 2001-02, 414, *T.B.B.R.* 2000, 688 and *A.J.T.* 2000-01, 787; Cass. AR C.04.0523.F 30 Jun. 2005, www.cass.be.
298. S. Stijns, *Leerboek Verbintenissenrecht 1* (Brugge: die Keure, 2016), 91–92; P. Wéry, *Droit des obligations, I, Théorie générale du contrat* (Brussels: Larcier, 2011), 243.
299. Cass. 9 Nov. 1987, *A.C.* 1987-88, 318, *Pas.* 1988, 298, *T.R.V.* 1988, 355 and *J.L.M.B.* 1988, 43.

the requirement is met.[300] Third, the party who commits the deceit must have had the intention to deceive – the deceit must deliberately mislead the other party into giving his approval in order to obtain an advantage.[301] Article 1116 OCC explicitly states that bad faith is not presumed so that a party who claims to have been deceived has to prove the bad faith of the other party, which proof can be provided by all legal means.[302] Fourth and finally, Article 1116 requires for the deceit to be such that the deceived party would not have contracted without the use of artifices.

214. In other words, the deceit must be of overriding importance: the deceived party would not have agreed to the contract without the deceit.[303] Such deceit is called principal deceit (*hoofdbedrog/dol principal*). If the deceit only led the deceived party to contract under more onerous conditions than otherwise, it is called incidental or additional deceit (*incidenteel bedrog/dol incident*) and will only lead to damages in case of precontractual fault from the deceiving party. This distinction, which is sustained in jurisprudence,[304] is the object of criticism by a part of the doctrine.

215. If the deceit is proven, the deceived party can demand for the contract to be declared null. If the nullity does not suffice to indemnify the deceived party, he can demand complementary damages on account of precontractual fault, being the deceit by the deceiver. It is also possible for him to accept the damages and to decide not to pursue nullity (*see infra* No. 236). In case of incidental deceit, nullity will not be obtained, yet damages because of *culpa in contrahendo* remain possible. However, it is also possible to demand the cancellation of the contract if this is the best form of reparation in nature.[305]

C. Improper Pressure (Violence)

216. Violence *(geweld/violence)* is a defect of consent caused by the application of moral or physical violence, or the threat of such violence, against a contract party, his honour or patrimony (Article 1112 OCC), or against his spouse, or relatives in descending or ascending line (Article 1113 OCC).[306]

217. Violence must meet three requirements. First, according to Article 1112 OCC, it must create the immediate fear of a considerable threat. This means that the

---

300. H. De Page, *Traité élémentaire de droit civil belge,* I (Brussels, Bruylant, 1962), No. 54; L. Cornelis, *Algemene theorie van de verbintenis* (Antwerp, Intersentia, 2000), No. 47.
301. S. Stijns, *Leerboek verbintenissenrecht 1* (Brugge, die Keure, 2016), 91–92.
302. Cass. 25 Feb. 2000, *Arr.Cass.* 2000, 478, *Pas.* 2000, 473, *R. Cass.* 2000, 369 and *RW* 2002-03, 37.
303. S. Stijns, *Leerboek Verbintenissenrecht 1* (Brugge: die Keure, 2016), 93; P. Wéry, *Droit des obligations, I, Théorie générale du contrat* (Brussels: Larcier, 2011), 245.
304. Cass. 21 Apr. 1988, *T.B.H* 1991, 203; Cass. 10 Feb. 1983, *A.C.* 1982-83, 755 and *Pas.* 1983, 665.
305. S. Stijns, *Leerboek Verbintenissenrecht 1* (Brugge: die Keure, 2016), 94.
306. E. Dirix, B. Tilleman & S. Lierman (eds), *De Valks Juridisch woordenboek* (Antwerp-Oxford: Intersentia, 2018), 96; S. Stijns, *Leerboek Verbintenissenrecht 1* (Brugge: die Keure, 2016), 94; T. Vansweevelt & B. Weyts, «Geldigheidsvereisten van de overeenkomst» in T. Vansweevelt and B. Weyts, *Handboek Verbintenissenrecht* (Antwerpen: Intersentia, 2019), 199.

violence or the threat of violence must be such as to impress a reasonable person (objective criterion) in the same circumstances (subjective criterion).[307] Article 1112 OCC explicitly mentions that age, sex and social position are taken into account. The threat may concern the other party himself, yet may also be against any third person with whom he may have an affective relationship (this is broader than the categories summed up in Article 1113 OCC), his patrimony, or his honour, i.e., his physical, material or moral integrity.[308] Second, violence must be determining for the conclusion of the contract. Like with deceit, there is a distinction to be made between principal and incidental violence (*see* No. 214, *supra*). Third, violence must be illegitimate. Compulsion which originates from the normal exercise of one's rights or authority is not illegitimate and is not considered a defect of consent.[309] Article 1114 OCC states explicitly that the fear or respect of parents or other blood relatives in ascending line, without the exercise of violence, cannot be considered a sufficient reason for a contract's nullity. The doctrine has broadened this to other authority figures, such as a teacher or employer. Nevertheless, violence in the relationship between employer and employee has been the subject of much jurisprudence. For example, an employer who threatens his employee with summary dismissal does not automatically commit violence.[310] It will however be considered violence in case the employer threatens to file a criminal complaint about facts that either did not happen or are not proportional to a criminal complaint, in order to convince an employee to resign voluntarily. The determining criterion is the reasonable behaviour of the employer.[311]

218. Violence must be proven by its victim, with all the legal means of proof. The ensuing nullity is relative, and may be complemented with damages.[312] In case the violence was exercised by a third party, the victim can claim tort damages from this third party if he manages to prove the violence falls within the scope of tort. Nullity of the contract will no longer be claimable in case the contract has been validated after the violence ended (Article 1115 OCC).

D. *Gross Disparity* (Laesio)

219. Lesion occurs when, in an onerous and commutative contract, the mutually contracted obligations are severely disproportionate. The economic disproportion must have been present at the conclusion of the contract.[313] Belgian law does not regard lesion as a general defect of consent, except for certain cases which have

307. S. Stijns, *Leerboek Verbintenissenrecht 1* (Brugge: die Keure, 2016), 95.
308. *Ibid.*, 95.
309. *Ibid.*, 96.
310. Cass. 7 Nov. 1977, *A.C.*1978, 288, *Pas.* 1978, 275, *R.W.* 1977-78, 1345 & *J.T.T.* 1978, 45.
311. Cass. 24 Mar. 2003, *J.L.M.B.* 2004, 1704.
312. S. Stijns, *Leerboek Verbintenissenrecht 1* (Brugge: die Keure, 2016), 98.
313. H. De Page, *Trait élémentaire de droit civil belge,* I (Brussels: Bruylant, 1962), No. 67; S. Stijns, W. van Gerven & P. Wéry, '*Chronique*', J.T. 1996, nr. 63; T. Vansweevelt & B. Weyts, «Geldigheidsvereisten van de overeenkomst» in T. Vansweevelt and B. Weyts, *Handboek Verbintenissenrecht* (Antwerpen: Intersentia, 2019), 205.

been specified by law (Article 1118 OCC). These are disparity for more than 7/12th in case of sale of immovables (Article 1674 OCC), disparity for more than 1/4th in case of division (Articles 887 and 1079 OCC), in case of *societas leoninas*, which is a partnership deed stipulating that either the whole of the benefits are allocated to one partner, either this partner is exempted from any share in the losses,[314] and in case of juridical acts committed by minors (Articles 1305 et al. OCC).

220. Qualified lesion (*gekwalificeerde benadeling/lésion qualifiée*) is a concept developed by jurisprudence and doctrine.[315] It can only be called upon if there is a severe disproportion within an onerous and commutative contract, as a consequence of abuse by the stronger party of circumstances of need, weakness or passion of the weaker party, or of abuse of their own position of power.[316] Consequently, three requirements must be met. First, there must be a severe disproportion between the mutual obligations, i.e., an actual or future harmful effect on one's patrimony.[317] Second, there must be abuse of the actual circumstances of inferiority of the aggrieved party, which may consist of personal circumstances, e.g., physical, moral or financial needs, inexperience or of an economical or financial superiority of the party committing the abuse, e.g., a monopoly position.[318] Finally, the abuse must have been determining: without it, the contract would not have been concluded, or it would have been concluded under more favourable conditions. Jurisprudence makes no distinction between principal and incidental lesion.[319]

221. The majority of the doctrine grounds the theory of qualified lesion on *culpa in contrahendo*, to be sanctioned as tort (*see* No. 77 *supra*), which implies the allocation of damages to the victim.[320] As such, the contract remains valid, although it could be nullified or moderated as a form of restitution in nature.[321]

---

314. Article 4:2 Companies and Associations Code (*Wetboek van Vennootschappen en verenigingen/Code des sociétés et des associations*) of 23 Mar. 2019, *Belgian Official Gazette* 4 Apr. 2019.
315. Cass. 9 Nov. 2012, *Arr. Cass.* 2012, 2491; *Not.Fisc.M.* 2013, 117, note H. Casman, *Pas.* 2012, 2183; *Rev.trim.dr.fam.* 2014, 833; *RW* 2012-13, 1415, note E. Adriaens; *TBBR* 2013, 168; *T.Fam.* 2013, 131; V. Hulpiau; *T.Not.* 2013, 356. *See* further S. Stijns, *Leerboek Verbintenissenrecht 1* (Brugge: die Keure, 2016), 97; P. Wéry, *Droit des obligations, I, Théorie générale du contrat* (Brussels: Larcier, 2011), 256.
316. S. Stijns, *Leerboek Verbintenissenrecht 1* (Brugge: die Keure, 2016), 98; L. Cornelis, *Algemene theorie van de verbintenis* (Antwerp: Intersentia, 2000), nr. 54 et al.; W. van Gerven en A. Van Oevelen, *Verbintenissenrecht* (Leuven: Acco, 2015), 125.
317. S. Stijns, *Leerboek Verbintenissenrecht 1* (Brugge: die Keure, 2016), 98–99.
318. *Ibid.*, 99.
319. *Ibid.* For more on this subject, also *see* E. Swaenepoel, *Toetsing van het contractuele evenwicht* (Antwerp: Intersentia, 2011).
320. P. Wéry, *Droit des obligations, I, Théorie générale du contrat* (Brussels: Larcier, 2011), 258.
321. S. Stijns, *Leerboek Verbintenissenrecht 1* (Brugge: die Keure, 2016), 100; P. Wéry, *Droit des obligations, I, Théorie générale du contrat* (Brussels: Larcier, 2011), 258.

§3. Cause

222. In order to be valid, a contract requires a cause (*oorzaak/cause*), which has to be lawful.[322] Although the requirement of cause has been the object of dissent within doctrine for a long time,[323] several recent judgments of the Court of Cassation confirm its necessity and define it as a dual concept.[324] The external cause (or the lawful cause) is the determining reason why a contract party decided to obligate himself. The internal cause (or object-cause) assesses the judicial, economic or social reasons for the parties to contract, i.e., its reason to exist or usefulness.[325] In the case of unilateral contracts, the internal cause is the intention to give (*animus donandi*). In the case of bilateral contracts (*see* No. 59 *supra*), the internal cause of one party's obligations is the other party's obligations.[326]

223. According to Article 1131 OCC, an obligation without cause, or with a false cause, cannot have consequences. This absence of cause may either be internal (if it has no use, no reason to exist) or external (in case its determining reason is erroneous). The sanction for the absence of cause is relative nullity (*see* No. 236 *infra*). The existence of cause must be determined at the moment the contract comes into being.[327] Consequentially the disappearance of cause after the conclusion of the contract does not affect its validity.

224. According to Article 1133 OCC, a contract's cause must be lawful. This means that the reason why the contract was concluded may not be contrary to rules of *openbare orde* or mandatory laws.[328] The sanction for a cause contrary to *openbare orde* is absolute nullity, while that for one contrary to mandatory law is relative nullity (*see* No. 236 *infra*).

225. Both innocent and guilty parties can demand the nullity of the contract. However, the innocent party can choose to invoke the '*in pari causa turpitudinis cessat repetitio*' principle (literally: 'in case of equal shameful behaviour, reclamations towards each other are impossible') to refuse the restitution of what was already performed. Furthermore, the behaviour of the guilty party may cause his

322. *See* Arts 1108, 1131 and 1133 OCC.
323. *See* W. van Gerven en A. Van Oevelen, *Verbintenissenrecht* (Leuven: Acco, 2015), 134; P. Wéry, *Droit des obligations, I, Théorie générale du contrat* (Brussels: Larcier, 2011), 280; T. Vansweevelt & B. Weyts, «Geldigheidsvereisten van de overeenkomst» in T. Vansweevelt and B. Weyts, *Handboek Verbintenissenrecht* (Antwerpen: Intersentia, 2019), 247.
324. Cass. 24 Sep, 2007, *RW* 2009-10, 1640 and *J.L.M.B.* 2008, 1171; Cass. 14 Mar. 2008, *RW* 2010-11, 21; Cass. 12 Dec. 2008, *RW* 2008-09, 1690; Cass. 7 May 2020, C.19.0423.N, *NJW* 2020, 500, note M. Meirlaen, *TBO* 2020, 355.
325. S. Stijns, *Leerboek Verbintenissenrecht 1* (Brugge: die Keure, 2016), 111–112.
326. E. Dirix, 'De meerpartijenovereenkomst', *T.P.R.* 1983, 777; I. Samoy, 'Pijnpunten bij het opstellen van consortium- en andere overeenkomsten met meer dan twee partijen' in S. Stijns (ed.), *Themiscahier Verbintenissenrecht* (Brugge: die Keure, 2006–2007), 66.
327. Cass. 12 Dec. 2008, *RW* 2008-09, 1690.
328. Cass. 7 May 2020, C.19.0423.N, *NJW* 2020, nr. 424, 500, note M. Meirlaen, *TBO* 2020, 355; S. Stijns, *Leerboek Verbintenissenrecht 1* (Brugge: die Keure, 2016), 118.

precontractual liability, thus making him liable for damages if fault, loss and causal link can be proven (*see* Nos 130 ff. *supra*).[329]

226. Exceptions to the requirement of a cause are only possible in the specific cases accepted by legislation or international commercial practices.[330] Abstract obligations are obligations which are separated, or abstracted from their cause. An example of such an abstract obligation is bank warranty on first demand. The bank's obligation to pay is abstracted from the underlying transactions (both the contract between the bank and the supplier of goods and the contract between the supplier and its buyer). The bank must respect its obligation to pay regardless of the underlying contracts and cannot call upon exceptions deriving from these underlying contracts.[331]

§4. Object

I. Concept

227. The object (*voorwerp/objet*) of a juridical act is the concrete legal consequence intended by parties.[332] There is no concept in Common Law which corresponds to object. In the case of contracts, this concrete legal consequence is the birth, change, transfer or end of one or several obligations.[333] Article 1126 OCC however stipulates that every contract's object is something a party binds themselves to give, to do, or not to do. As such, the law does not make a clear distinction between the object of a contract and the object of an obligation, and even mixes up both concepts.[334] Recent doctrine attempts to make a distinction between these two. While the object of the contract is the intended legal consequence(s), the object of the obligation is the promised performance (to give, to do or not to do).[335] The condition of substantive validity which must be met in order to have a valid object is the object of the obligation, i.e., the promised performance.[336]

329. S. Stijns, *Leerboek Verbintenissenrecht 1* (Brugge: die Keure, 2016), 119.
330. *Ibid.*, 121–122.
331. *Ibid.*, 112.
332. R. Dekkers & A. Verbeke, *Handboek Burgerlijk Recht*, III (Antwerp: Intersentia: 2007), 39; S. Stijns, *Leerboek Verbintenissenrecht 1* (Brugge: die Keure, 2016), 103; W. van Gerven en A. Van Oevelen, *Verbintenissenrecht* (Leuven: Acco, 2015), 130–131; P. Van Ommeslaghe, *Les obligations vol. 1* in *Traité de droit civil, tome II* (Brussels: Bruylant, 2013), 303.
333. S. Stijns, *Leerboek Verbintenissenrecht 1* (Brugge: die Keure, 2016), 103.
334. Articles 1108, 1126, 1127 & 1128 OCC refer to the object of the contract, while Arts 1129 & 1130 refer to the object of the obligation.
335. S. Stijns, *Leerboek Verbintenissenrecht 1* (Brugge: die Keure, 2016), 104.
336. L. Cornelis, *Algemene theorie van de verbintenis* (Antwerp: Intersentia, 2000), No. 106.

II. Requirements

228. The object must exist, or at least its existence must be possible. Article 1130 OCC stipulates that future things can be the object of an obligation. Impossible performances (e.g., sale of goods which have already been destroyed) cannot be object of obligations.

229. Article 1128 OCC also states that things which are outside *commercium*, i.e., which cannot be dealt with in a private legal transaction, cannot constitute the object of an agreement. For example, neither property of public domain[337] nor a public office can be the subject matter of a contract. In principle, personality rights are also outside the sphere of *commercium*.[338]

230. Parties must know what they obligate themselves to. Article 1129 OCC demands for a thing to be determined towards its kind. Its amount may be uncertain, but should at least be determinable. Jurisprudence considers this requirement met in case the object 'can be determined from objective data which are independent from the parties will'[339] or when 'the contract includes objective elements which allow for the object to be determined without requiring a new consensus between parties'.[340] Parties may however agree on a third party to determine the object.[341] Most of the recent doctrine also accepts for the object to depend upon the decision of one of the contract parties.[342] This possibility is grounded on the theory of the autonomy of will. However, this principle knows several exceptions (e.g., in labour law, clauses granting the employer the right to unilaterally alter contractual conditions are considered null[343]) and is nuanced by good faith (*see* No. 101 *supra*) and the doctrine of abuse of rights (*see* No. 103 *supra*).

231. Like cause, object should not be contrary to public order or mandatory laws. The relevant criterion is whether the object causes or maintains an unlawful situation.[344]

---

337. Cass. 25 Sep. 2000, *Arr.Cass.* 2000, 1428, *Pas.* 2000, 1399 & *R.W.* 2002-03, 775.
338. This however does not prevent the (limited) possibility to contract about the protected personality right or personality component (in the interest of the person or another person's personality rights), e.g., in case of donation of blood, organs or cells. Specific rules apply to this kind of contracts.
339. Cass. 20 May 1994, *Arr.Cass.* 1994, 507, & *Pas.* 1994, 492; Cass. 21 Sep. 1987, *Arr.Cass.* 1987-88, 84, *Pas.* 1988, 77 & *R.W.* 1988-89, 1325.
340. Cass. 21 Feb. 1991, *Arr.Cass.* 1990-91, 679 & *Pas.* 1991, 604; Cass. 25 Sep, 2000, *Arr.Cass.* 2000, 1428, *Pas.* 2000, 1399 & *R.W.* 2002-03, 775; Cass. 13 juni 2005, *Arr. Cass.* 2005, 1312, *Pas.* 2005, 1305, *RW* 2008-09, 300 and *JTT* 2006, 29.
341. For example, Art. 1592 CC in case of price determination in sale. *See also*: Cass. 31 Oct. 2008, *R.W.* 2009-10, 1258–1261.
342. S. Stijns, *Leerboek Verbintenissenrecht 1* (Brugge: die Keure, 2016), 106–107; W. van Gerven en A. Van Oevelen, *Verbintenissenrecht* (Leuven: Acco, 2015), 132; P. Wéry, *Droit des obligations, I, Théorie générale du contrat* (Brussels: Larcier, 2011), 278.
343. Article 25 of the Law of 3 Jul. 1978 on Labour Contracts (*Arbeidsovereenkomstenwet/Loi relative aux contrats de travail*), *Belgian Official Gazette* 22 Aug. 1978.
344. Cass. 7 Nov. 2019, C.19.0061.N, NJW 2019, 895, note M. Meirlaen, S. Stijns, *Leerboek Verbintenissenrecht 1* (Brugge: die Keure, 2016), 107–108; P. Wéry, *Droit des obligations, I, Théorie générale du contrat* (Brussels: Larcier, 2011), 274.

III. Consequences

232. The absence of a (determinable) object or the presence of an object contrary to public order results in absolute nullity. In case the object is contrary to mandatory law, the nullity is relative (about this distinction, *see infra*, No. 236).

IV. Theory of the Dissolution in Case of Disappearance of the Object

233. Unlike cause, object must not only be present at the moment of the conclusion of the contract but also must continue to exist for the entire duration of the contract.[345] Dissolution (*verval/caducité*) is a way for a validly concluded contract to end, when one of the conditions for the contract's validity disappears during its execution, resulting in the impossibility to execute this contract in kind. In regard to the disappearance of a contract's object, this doctrine has been accepted by jurisprudence since the judgment of the *Court of Cassation* of 28 November 1980.[346] In this judgment, a lease contract was automatically considered dissolved due to the material destruction of the leased goods, resulting in the impossibility to be executed.

V. Initial Impossibility

234. Belgian law does not have a separate doctrine on initial impossibility. However, similar results are achieved by the requirement for a contract's object to be possible. If it is impossible from the beginning, the contract is considered to lack an object and will lead to nullity (*see* No. 228 *supra*).

§5. Consequences of a Defect of Consent or a Lack of Substantive Validity: Nullity

I. Concept and Characteristics

235. When one or more conditions of substantive validity are lacking, the contract becomes null. Nullity only sanctions issues concerning the formation of contracts, as opposed to problems arising after their formation. It should not be confused with termination, one of the possible sanctions in case of problems regarding the execution of an otherwise validly formed contract (*see* Nos 388 ff. *infra*). Both sanctions can never go together.[347] In principle, nullity is retroactive, which means that a null contract is considered without effect *ab initio*, and that each party

345. T. Vansweevelt & B. Weyts, «Geldigheidsvereisten van de overeenkomst» in T. Vansweevelt and B. Weyts, *Handboek Verbintenissenrecht* (Antwerpen: Intersentia, 2019), 218, nr. 341.
346. Cass. 28 Nov. 1980, *A.C.* 1980-81, 352, *Pas.* 1981, 369; Cass. 2 Feb. 2018, C.17.0055.F, *JT* 2018, nr. 6739, 624, *TBBR* 2018, 519, note P.A. Foriers.
347. S. Stijns, *Leerboek Verbintenissenrecht 1* (Brugge: die Keure, 2016), 136.

must make restitution for what they have received. Only a judge can declare a contract null. The parties are not allowed to do this without a judge's intervention.

236. Nullity may be absolute or relative, according to the type of law that has been breached.[348] If it is a law of public order (*see* No. 46 *supra*), the contract will be sanctioned with absolute nullity, while with an imperative law, the nullity will be relative. The most important consequences of this distinction are the following. From the outset, however, it needs to be stressed that this distinction has lost much of its practical relevance.

The relevance of the distinction between absolute and relative nullity can be located on three levels. First, in case of absolute nullity, any interested party can invoke it, including the prosecution and even the court ex officio – without the parties calling for it – while in case of relative nullity, only the person for whose protection the law has established the nullity can do so. Second, absolute nullity can be invoked at any stage of the procedure, while relative nullity must be called upon at the start of it. A relative nullity which is not mentioned at the start of proceedings will not be taken into account by the judge. Third, a legal relation sanctioned by a relative nullity can be validated by confirmation afterwards, while one sanctioned by an absolute nullity can never be confirmed.

However, the distinction between both types of nullity must be strongly relativised. As the judge is obliged to decide a case based on the applicable legal norms,[349] he must rely on the applicable legal norms even if they have not been invoked by the parties. In this obligation, he is only limited to the extent that he must honour the right to a fair trial and may not rule *ultra petita*.[350] By consequence, a judge must invoke also the relative nullity ex officio – safe under the aforementioned limits to this obligation.

II. Modulations of the Nullity Sanction

237. Nullity being a drastic sanction, the majority of the doctrine has been striving for the modulation or flexibility of nullity for decades. According to them, the nullity sanction should not reach further than required by its goal.[351] Different methods are used in order to adapt the sanction to the severity of the breach, besides the blurred edges between relative and absolute nullity described hereabove.

---

348. R. Dekkers & A. Verbeke, *Handboek Burgerlijk Recht*, III (Antwerp: Intersentia: 2007), 109; F. Peeraer, 'Nietigheid', in B. Weyts and T. Vansweevelt, *Handboek Verbintenissenrecht* (Mortsle, Intersentia, 2019), 483; S. Stijns, *Leerboek Verbintenissenrecht 1* (Brugge: die Keure, 2016), 138; W. van Gerven en A. Van Oevelen, *Verbintenissenrecht* (Leuven: Acco, 2015), 145; P. Wéry, *Droit des obligations, I, Théorie générale du contrat* (Brussels: Larcier, 2011), 317.
349. Cass. 14 Apr. 2005, *Arr.Cass.* 2005, 868, concl. P. De Koster, *JT* 2005, 659, note J. Van Compernolle, *err. JT* 2005, 796; *JLMB* 2005, 856, note G. de Leval, *Pas.* 2005, 862, concl.; P. De Koster; *RABG* 2005, 1663, note R. Verbeke.
350. S. Stijns, *Leerboek Verbintenissenrecht 1* (Brugge: die Keure, 2016), 139.
351. *Ibid.*, 140.

238. First, *damages* may be added to the nullity sanction when a precontractual fault has been made and the ensuing loss cannot be undone by the sole nullity of the contract. In that case, it is a complementary sanction, which is cumulated with the nullity. It is also possible for damages to be the only sanction for a precontractual fault, i.e., when the conditions for nullity are not met (*see* No. 129 *supra*). This is the case for incidental deceit or violence. Finally, in the case of a relative nullity and a *culpa in contrahendo*, it is possible for the party who suffered loss to choose between two alternatives: nullity or damages. Indeed, he can renounce to invoke the relative nullity and accept for the contract to remain, provided that he obtains damages.[352]

239. Second, it is possible for nullity to be *partial*.[353] A judge can limit nullity to only one or more clauses of the contract, as long as these clauses do not form an unbreakable or indivisible unity with the rest of the contract. In the latter case, the judge will have to declare the entire contract null.[354] Connected to the partial nullification is the power of the judge to moderate. In that case, the unlawful element is not nullified, but reduced.[355]

240. Third, the courts can *convert* the intended but null contract into a valid one, similar to the null contract in both contents and effects. This new contract should reasonably be wanted by the parties if they had been aware of the nullity of the initial one. Belgian law so far lacks systematics about conversion, but some specific laws mention the possibility. The doctrine has not reached a consensus yet as to cases where the law does not elaborate on conversion.[356] Conversion should not be confused with the common law conversion in tort or equity.

241. Finally, some techniques allow to *moderate* the effect of the principle of restitution. First, in the case of contracts with consecutive or continuous execution, restitution is often impossible, or parties have performed mutually. As retroactivity is quite inconvenient in such cases, some doctrine advocates non-retroactivity or undoing for the future only.[357] Second, the Latin proverb '*in pari causa turpitudinis cessat repetitio*' (*see* No. 225 *supra*) allows for the judge to refuse the restitution of

---

352. *Ibid.*, 141–142.
353. Cass. 9 Sep. 2019, *DAOR* 2019, 43, note D. Philippe; *RABG* 2019, 1790; *RW* 2019-20, 1534; *TBH* 2020, 513, note S. Lagasse; Cass. 23 Nov. 2017, *RW* 2018-19, 704; *TBBR* 2018, 208, note F. Peeraer; *TBH* 2018, 298; *TBO* 2018, 301; Cass. 14 Sep. 2017, *TBBR* 2018, 296, note G. De Pierpont, Y. Ninane; *TRVRPS* 2018, 123, note B. Bellen; Cass. 25 Jun. 2015, *RCJB* 2016, 387, note P. Wéry; Cass. 23 Jan. 2015, *RW* 2015-16, 1188, note F. Peeraer.
354. F. Peeraer, 'Nietigheid', in B. Weyts and T. Vansweevelt, *Handboek Verbintenissenrecht* (Mortsle, Intersentia, 2019), 501–506; S. Stijns, *Leerboek Verbintenissenrecht 1* (Brugge: die Keure, 2016), 142–144; P. Wéry, *Droit des obligations, I, Théorie générale du contrat* (Brussels: Larcier, 2011), 325.
355. F. Peeraer, 'Nietigheid', in B. Weyts and T. Vansweevelt, *Handboek Verbintenissenrecht* (Mortsle, Intersentia, 2019), 502; S. Stijns, *Leerboek Verbintenissenrecht 1* (Brugge: die Keure, 2016), 144–145.
356. *Ibid.*, 501–506; *Ibid.*, 145–147.
357. S. Stijns, *Leerboek Verbintenissenrecht 1* (Brugge: die Keure, 2016), 147; P. Wéry, *Droit des obligations, I, Théorie générale du contrat* (Brussels: Larcier, 2011), 341.

what was performed in violation of public order (according to a part of the doctrine, this is also possible for violations of imperative laws).[358] Third, although the nullity sanction forces the parties to give back what they have received, this restitution may be done either in nature or by equivalent, which will usually mean that one has to pay damages to the other. It is also possible for parties to stipulate that nullity will only have effects *ex nunc*.

III. Damages

242. As stated in No. 238 *supra*, *damages* may be added to the nullity sanction when a precontractual fault has been made and the ensuing loss cannot be undone by the sole nullity of the contract. In that case, it is a complementary sanction, which is cumulated with the nullity. The requirements for precontractual liability are treated in Nos 129 ff. *supra*.

358. *Ibid.*, 147–148; *Ibid:*.

Chapter 3. The Contents of a Contract

§1. Different Clauses

I. Ascertaining Express Terms

243. Contracts are normally made up of a number of terms, some of which are considered of major importance and some of which are considered of lesser importance. However, unlike English law, Belgian law does not make a distinction between conditions, warranties and innominate terms, or between terms and representations. Neither does it know the concept of collateral contract.

II. Implied Terms

244. Article 1135 OCC states that 'agreements are binding not only in their express terms but also in accordance with the requirements of equity, usage and the law'. Most rules regarding obligations are suppletive, i.e., non-mandatory (*see* No. 47 *supra*). Parties have the power to deviate from those rules in their contract. However, if the contract does not mention deviations on a certain subject (e.g., no terms concerning liability for breach), the suppletive laws on the subject are implied to be applicable. This somewhat parallels common law's use of implied terms. Also, while parties may deviate from suppletive laws, terms which do not comply with public order or imperative laws can be nullified (*see* Nos 46 and 236 *supra*). These rules are not only implied but even take priority on the terms of the contract.

245. In addition, the complementing function of good faith based on Article 1134, 3rd section OCC (*see* No. 102 *supra*) imposes several additional duties on parties, e.g., the duty of information, the duty for the aggrieved party to reasonably limit the damages,[359] and the duty to renegotiate in the case of a long-term contract.

III. Exemption Clauses

A. Concept and Qualification of Exemption Clauses

246. An exemption clause (*exoneratieclausule* or *bevrijdingsbeding/clause exonératoire*) is a contract term where a party limits or excludes his liability towards the other party.[360] As most rules concerning liability are suppletive,[361] this type of clause is considered valid.[362] They are, however, submitted to certain restrictions (*see* Nos 250–252 *infra*).

359. Cass. 14 May 1992, *Arr.Cass.* 1991-92, 855 & *Pas.* 1992, 798; Cass. 17 May 2001, *Pas.* 2001, 889.

360. E. Dirix, B. Tilleman & S. Lierman (eds), *De Valks Juridisch woordenboek* (Antwerp-Oxford: Intersentia, 2018), 162. For more on this subject, *see*: E. Dirix, 'Exoneratiebedingen', *T.P.R.* (1988), 1171 et seq.; J. Herbots, 'De exoneratiebedingen in het gemeen recht' in *Exoneratiebedingen*

247. Often, to escape these restrictions, parties word an exemption clause as to resemble a clause of another nature. Therefore, one must evaluate whether the clause intends to limit liability or results in a limitation of liability, in which case it is considered as an exemption clause and the restrictions apply. Determining whether a clause is a disguised exemption clause is not always an easy task in practice. This is particularly difficult with terms which merely detail the contents of a contract or the scope of the obligations (*inhoudbepalend beding/clause déterminant le contenu obligationel*). Although such clauses are perfectly valid and are not submitted to the restrictions applicable to exemption clauses, they may 'hide' an exemption clause if their goal or result is to limit liability, in which case these restrictions do apply.[363]

B. Acceptance

248. In order to be valid, an exemption clause must have been accepted by the party against whom it is called upon. The normal conditions for acceptance apply (*see* No. 123 *supra*). Acceptance may be silent or explicit. It can only be applicable if the contract parties were informed of it (or could take notice of it) before or at the moment of the conclusion of the contract.[364] For example, when the exemption clause is written on a board which is only seen after the conclusion of the contract, it will not be considered as accepted and will not be applicable.[365] If this board is visible before the conclusion of the contract, the clause must be clear and legible in order to be considered accepted.

(Brugge: die Keure, 1993), 7 et seq.; M. Fontaine & G. Viney (eds), *Les sanctions de l'inexécution des obligations contractuelles* (Brussels: Bruylant, 2001); O. Vanden Berghe, 'Exoneratiebedingen in het gemeen recht en in het consumentenrecht' in *Contractuele clausules rond de (niet-)uitvoering en de beëindiging van contracten*, eds. S. Stijns and K. Vanderschot (Antwerp: Intersentia, 2006), 41–75; O. Vanden Berghe & M. Hostens, 'Exoneratieclausules' in G-L Ballon et al. (eds), *Gemeenrechtelijke clausules Vol I. & II.* (Antwerpen: Intersentia, 2013).

361. W. van Gerven en A. Van Oevelen, *Verbintenissenrecht* (Leuven: Acco, 2015), 176 et seq.; P. Wéry, *Droit des obligations, I, Théorie générale du contrat* (Brussels: Larcier, 2011), 736.

362. Cass. 23 Nov. 1987, *Arr.Cass.* 1987-88, 371 and *Pas.* 1988, 347; L. Cornelis, *Algemene theorie van de verbintenis* (Antwerp: Intersentia, 2000), No. 472.

363. S. Stijns, *Leerboek Verbintenissenrecht 1* (Brugge: die Keure, 2016), 173; W. van Gerven en A. Van Oevelen, *Verbintenissenrecht* (Leuven: Acco, 2015), 177; P. Wéry, *Droit des obligations, I, Théorie générale du contrat* (Brussels: Larcier, 2011), 737.

364. L. Cornelis, *Algemene theorie van de verbintenis* (Antwerp: Intersentia, 2000), No. 472; S. Stijns, *Leerboek Verbintenissenrecht 1* (Brugge: die Keure, 2016), 173–174; W. van Gerven en A. Van Oevelen, *Verbintenissenrecht* (Leuven: Acco, 2015), 178; O. Vanden Berghe & M. Hostens, 'Exoneratieclausules' in G-L Ballon et al. (eds), *Gemeenrechtelijke clausules Vol I. & II.* (Antwerpen: Intersentia, 2013), 1327; P. Wéry, *Droit des obligations, I, Théorie générale du contrat* (Brussels: Larcier, 2011), 739.

365. S. Stijns, *Leerboek Verbintenissenrecht 1* (Brugge: die Keure, 2016), 174.

C. Interpretation

249. The *Court of Cassation* judged that an exemption clause must be interpreted restrictively.[366] Consequentially, an exemption clause which is phrased in general terms does not include exemption for gross negligence (*zware fout/faute lourde*). Thus, exemption for gross negligence must be formulated explicitly or be an inevitable consequence of its formulation.[367] Also, by virtue of the general interpretation rule of Article 1162 OCC, in case of sustained doubt about its scope, such clause must be interpreted against the party who has stipulated and in favour of the party who has bound himself.

D. Validity

250. As most rules concerning liability are suppletive,[368] exemption clauses are considered valid in Belgian law.[369] They are, however, submitted to certain restrictions. As is the case for any contract terms, exemption clauses cannot validly deviate from mandatory laws and public order/*ordre public*. For example, Article VI.83, 25° CEL forbids terms which limit or exclude an enterprise's liability for death or physical injury to the consumer due to an action or inaction of this enterprise. Another example is Article 10 §1 of the Law of 25 February 1991 on products liability, which states that the producer cannot exclude or limit his liability towards the victim of a flaw in the product (except when the fault of the victim or of a person for whom he is responsible contributed to the damage).[370]

251. Another limitation to exemption clauses is that the debtor cannot liberate himself from liability for personal fraud.[371] However, there is no unanimity on the meaning of fraud in this context, more specifically on the question of whether or not the wilful failure to perform must have been accompanied by an intention to

366. Cass. 22 Mar. 1979, *Arr.Cass.* 1978-79, 860 and *Pas.* 1979, 863.
367. S. Stijns, *Leerboek Verbintenissenrecht 1* (Brugge: die Keure, 2016), 174; W. van Gerven en A. Van Oevelen, *Verbintenissenrecht* (Leuven: Acco, 2015), 178; O. Vanden Berghe & M. Hostens, 'Exoneratieclausules' in G-L Ballon et al. (eds), *Gemeenrechtelijke clausules Vol I. & II.* (Antwerpen: Intersentia, 2013), 1339–1340; P. Wéry, *Droit des obligations, I, Théorie générale du contrat* (Brussels: Larcier, 2011), 739.
368. W. van Gerven en A. Van Oevelen, *Verbintenissenrecht* (Leuven: Acco, 2015), 176 et seq.; P. Wéry, *Droit des obligations, I, Théorie générale du contrat* (Brussels: Larcier, 2011), 740.
369. Cass. 23 Nov. 1987, *Arr.Cass.* 1987-88, 371 and *Pas.* 1988, 347; L. Cornelis, *Algemene theorie van de verbintenis* (Antwerp: Intersentia, 2000), No. 472; O. Vanden Berghe & M. Hostens, 'Exoneratieclausules' in G-L Ballon et al. (eds), *Gemeenrechtelijke clausules Vol I. & II.* (Antwerpen: Intersentia, 2013), 1328.
370. *Wet betreffende de aansprakelijkheid voor produkten met gebreken/Loi relative à la responsabilité du fait des produits défectueux, Belgian Official Gazette* 22 Mar. 1991.
371. M. Coipel, *Eléments de théorie générale des contrats* (Diegem: Story-Scientia, 1999), No. 276; S. Stijns, *Leerboek Verbintenissenrecht 1* (Brugge: die Keure, 2016), 176; O. Vanden Berghe & M. Hostens, 'Exoneratieclausules' in G-L Ballon et al. (eds), *Gemeenrechtelijke clausules Vol I. & II.* (Antwerpen: Intersentia, 2013), 1333; W. van Gerven en A. Van Oevelen, *Verbintenissenrecht* (Leuven: Acco, 2015), 181; P. Wéry, *Droit des obligations, I, Théorie générale du contrat* (Brussels: Larcier, 2011), 741.

cause harm to the other party. The majority of the doctrine considers that a wilful failure, regardless of additional intentions, suffices to consider a behaviour fraud. On the other hand, the *Court of Cassation* held in 1959 that an exemption clause for one's own gross negligence was valid.[372] The difference between gross negligence and fraud is that fraud is intentional.[373] The same judgment stated that exemption for wilful failure to perform or gross negligence of one's employees was valid. Consequentially, it is profitable for a debtor to delegate performance to helpers, rather than performing himself, as a broader exemption is then permitted. It should however be noted that, by virtue of Article VI.83, 13° CEL, exemption from one's own gross negligence or gross negligence of one's employees or agents is forbidden in contracts between a consumer and an enterprise.[374]

252. Quite logically, the clause may not 'erode' or take away the meaning of the obligations of the defendant.[375] One may not, at the same time, take an obligation upon himself and exempt himself from any liability for breach of contract.[376]

E. Abuse of Exemption?

253. Like other contractual rights, the exercise of valid exemption clauses is submitted to the requirement of good faith and the prohibition of abuse of rights (*see* Nos 101 et seq.). It could, e.g., be considered against good faith to call upon terms which exempt the debtor from liability for his own gross negligence[377] or fraud by his auxiliaries.[378]

IV. Penalty Clauses

A. Concept and Function

254. Article 1226 OCC defines a penalty clause (*strafbeding/clause pénale*) as a clause whereby a person obligates herself to pay a fixed sum in case of non-performance of the contract, as a compensation for the damage caused by the non-performance. Such a clause might serve two goals. First, it aims to compensate,

372. Cass. 25 Sep. 1959, *Arr.Cass.* 1960, 86, *Pas.* 1960, 113 and *R.C.J.B.* 1960, 10, note J. Dabin.
373. Cass. 7 Mar. 1988, *Arr.Cass.* 1987-88, 882 and *Pas* 1988, 812.
374. *See* No. 75 *supra* for a definition of 'consumer'.
375. Cass. 25 Sep. 1959, *Arr.Cass.* 1960, 86 and *Pas.* 1960, 113; Cass. 23 Nov. 1987, *Arr.Cass.* 1987-88, 371 and *Pas.* 1988, 347; Cass. 27 Sep. 1990, *Arr.Cass.* 1990-91, 88 and *Pas.* 1991, 82; Cass. 26 Mar. 2004, *Arr. Cass.* 2004, 537, *Pas.* 2004, 513, *RW* 2007-08, 93.
376. S. Stijns, *Leerboek Verbintenissenrecht 1* (Brugge: die Keure, 2016), 178–179; W. van Gerven en A. Van Oevelen, *Verbintenissenrecht* (Leuven: Acco, 2015), 180; P. Wéry, *Droit des obligations, I, Théorie générale du contrat* (Brussels: Larcier, 2011), 743. *Contra:* L. Cornelis, *Algemene theorie van de verbintenis* (Antwerp: Intersentia, 2000), No. 479.
377. S. Stijns, *Leerboek Verbintenissenrecht 1* (Brugge: die Keure, 2016), 179; W. van Gerven en A. Van Oevelen, *Verbintenissenrecht* (Leuven: Acco, 2015), 181; P. Wéry, *Droit des obligations, I, Théorie générale du contrat* (Brussels: Larcier, 2011), 742.
378. S. Stijns, *Leerboek Verbintenissenrecht 1* (Brugge: die Keure, 2016), 180.

which is considered advantageous for both parties, as it allows to liquidate damages in advance and thereby obviate the need for possibly difficult calculations and the consequent delays.[379] Furthermore, such a term frees the parties from the need to prove the existence and the scope of the damages, as a fixed sum is determined in advance. Second, it may also allow for the creditor to exert pressure on the debtor. Belgian law only accepts the first function, which has repeatedly been confirmed by the *Court of Cassation*,[380] whose jurisprudence was eventually confirmed by the legislator in 1998.[381]

B. Qualification: Difference with Termination Clauses

255. Not every term which stipulates a fixed compensation is considered a penalty clause. For example, termination clauses (*éénzijdig opzegbeding/clause de résiliation*) should not be confused with penalty clauses.[382] A termination clause allows for a party to terminate a contract prematurely and unilaterally, against the payment of a fixed sum to the other party. In contrast to what is the case with penalty clauses, the payment does not aim to compensate for the loss due to non-performance, but is, in fact, granted in return for the right to end a contract prematurely.[383] The premature termination comes down to the exercise of a contractual right, and does not constitute a breach for which a compensation is stipulated.[384] Clauses which allow for the debtor to free himself by the performance of another obligation than the primary obligation are not considered penalty clauses either.

379. E. Van Den Haute, 'Schadebedingen' in G-L Ballon et al. (eds), *Gemeenrechtelijke clausules Vol I. & II.* (Antwerpen: Intersentia, 2013), 1397.

380. Cass. 17 Apr. 1970, *Arr.Cass.* 1970, 754 and *Pas.* 1970, 711; Cass. 24 Nov. 1972, *Arr.Cass.* 1973, 302 and *Pas.* 1973, 297; Cass. 8 Feb. 1974, *Arr.Cass.* 1974, 624 and *Pas.* 1974, 597; Cass. 28 Nov. 1991, *Arr.Cass.* 1991-92, 282 and *Pas.* 1992, 240.

381. This was done in the Law of 23 Nov. 1998 for the adaptation of the OCC regarding penalty clauses and moratory interests, *Belgian Official Gazette* 13 Jan. 1999. Peculiarly, the original intention of L. Willem, who put the initial proposition of law into the Chamber, was to grant penalty clauses the role of a 'reasonable lever' besides their compensation goal (*see* Toelichting bij wetsvoorstel L. Willems, Parl. St., Kamer, 1997–1998, No. 1373/1, p. 3).

382. For more on termination clauses, *see* F. Vermander, *De opzegging van overeenkomsten, Ph.D. Thesis* (Mortsel: Intersentia, 2014), 1060.

383. Cass 8 Dec. 1988, *Arr.Cass.* 1988-89, 427 and *Pas.* 1989, 389; Cass 6 Dec. 1996, *Arr.Cass.* 1996, 1169 and *Pas.* 1996, 1241; Cass. 22 Oktober 1999, *Arr.Cass.* 1999, 1318 and *Pas* 1999, 1373; Cass. 6 Sep. 2002, *Pas.* 2002, 1546; Cass. 28 Apr. 2011, *Pas.* 2011, 1191, *TBBR*, 2013, 88, note P. Wéry, *Bank Fin.R* 2012, 120, note J. Baeck and *JLMB* 2011, 1017.

384. S. Stijns, *Leerboek Verbintenissenrecht 1* (Brugge: die Keure, 2016), 195–196.

C. Legality and Restriction of Exaggerate Penalty Clauses

256. Penalty clauses are, in principle, lawful. The existence of such a clause does not prevent the creditor from suing for performance. However, one cannot demand both performance and liquidated damages for the same breach except in so far as the damages are for delay.

257. Penalty clauses which stipulate a fixed sum so high that it comes down to a private fine, so that the non-performance is advantageous for the creditor, are forbidden. The *Court of Cassation* has declared such clauses absolutely null with its judgment of 17 April 1970 on the ground that they are contrary to public order.[385] As stated before, the *Court of Cassation*[386] and the legislator chose to reject the possibility to exert pressure as a function of penalty clauses. A penalty clause must respect the criterion of potential damage: the fixed sum cannot be higher than the damage the creditor may suffer in case of non-performance.[387]

The law of 23 November 1998[388] recognised the illegality of such clauses, but replaced the nullity sanction with the moderation of the clause. Article 1231, paragraph 1 OCC now states that, on request of the debtor or on his own initiative, the judge can reduce the penalty sum when that sum evidently exceeds the foreseeable damage in case of non-performance. In such case, the judge cannot reduce the compensation below the amount which would have been due in case no penalty clause had been stipulated. In other words, exaggerated penalty clauses can be moderated within the boundaries of, on one side, the maximum damage the parties could foresee to be caused by non-performance at the moment the contract started and, on the other side, the actual damage caused by the non-performance in this particular case. In order to enjoy this lower limit, the creditor must prove his actual damage.[389]

258. Similar rules apply to obligations whose object is the payment of a sum of money. Article 1153 CC *in fine* states that, if such is requested by the debtor, the judge can reduce the penalty sum when that sum evidently exceeds the actual damage caused by the late payment. Thus, a literal reading of this article shows a different criterion than Article 1231 OCC, where reduction of the penalty sum is only possible when the stipulated sum exceeds the foreseeable damage. However, the doctrine pleads for a more teleological reading of Article 1153 OCC, according to which the criterion is the foreseeable damage in case of late payment as well. Also, the lower limit for the reduction of the fixed interest is the legal interest.

385. Cass. 17 Apr. 1970, *Arr.Cass.* 1970, 754 and *Pas.* 1970, 711; Cass. 24 Nov. 1972, *Arr.Cass.* 1973, 302 and *Pas.* 1973, 297; Cass. 8 Feb. 1974, *Arr.Cass.* 1974, 624 and *Pas.* 1974, 597; Cass. 28 Nov. 1991, *Arr.Cass.* 1991-92, 282 and *Pas.* 1992, 240.

386. Cass. 17 Apr. 1970, *Arr.Cass.* 1970, 754 and *Pas.* 1970, 711; Cass. 24 Nov. 1972, *Arr.Cass.* 1973, 302 and *Pas.* 1973, 297; Cass. 8 Feb. 1974, *Arr.Cass.* 1974, 624 and *Pas.* 1974, 597; Cass. 28 Nov. 1991, *Arr.Cass.* 1991-92, 282 and *Pas.* 1992, 240.

387. Cass. 21 Nov. 1985, *Arr.Cass.* 1985-86, 404 and *Pas.* 1986, 347; Cass. 2 Dec. 1983, *Arr.Cass.* 1983-84, 398 and *Pas.* 1984, 371.

388. Law of 23 Nov. 1998 *tot wijziging, wat het strafbeding en de moratoire interest betreft, van het Burgerlijk wetboek/modifiant le Code civil en ce qui concerne la clause pénale et les intérêts moratoires, Belgian Official Gazette* 13 Jan. 1999.

389. S. Stijns, *Leerboek Verbintenissenrecht 1* (Brugge: die Keure, 2016), 197–198.

259. In the case of consumer contracts, stricter rules apply.[390] Article VI.83,24° CEL forbids clauses which provide a compensation sum in case of non-performance by the consumer which is disproportionate to the damage which could be suffered by the enterprise. Article VI.83,17° CEL also imposes reciprocity for penalty clauses, as it forbids penalty clauses against the consumer unless an equivalent clause against the enterprise is stipulated as well. Penalty clauses that breach any of these articles are void. Also, as discussed in Nos 432–433 *infra*, specific rules apply to transactions between companies, where it is also possible for the judge to raise the stipulated interests instead of lowering them.

D. Penalty Reduction in Case of Partial Performance and Control on Abuse of Rights

260. If a penalty clause respects the aforementioned boundaries, the judge must, in principle, respect its obligatory force. However, according to Article 1231, paragraph 2 OCC, if the obligations of the contract have been performed, albeit only partially, it is still possible for the judge to reduce the penalty.

261. Also, as judged by the *Court of Cassation* in 1988, even if a penalty clause meets the requirements to be considered valid, it is still possible to demand its reduction to a 'normal use' in case of abuse of rights by the creditor (*see* Nos 103 et seq. *supra*).[391] Although the law has since been modified, this jurisprudence remains valid, as the possibility for a judge to moderate the exercise of a right which has been abused differs from the right to moderate exaggerated penalty clauses.[392] Moderation due to abuse of rights may exceed the actual damage and even result in the general ban from calling upon the clause.[393] This may thus result in an impossibility for the creditor to call upon the penalty clause altogether.[394]

V. Arbitration Clauses

262. Arbitrage (*arbitrage*) is jurisdiction by judges who were not appointed by authorities, i.e., private persons who are designated by one or several parties to a

390. Consumer contracts are defined as contracts between an enterprise and a consumer. In this regard, a consumer is 'any natural or legal person who acquires or uses products brought upon the market for exclusively non-professional goals' (*see* E. Dirix, B. Tilleman & S. Lierman (eds), *De Valks Juridisch woordenboek* (Antwerp-Oxford: Intersentia, 2018), 104–105).
391. Cass. 18 Feb. 1988, *Arr.Cass.* 1987-88, 709 and *Pas.* 1988, 728.
392. S. Stijns, *Leerboek Verbintenissenrecht 1* (Brugge: die Keure, 2016), 199; W. van Gerven en A. Van Oevelen, *Verbintenissenrecht* (Leuven: Acco, 2015), 120; P. Wéry, *Droit des obligations, I, Théorie générale du contrat* (Brussels: Larcier, 2011), 710. Contra: L. Cornelis, *Algemene theorie van de verbintenis* (Antwerp: Intersentia, 2000), No. 510.
393. Cass. 8 Feb. 2001, *Arr.Cass.* 2001, 245 & *Pas.* 2001, 244; Cass. 1 Oct. 2010, *Pas* 2010, 2470, *RW* 2011-12, 142, note S. Jansen and S. Stijns, *TBBR* 2012, 387, note P. Bazier and *TBH* 2011, 77.
394. S. Stijns, *Leerboek Verbintenissenrecht 1* (Brugge: die Keure, 2016), 200.

dispute or by other arbitrators who were designed in that dispute in order to solve it.[395] The rules on arbitrage are laid down in Articles 1676–1723 of the Judicial Code.[396]

In principle, arbitration clauses (*arbitrageclausule/clause d'arbitrage*), i.e., clauses providing for the arbitration of future controversies arising out of a contract, are considered valid. There are some exceptions; e.g., disputes regarding labour contracts may not be subjected to arbitrage (*see* Articles 1678, 2 al. and 578 of the Judicial Code).

According to Article 1677 Judicial Code, arbitration contracts and clauses must be made in writing signed by the parties or in another binding document in which their intention of submitting the controversy to arbitration is clear. There are no other rules concerning the form of arbitration clauses.

If a dispute submitted to arbitrage is brought before a judge, he must declare himself incompetent to adjudicate this dispute *if this is demanded* by a party (Article 1679 Judicial Code). In other words, if the defendant fails to demand dismissal at the beginning of an ordinary action, the arbitrage clause is waived. Also, an arbitration clause may be waived by the joint action of both parties. However, even when the application of an arbitration clause is due, a party may still demand provisional relief or protective measures from a judge (Article 1679 Judicial Code).

VI. Replacement Clauses

263. A replacement clause (*vervangingsclausule/clause de remplacement*) is a clause by which the creditor is relieved from the duty to obtain a mandate from a court to replace the debtor at the debtor's expense (also *see* No. 418 *infra*). In principle, such clause is considered valid. The Court of Cassation recently ruled that the creditor can replace his debtor without a mandate from a court even in the absence of a replacement clause, provided exceptional circumstances justify such a replacement without prior judicial mandate.[397]

§2. Interpretation

264. The interpretation of a contract is a legal technique whereby a judge tries to determine the meaning of an unclear contract or clause about which a dispute has arisen between parties, in application of Articles 1156–1164 OCC. In other words, there has to be an ambiguity, as a clear contract or clause does not need to be interpreted, and the judge must apply the aforementioned articles.[398]

395. K. Cox, 'Arbitragebedingen', in G-L Ballon et al. (eds), *Gemeenrechtelijke clausules Vol I. & II.* (Antwerpen: Intersentia, 2013), 1674; E. Dirix, B. Tilleman & S. Lierman (eds), *De Valks Juridisch woordenboek* (Antwerp-Oxford: Intersentia, 2010), 33.
396. *Gerechtelijk Wetboek/Code Judiciaire* of 10 Oct. 1967, *Belgian Official Gazette* 31 Oct. 1967.
397. Cass. 22 Jun. 2020, C.18.0357.N, *TBBR* 2020, 583, note S. De Rey.
398. W. Buelens, 'Gevolgen van de overeenkomst voor de contractspartijen' in B. Weyts and T. Vansweevelt, *Handboek Verbintenissenrecht* (Mortsle, Intersentia, 2019), 261.

265. Unlike Dutch law, Belgian law does not recognise good faith as an element of interpretation.[399] The will of parties prevails over what the parties *ought to* want. Good faith is only subsidiary to the will of the parties.[400] As such, while good faith has implications on the completion and execution of a contract (*see* Nos 101 *supra*), it cannot substitute the will of the parties when it comes to the *meaning* of a contract.

I. Point of Departure: Article 1156 of the Civil Code

266. Article 1156 OCC stipulates that the court must determine the mutual intention of the contracting parties, rather than the literal interpretation of the wording of the contract.[401] When doing this, it can take both internal and external elements into account.[402] Internal elements are elements *within* the written document describing the contract. While most contracts do not have formal requirements, parties will usually still draw up a document as a proof of the contract. The *Court of Cassation* has decided that whenever there is a written document, the judge has to determine the intended meaning of this document.[403] External elements are elements which are independent from the written document describing the contract (*outside* the contract), e.g., the execution of the contract, precontractual documents, publicity, the execution of previous contracts between the same parties, etc.[404] The interpretation of a contract belongs to appreciative powers of the judge, and can therefore not be challenged before the *Court of Cassation.*[405]

267. These appreciative powers have three boundaries. First, the judge may not infringe on the probative effect (*bewijskracht/foi due aux actes*) of a written document. In other words, they may not give the document a meaning which is incompatible with the terms of the document itself.[406] Second, the judge may not breach the binding power of the contract: he may not alter nor complement the contract. Third, the courts must apply the rules of legal interpretation.[407]

399. About the interpretation of contracts according to Dutch law, *see* N. Kornet, *Contract Interpretation and Gap Filling: Comparative and Theoretical Perspectives* (Maastricht: Intersentia, 2006).
400. S. Stijns, *Leerboek Verbintenissenrecht 1* (Brugge: die Keure, 2016), 63–65.
401. Cass. 22 Oct. 1982, *Arr.Cass.* 1982-83, 283 & *Pas.* 1983, 256.
402. P. Wéry, *Droit des obligations, I, Théorie générale du contrat* (Brussels: Larcier, 2011), 396.
403. Cass. 24 Mar. 1988, *Arr.Cass.* 1987-88, 972 & *Pas.* 1988, 894.
404. Cass. 24 Sep. 1987, *Arr.Cass.* 1987-88, 116 & *Pas.* 1988, 112; W. Buelens, 'Gevolgen van de overeenkomst voor de contractspartijen' in B. Weyts and T. Vansweevelt, *Handboek Verbintenissenrecht* (Mortsle, Intersentia, 2019), 264; P. Wéry, *Droit des obligations, I, Théorie générale du contrat* (Brussels: Larcier, 2011), 395.
405. R. Dekkers & A. Verbeke, *Handboek Burgerlijk Recht*, III (Antwerp: Intersentia: 2007), 65; P. Van Ommeslaghe, *Les obligations vol. 1* in *Traité de droit civil, tome II* (Brussels: Bruylant, 2013), 606.
406. P. Wéry, *Droit des obligations, I, Théorie générale du contrat* (Brussels: Larcier, 2011), 397.
407. S. Stijns, *Leerboek Verbintenissenrecht 1* (Brugge: die Keure, 2016), 59–61.

II. Other Interpretation Rules

268. Articles 1157–1164 OCC further complete the principle stated in Article 1156 OCC. According to Article 1157 OCC, if a clause is ambiguous, it must rather be interpreted in such a way as to have consequences, rather than a way where it does not. Article 1158 OCC stipulates that terms which may be interpreted in two different ways have to be understood in the way that corresponds best to the contents of the contract. Article 1159 OCC states that ambiguous words have to be interpreted according to what is usual in the district where the contract was concluded. According to Article 1160 OCC, the contract must be completed with the usual clauses, even if they are not mentioned in it. The noteworthy Article 1162 OCC stipulates that when it is impossible to determine the meaning of an ambiguous contract or clause ('constant doubt') with the internal and external elements of the written document, the judge must interpret the contract against the party who has stipulated and in favour of the party who has bound himself.

269. Article VI.37, §2 CEL goes even further in favour of the consumer: in case of doubt about the meaning of a clause, the interpretation which is the most advantageous for the consumer must be chosen.

270. Jurisprudence also applies a strict or even restrictive interpretation to clauses which deviate from what is provided by the law. A restrictive interpretation (*restrictieve interpretatie/interprétation restrictive*) means that the application of the clause is reduced to a minimum. On the other hand, a strict interpretation (*strikte interpretatie/interprétation stricte*) means that the clause does not get restricted nor extended. It is interpreted according to its exact wording.[408]

§3. Conditional Contracts

I. Concept

271. Obligations do not always create the right for the creditor to demand performance immediately. Indeed, parties may determine the moment when the legal consequences of obligations will start by including a condition or a term. Thus, they may determine that performance will depend on the occurrence of a future certain (term) or uncertain event (condition).

272. Article 1168 OCC describes an obligation as 'conditional, when it depends on a future and uncertain event, either because the obligation is suspended until the

408. W. Buelens, 'Gevolgen van de overeenkomst voor de contractspartijen' in B. Weyts and T. Vansweevelt, *Handboek Verbintenissenrecht* (Mortsle, Intersentia, 2019), 290; S. Stijns, *Leerboek Verbintenissenrecht 1* (Brugge: die Keure, 2016), 61; P. Wéry, *Droit des obligations, I, Théorie générale du contrat* (Brussels: Larcier, 2011), 400.

event happens, or because it will be cancelled depending on whether the event happens or not'. Thus, a condition (*voorwaarde/condition*) is a modality of (an) obligation(s) whose object is an event whose future realisation is uncertain.[409] A typical example is the obligation to buy an apartment on the condition that a bank loan will be obtained to finance the purchase. Conditions should not be confused with stipulations of time or 'terms' (*tijdsbepaling/terme*). A term is like a condition in that the event to which it refers is in the future, but it differs in that the event is certain to occur (although the moment at which it will occur may not be certain).[410]

273. According to Article 1172 OCC, any condition which constitutes something impossible, or is contrary to *goede zeden/bonne moeurs* or forbidden by law, is void and makes the contract which depends on it void. Article 1173 OCC states that the condition not to do something that is impossible does not make the obligation depending on this condition void. The question of whether something is impossible is considered at the time the obligation is concluded, not afterwards.[411]

274. A distinction is made between resolutive (ontbindende voorwaarde/condition résolutoire) and suspensive conditions (opschortende voorwaarde/condition suspensive).

II. The Resolutive Condition

A. Concept

275. According to Article 1183 OCC, in case of a resolutive condition (*ontbindende voorwaarde/condition résolutoire*), if the stipulated event happens, the obligation is terminated and things are restored in the same state as if no obligation had ever existed (e.g., a concert that will be cancelled if the artist is sick). If the creditor received anything, he must give it back if the resolutive condition takes place. Resolutive conditions are created by the will of the parties.[412] They resolve the obligation automatically as soon as the stipulated event happens. Article 1183 OCC explicitly states that it restores things 'in the same state as if no obligation had ever existed'.

B. Validity

276. Resolutive conditions are, in principle, considered valid. However, parties may try to use resolutive conditions in order to circumvent mandatory rules which

409. E. Dirix, B. Tilleman & S. Lierman (eds), *De Valks Juridisch woordenboek* (Antwerp-Oxford: Intersentia, 2018), 500.
410. S. Stijns, *Leerboek Verbintenissenrecht 2* (Brugge: die Keure, 2020), 5.
411. L. Cornelis, *Algemene theorie van de verbintenis* (Antwerp: Intersentia, 2000), No. 165.
412. S. Stijns, *Leerboek Verbintenissenrecht 2* (Brugge: die Keure, 2020), 11.

aim to protect weaker parties, in which case they are considered null.[413] For example, the Law of 3 July 1978 on Labour Contracts forbids resolutive conditions regarding the marriage or pregnancy of an employee.[414]

C. Effects

277. The effect of a condition depends on whether it must still occur (‘*pendente conditione*’), it already occurred (‘*eveniente conditione*’) or it is established that the condition will not be fulfilled (‘*deficiente conditione*’).

278. Pendente conditione, the obligation is fully effective and enforceable. It is possible for the parties to stipulate that the condition will be a future, uncertain event which must happen within a certain amount of time. Indeed, if such a time limit is lacking, it may be very hard for parties to prove that the condition has remained unfulfilled.[415]

279. Eveniente conditione, Article 1179 OCC provides that on the occurrence of the event, the fulfilled condition has a retroactive effect until the day when the obligation was contracted. Consequentially, the obligation is terminated and everything that has been done in the period before it was fulfilled must be undone. In the example of a donation of a house until such time as the donor marries, any intervening alienation or burdening of the property will be invalidated. This effect can be quite inconvenient, and therefore, it is interpreted restrictively. Thus, a distinction is made between juridical acts which remove a thing from their owner's patrimony (*daad van beschikking/acte de disposition*), which are, in principle, to be undone, and actions which are necessary or useful to preserve a thing and augment its profit (*daad van beheer/acte de gestion*), which remain acquired.[416] The rights of bona fide third parties are protected by publicity measures for immovables (Article 1 of the Law on Mortgage) and by Article 2279 OCC for movables (Article 2279 OCC states the principle that ‘possession counts as title’ for movables, which means that unless proven otherwise, the person who has a movable under his power is considered to be that thing's owner). Furthermore, parties may stipulate to exclude retroactivity.

280. Deficiente conditione, the right of the creditor becomes permanent. However, as stated before, it may be hard to prove that a condition is unfulfilled when no time limit has been stipulated. According to Article 1176 OCC, when an obligation has been contracted under the condition that an event happens within a fixed time, the condition is considered unfulfilled when the time expires without the event

413. *Ibid.*, 11; S. Stijns, W. van Gerven & P. Wéry, ‘Chronique’, *J.T.* 1999, No. 4.
414. *Wet betreffende de arbeidsovereenkomsten/Loi relative aux contrats de travail, Belgian Official Gazette* 22 Jul. 1978.
415. S. Stijns, *Leerboek Verbintenissenrecht 2* (Brugge: die Keure, 2020), 13.
416. E. Dirix, B. Tilleman & S. Lierman (eds), *De Valks Juridisch woordenboek* (Antwerp-Oxford: Intersentia, 2018), 113.

having happened. If there is no time fixed, the condition may always be fulfilled, and it is considered to be unfulfilled only when it has become certain that the event will not happen. According to Article 1177 OCC, when an obligation has been contracted under the condition that an event will not happen within a fixed time, the condition is fulfilled when the time expires without the event having happened; this is also true if it is certain that the event will not happen before the time expires, and if there is no determined time, it is fulfilled only when it is certain that the event will not happen.

III. The Suspensive Condition

A. Concept

281. According to Article 1181 OCC, in case of a suspensive condition (*opschortende voorwaarde/condition suspensive*), the obligation is suspended until the event happens (e.g., the condition in a contract between an artist and a concert organiser that states that the contract is suspended until the organiser has obtained the necessary permissions from the local authorities). The conditional obligation starts to exist before the fulfilment of the condition, but its performance is suspended.[417]

B. Validity

282. The validity of suspensive conditions depends on the type of condition. According to Article 1174 OCC, a suspensive condition which depends solely on the will of the *debtor* (a 'purely potestative condition') is void. On the other hand, conditions which depend on chance and are not in the power of any party ('casual conditions') and conditions which depend both on the will of one of the parties and on other factors independent from his will ('mixed' or 'common potestative conditions') are considered valid.

C. Effects

283. The effect of a suspensive condition depends on whether it must still occur (*pendente conditione*), it already occurred (*eveniente conditione*) or it is established that the condition will not be fulfilled (*deficiente conditione*).

284. Pendente conditione, the obligation exists, but its performance is suspended. The debtor does not owe anything to the creditor, and does not (yet) have to perform. The obligation cannot be enforced, if money is paid by mistake, it can be recovered, and if the obligation concerns some kind of transfer of property, it

417. Cass. 5 Jun. 1981, *Arr.Cass.* 1980-81, 1157 & *Pas.* 1981, 1149.

does not get transferred yet (consequentially, the risk remains with the debtor/owner).[418] However, the creditor may take steps to protect his rights (e.g., register a mortgage). Also, the debtor is not allowed to attempt to prevent the normal fulfilment of the condition. Article 1178 OCC provides that, if he does, the condition will be considered fulfilled. If this is the case, the creditor will be entitled to demand execution or termination and damages (*see* Nos 415 ff. *infra*). It is possible for parties to stipulate a term within which the event must occur in order to be taken into account. In that case, if the event fails to happen within that term, the condition will be considered unfulfilled. If parties do not stipulate such a term, the event is, in principle, unlimited in time and the condition can only be considered unfulfilled if it is *reasonably* established that it will not take place.[419]

285. Eveniente conditione, the obligation becomes effective and must be performed.[420]

286. Deficiente conditione, the conditional obligation will never have effect and the contract will become without object, and, consequentially, be dissolved.[421] It ceases to exist. This dissolution only has effect for the future.[422]

---

418. W. van Gerven en A. Van Oevelen, *Verbintenissenrecht* (Leuven: Acco, 2015), 541.
419. Cass. 25 May 2007, *RW* 2007-08, 1034.
420. S. Stijns, *Leerboek verbintenissenrecht 2* (Brugge: die Keure, 2020), 19.
421. L. Cornelis, *Algemene theorie van de verbintenis* (Antwerp: Intersentia, 2000), No. 162; S. Stijns, *Leerboek verbintenissenrecht 2* (Brugge: die Keure, 2020), 20.
422. Cass. 27 Jun. 2008, *JLMB* 2009, 105, note.

Chapter 4. Privity of Contract

§1. The Rule of Privity of Contract

I. Third Parties and the Contract: Main Principles and Concepts

A. *Internal and External Effects of a Contract*

287. Article 1165 OCC provides that 'agreements only have effect between the parties; they impose no burden on third parties and only grant them benefits in the case provided for in Article 1121'. Originally, this article was given a literal interpretation: contracts only bind the contracting parties and have no effect on third parties. However, this view has shifted gradually since the twentieth century, as, on consideration, a contract does have consequences for third parties due to its mere existence.[423] A distinction must be made between the internal effects of a contract and the external effects of a contract.

288. The internal effects of a contract are the obligations imposed by the contracts upon the parties, i.e., the rights and duties resulting from it. These are relative (*relatief/relatif*), as they are limited to the contracting parties and do not affect third parties, as stated by Article 1165 OCC. Consequentially, a third party derives no duties to perform from the contract, and, in principle, cannot claim its execution by one of the contracting parties. However, where rights (as opposed to duties) are concerned, there are two exceptions to the relativity of the internal effects of a contract. First, one may stipulate for the benefit of a third party (*see* Nos 310 ff. *infra*). Second, in certain cases, the law confers upon a third party the right to enforce a contract to which he is not a party (the 'direct action', *see* Nos 314 ff. *infra*). Although a contract may grant rights to third parties, it can never impose duties on them.[424] Although certain figures may create another impression, we will see in Nos 306–309 *infra* that, in fact, they are not exceptions but applications of the rule that one cannot impose duties on third parties.

289. The external effects of a contract are the existence of this contract as a fact and the existence of its effects for the contracting parties. External effects are opposable (*tegenwerpelijk/opposable*) to third parties, as the contract and its consequences for the contracting parties are facts whose existence cannot be ignored nor

423. Cass. 27 May 1909, *Pas.* 1909, 273; Cass. 14 Nov. 1986, *Arr.Cass.* 1986-87, 357 and *Pas.* 1987, 331; Cass. 18 May 1989, *Arr.Cass.* 1988-89, 1098 and *Pas.* 1989, 990; Cass. 25 Apr. 2003, A.R. C.01.0607.N; Cass 9 May 2003, A.R. C010010N; Cass. 29 Oct. 2004, A.R. C030284N, www-.cass.be.

424. Cass. 18 Apr. 1997, *Arr.Cass.* 1997, 458 and *Pas.* 1997, 475; Cass. 22 Jan. 1990, *Arr.Cass.* 1989-90, 666 and *Pas.* 1990, 598.

denied by third parties.[425,426] There are two exceptions to the principle of opposability of external effects: the Paulian action (*see* Nos 301–303 *infra*) and the simulation action (*see* Nos 304 *infra*).

290. It should be noted that the opposability of a contract also implies the opposability of each clause from this contract.[427] This means that an exemption clause may be opposed to third parties, but may also be invoked by third parties. For example, a building contractor who has to defend himself against a claim from his principal, against whom the buyer of an apartment filed a claim, can invoke the existence of an exemption clause in the sale contract between the principal and the buyer. Due to the existence of the clause, the principal cannot be held liable.[428] However, due to the relativity of the contract, the third party is not awarded rights and is not freed by the exemption clause.[429] For instance, a land surveyor who made a mistake regarding the size of a piece of land cannot be exonerated by a clause between the seller and the buyer of the land which provides that 'the seller does not guarantee the correctness of the size mentioned in the sale contract'.[430]

B. Parties and Third Parties

291. The CC lacks a definition of 'third party'. The doctrine defines it as 'anyone who is not a contracting party nor the legal successor of a contracting party'.[431] Consequentially, in order to determine who is a third party, one must first determine who is a contracting party and from this deduce *a contrario* who is not.

292. Anyone who was present when the contract was concluded and gave his consent in his own name and for his own account is considered a party and is bound by the contractual obligations. This is also the case for those who were validly represented by an agent at the conclusion of the contract. One may also become a party as a consequence of unauthorised representation, i.e., if the agent acts without authority, or exceeds the limits of his authority. This will be the case when the principal ratifies the unauthorised act or when the doctrine of an apparent mandate is

425. Cass. 14 Nov. 1986, *Arr.Cass.* 1986-87, 357 and *Pas.* 1987, 331; Cass. 18 May 1989, *Arr.Cass.* 1988-89, 1098 and *Pas.* 1989, 990.
426. N. Carette & V. Withofs, 'Gevolgen voor derden van de overeenkomst' in B. Weyts and T. Vansweevelt, *Handboek Verbintenissenrecht* (Mortsle, Intersentia, 2019), 593; L. Cornelis, *Algemene theorie van de verbintenis* (Antwerp: Intersentia, 2000), No. 282; S. Stijns, *Leerboek Verbintenissenrecht 1* (Brugge: die Keure, 2016), 228; W. van Gerven en A. Van Oevelen, *Verbintenissenrecht* (Leuven: Acco, 2015), 224 et seq.; P. Van Ommeslaghe, *Les obligations vol. 1* in *Traité de droit civil, tome II* (Brussels: Bruylant, 2013), 645 and 657; P. Wéry, *Droit des obligations, I, Théorie générale du contrat* (Brussels: Larcier, 2011), 861.
427. S. Stijns, *Leerboek Verbintenissenrecht 1* (Brugge: die Keure, 2016), 242.
428. Cass. 22 Apr. 1977, *Arr.Cass.* 1977, 868 & *Pas.* 1977, 860.
429. S. Stijns, *Leerboek Verbintenissenrecht 1* (Brugge: die Keure, 2016), 242.
430. Cass. 27 Sep. 1974, *Arr.Cass.* 1975, 125 & *Pas.* 1975, 113.
431. N. Carette & V. Withofs, 'Gevolgen voor derden van de overeenkomst' in B. Weyts and T. Vansweevelt, *Handboek Verbintenissenrecht* (Mortsle, Intersentia, 2019), 594; E. Dirix, B. Tilleman & S. Lierman (eds), *De Valks Juridisch woordenboek* (Antwerp-Oxford: Intersentia, 2018), 121.

successfully invoked. According to the doctrine of apparent mandate (*see* No. 346 *infra*), a principal can be considered to be bound on account of an apparent agency, not only when he made this appearance possible by his negligence but also when, without negligence on the part of the principal, third parties could reasonably believe in the power of agency of the apparent agent.[432]

293. One may also start out as a third party, but later become a contracting party by succeeding to a contracting party. Article 1122 OCC states that one is 'considered to contract for oneself and for one's heirs and successors'. Thus, persons who inherit the whole or an abstract fraction of a contracting party's patrimony are put on par with this party. In the case of physical persons, this may happen in the case of death of a contracting party. In the case of legal persons, this may happen in the case of fusion. According to Article 682,3° of the Code on societies, every obligation or contract of an absorbed society is assumed by the absorbing society.[433] It should however be pointed out that, for physical and legal persons alike, there are exceptions to this rule, most notably in the case of *intuitu personae* contracts.[434] What happens when a person does not obtain the whole or an abstract fraction of a contracting party's patrimony, but only one specific good (e.g., through a sale or a gift)? According to the theory of the qualitative rights (*kwalitatieve rechten/droits qualitatifs*), this person will automatically hold the rights of his predecessor which are closely connected with the good he obtained. However, he will not be bound by the obligations or debts of his predecessor. For instance, the claim against the original seller based on his duty to guarantee the absence of hidden defects is transferred to the successive buyers of the good.

294. One may also become a party to a pre-existing contract through accession.[435] All the parties, i.e., all the original parties to the original agreement and the new acceding party, must express their will to accept the accession. In principle, a new acceding party is bound by the contract in the same way as the original parties. Indeed, he becomes a party himself and thus obtains the rights and becomes bound by the duties ensuing from the contract.[436]

---

432. For more on this subject, *see* I. Samoy, 'Unauthorised Agency in Belgian Law' in *The Unauthorised Agent*, ed. D. Busch and L.J. Macgregor (Cambridge: University Press, 2009), 3. Following conditions must be met in order to successfully invoke the doctrine of apparent mandate: (1) an appearance of (sufficient) authority to represent, (2) a legitimate faith or belief of the third party in the existence of (sufficient) authority to represent, (3) the imputability of the apparent authority to the principal, (4) a (risk of) damage for the third party, and (5) the legislator may not have excluded or limited the application of the doctrine of beliefs.
433. *Wetboek van Vennootschappen/Code des sociétés* of 7 May 1999, *Belgian Official Gazette*, 6 Aug. 1999.
434. *See* P. Wéry, *Droit des obligations, I, Théorie générale du contrat* (Brussels: Larcier, 2011), 798.
435. P. Wéry, *Droit des obligations, I, Théorie générale du contrat* (Brussels: Larcier, 2011), 798.
436. For more on this subject, *see*: T. Dang Vu, & I. Samoy, 'Dynamic Conclusion of the Contract and Proof' in *Consortium Agreements for Research Projects. Multiparty Agreements under Belgian Contract Law*, ed. I. Samoy (Cambridge: Intersentia, 2011), in preparation (ISBN n° 978-94-000-0196-1); I. Samoy, 'Pijnpunten bij het opstellen van consortium- en andere overeenkomsten met meer dan twee partijen', in *Themis-cahier Verbintenissenrecht*, ed. S. Stijns (Brugge: die Keure, 2006–2007), 63.

295. Another way to become a party after the conclusion of a pre-existing contract is due to a transfer of (a part of) the contract.[437] If the transfer of the contract was complete, the cedent is released from the contract and the cessionary replaces him as a contracting party (*see* No. 329 *infra*). If it was incomplete (*see* No. 329 *infra*), the transferring party remains bound by the contract.

II. Opposability of the External Effects of a Contract to Third Parties

A. Conditions

296. Following conditions must be met for a contract to be opposable to third parties. First, there must be a valid contract between parties. Second, the person who wants to call upon the contract must prove its existence. Third parties and parties can prove the contract with all legal means of proof (*see* No. 189 *supra*) (Article 8.14 CC). Contracting parties, contrary to third parties, have to respect the requirements concerning the fixed date of the act (Article 8.22 CC).

297. In certain cases, the law requires additional formalities in order for a juridical act to be opposable to third parties. In general, it is not necessary for the third party to have knowledge of the contract in order for it to be opposable. However, for certain types of contracts, the law imposed publicity as a supplementary condition for opposability, e.g., for the sale of immovables. If a formality for opposability has not been respected, the contract will not be opposable to third parties, unless they have knowledge of the contract and are not bona fide.[438] Also, even if the formalities are not respected, a third party keeps the right to invoke the contract if it is in his interest.[439]

B. Complicity of a Third Party to Breach of a Contract

298. Opposability affects the behaviour of third parties, resulting in liability for a third party who cooperates to the breach of a contract. The theory of complicity of a third party to a breach of a contract determines the requirements for liability due to the failure to take another's contract into account. As a third party is, by definition, not a contracting party, liability for one's complicity to breach of a contract is extracontractual, and finds its ground in Articles 1382 et seq. OCC (*see* No. 77 *supra*). The situation aimed at is that where two (or more) parties, A and B, have a contract, and a third party C concludes another contract with B, due to which B breaches his contract with A and thus incurs contractual liability towards A. Yet can A claim compensation from C as well? A typical example is the brewer who has an

437. P. Wéry, *Droit des obligations, I, Théorie générale du contrat* (Brussels: Larcier, 2011), 793 et seq.
438. S. Stijns, *Leerboek Verbintenissenrecht 1* (Brugge: die Keure, 2016), 239.
439. L. Cornelis, *Algemene theorie van de verbintenis* (Antwerp: Intersentia, 2000), No. 303; S. Stijns, W. van Gerven & P. Wéry, 'Chronique', *J.T.* (1996): No. 174.

exclusivity contract with the owner of a pub, where the owner of the pub binds himself to buy all his beer from this brewer. It sometimes happens for the owner of the pub to breach his contract by acquiring some beer from another brewer. As this is a clear breach of his contract with the first brewer, the pub owner will be liable contractually. The question is whether the first brewer can also hold the second brewer liable for his role in the breach.

299. The victim of a third party's complicity to breach of contract must prove the third party's fault, the damage and the causal link between both. Following requirements must be met to prove the fault of the third party:[440] (1) there must be a valid contractual obligation from B towards A; (2) this contractual obligation is breached by B; (3), the third party had or should have had knowledge of the contractual situation between A and B and (4) the third party willingly cooperated to the breach of contract; i.e., he had knowledge of the contract and of its breach.

300. The compensation for the damages may either be in kind or by equivalent (*see* Nos 137–138 *supra*). Compensation in kind aims to place A back in the situation where he would have been without the complicity to breach of contract, which is realised by cancelling the contract between B and C. Compensation by equivalent is often pecuniary damages. A can demand compensation from both B and C, who may be condemned *in solidum* and both be held to the compensation of the entire damage (*see* No. 328 *infra*).[441]

C. *Exceptions*

1. The Paulian Action

301. According to Article 1167 OCC, a creditor may, in his own name, oppose actions committed by his debtor which fraudulently infringe on his rights. The Paulian action (*pauliaanse vordering/action paulienne*), whose name is derived from the *actio Pauliana* of the Roman law, is the demand made by a creditor to obtain the non-opposability of juridical acts that were committed by his debtor and which fraudulently infringe on his recourses to retrieval.[442] It should be noted that a demand is required, and that non-opposability is not automatical. The Paulian action can also be invoked against a third party who acquired the fraudulent good

440. N. Carette & V. Withofs, 'Gevolgen voor derden van de overeenkomst' in B. Weyts and T. Vansweevelt, *Handboek Verbintenissenrecht* (Mortsle, Intersentia, 2019), 657; E. Dirix & A. Van Oevelen, 'Kroniek', *R.W.* (1992–1993): 1252; S. Stijns, *Leerboek Verbintenissenrecht 1* (Brugge: die Keure, 2016), 246; W. van Gerven en A. Van Oevelen, *Verbintenissenrecht* (Leuven: Acco, 2015), 229; P. Wéry, *Droit des obligations, I, Théorie générale du contrat* (Brussels: Larcier, 2011), 874.
441. Cass. 19 Dec. 2019, C.19.0167.N, *RW* 2020-21, 56, note S. Baeyens.
442. E. Dirix, B. Tilleman & S. Lierman (eds), *De Valks Juridisch woordenboek* (Antwerp-Oxford: Intersentia, 2018), 349.

from the third party who participated in the fraudulent action if the requirements for a Paulian action are met towards both the original third party and the new acquirer.[443]

302. The effect of a successful Paulian action is the non-opposability of the contract. This means that, on the one hand, the creditor will be enabled to act as if the fraudulent contract does not exist against him.[444] However, on the other hand, the contract is not cancelled and it remains valid between contracting parties and towards all other third parties who did not file a (successful) Paulian action.[445]

303. In order for a Paulian action to be successful, following cumulative requirements must be met.[446] First, one has to be creditor of a claim of an earlier date than the juridical act which is challenged.[447] Anteriority of the claim must be proven according to the system of proof applicable to juridical acts (*see* No. 183 *supra*).[448] There is one exception to this rule: when the challenged juridical act was committed with the sole intention to escape the recovery by future creditors, anteriority is not required.[449] Second, the creditor must have suffered prejudice. The prejudice is the fact that the creditor cannot recover on the patrimony of the debtor, or can only do so at a higher cost.[450] For this requirement to be met, it suffices to prove that the juridical act led to an impoverishment of the debtor or a diminution of the possibilities for recovery of the creditor.[451] Third, the prejudice suffered by the creditor must be the effect of a fraudulent action by the debtor. This does not imply the intent to deceive, but requires knowledge on the debtor's part that he is impoverishing

443. Cass. 9 Feb. 2006, *Pas.* 2006, 336.

444. Cass. 8 Jun. 2020, C.19.0641.F, *TIBR* 2020, nr. 2, RS-148. N. Carette & V. Withofs, 'Gevolgen voor derden van de overeenkomst' in B. Weyts and T. Vansweevelt, *Handboek Verbintenissenrecht* (Mortsle, Intersentia, 2019), 663; L. Cornelis, *Algemene theorie van de verbintenis* (Antwerp: Intersentia, 2000), No. 307; E. Dirix & A. Van Oevelen, 'Kroniek', *R.W.* (1992–1993): 1254; R. Kruithof e.a., 'Overzicht', *T.P.R.* (1994): Nos 361 & 369; S. Stijns, *Leerboek Verbintenissenrecht 1* (Brugge: die Keure, 2016), 248; W. van Gerven en A. Van Oevelen, *Verbintenissenrecht* (Leuven: Acco, 2015), 231.

445. H. De Page, *Traité élémentaire de droit civil belge, III* (Brussels: Bruylant, 1967), No. 203; E. Dirix & A. Van Oevelen, 'Kroniek', *R.W.* (1992–1993): 1255; R. Kruithof e.a., 'Overzicht', *T.P.R.* (1994): No. 369, S. Stijns, *Leerboek Verbintenissenrecht 1* (Brugge: die Keure, 2016), 249; W. van Gerven en A. Van Oevelen, *Verbintenissenrecht* (Leuven: Acco, 2015), 231–232.

446. N. Carette & V. Withofs, 'Gevolgen voor derden van de overeenkomst' in B. Weyts and T. Vansweevelt, *Handboek Verbintenissenrecht* (Mortsle, Intersentia, 2019), 666; S. Stijns, *Leerboek Verbintenissenrecht 1* (Brugge: die Keure, 2016), 249; W. van Gerven en A. Van Oevelen, *Verbintenissenrecht* (Leuven: Acco, 2015), 229–231; P. Wéry, *Droit des obligations, I, Théorie générale du contrat* (Brussels: Larcier, 2011), 873–874.

447. Cass. 3 Oct. 1985, *Arr.Cass.* 1985-86, 117 and *Pas.* 1986, 100; Cass. 5 Jan. 2006, www.cass.be; Cass. 20 Mar. 2008, *Pas.* 2008, 776.

448. H. De Page, *Traité élémentaire de droit civil belge, III* (Brussels: Bruylant, 1967), No. 227.

449. *Ibid.*, No. 228; R. Kruithof e.a., 'Overzicht', *T.P.R.* (1994): No. 363; S. Stijns, W. van Gerven & P. Wéry, 'Chronique', *J.T.* (1996): No. 180; S. Stijns, *Leerboek Verbintenissenrecht 1* (Brugge: die Keure, 2016), 249.

450. S. Stijns, W. van Gerven & P. Wéry, 'Chronique', *J.T.* (1996): No. 180; S. Stijns, *Leerboek Verbintenissenrecht 1* (Brugge: die Keure, 2016), 250.

451. R. Kruithof e.a., 'Overzicht', *T.P.R.* (1994): No. 364; S. Stijns, *Leerboek Verbintenissenrecht 1* (Brugge: die Keure, 2016), 250; W. van Gerven en A. Van Oevelen, *Verbintenissenrecht* (Leuven: Acco, 2015), 230.

himself or increasing his insolvency to the prejudice of the creditor.[452] According to the *Court of Cassation*, 'it suffices for the creditor to prove that the action was abnormal and that the debtor acted with the knowledge that his creditors would be prejudiced'.[453] Fourth, in case of a reciprocal contract between third party and debtor, the third party must know that the debtor impoverishes himself by his fraudulent action and thus prejudices his creditor.[454] If, however, the contract between the third party and the debtor is gratuitous, this knowledge is unnecessary.[455]

2. Simulation

a. Concept and Types

304. Simulation (*veinzing/simulation*) aims at the situation where parties willingly pretend that they have a certain contract or other juridical act in public while they secretly contract otherwise. Thus, parties in fact conclude two contracts: the apparent or public contract (*schijnovereenkomst/acte apparent*) and the hidden contract or counter letter (*tegenbrief/contre-lettre*).[456]

b. Effects

305. Article 1321 OCC states that 'counter letters are effective only between the contracting parties; they are not effective against third parties'. Thus, the contracting parties are bound towards each other by the hidden contract.[457] This contract is proven by the counter letter. However, the hidden contract is not opposable to third parties. Third parties may choose to accept the existence of the apparent contract or of the hidden contract.[458] The possibility to call upon the apparent contract is an

---

452. E. Dirix & A. Van Oevelen, 'Kroniek', *R.W.* (1992-93): 1254; R. Kruithof e.a., 'Overzicht', *T.P.R.* (1994): No. 365; S. Stijns, *Leerboek Verbintenissenrecht 1* (Brugge: die Keure, 2016), 250; W. van Gerven en A. Van Oevelen, *Verbintenissenrecht* (Leuven: Acco, 2015), 231.
453. For example, Cass. 15 Mar. 1985, *Arr.Cass.* 1984-85, 969 and *Pas.* 1985, 875; Cass. 29 Oct. 1989, *Arr.Cass.* 1989-90, 282 and *Pas.* 1990, 248.
454. H. De Page, *Traité élémentaire de droit civil belge, III* (Brussels: Bruylant, 1967), No. 206; E. Dirix & A. Van Oevelen, 'Kroniek', *R.W.* (1992-93), 1255; R. Kruithof e.a., 'Overzicht', *T.P.R.* (1994): No. 366; S. Stijns, *Leerboek Verbintenissenrecht 1* (Brugge: die Keure, 2016), 215; W. van Gerven en A. Van Oevelen, *Verbintenissenrecht* (Leuven: Acco, 2015), 231.
455. H. De Page, *Traité élémentaire de droit civil belge, III* (Brussels: Bruylant, 1967), No. 207; R. Kruithof e.a., 'Overzicht', *T.P.R.* (1994): No. 366; S. Stijns, W. van Gerven & P. Wéry, 'Chronique', *J.T.* 1996, No. 180; S. Stijns, *Leerboek Verbintenissenrecht 1* (Brugge: die Keure, 2016), 251; P. Wéry, *Droit des obligations, I, Théorie générale du contrat* (Brussels: Larcier, 2011), 874–875.
456. Cass. 22 May 2020, F.19.0099.F, *Rec.gén. enr.* Not. 2020, book 7, 330, note P. De Page.
457. L. Cornelis, *Algemene theorie van de verbintenis* (Antwerp: Intersentia, 2000), No. 42; H. De Page, *Traité élémentaire de droit civil belge, III* (Brussels: Bruylant, 1967), No. 626; R. Kruithof e.a., 'Overzicht', *T.P.R.* (1994): Nos 104–106; S. Stijns, *Leerboek Verbintenissenrecht 1* (Brugge: die Keure, 2016), 252; W. van Gerven en A. Van Oevelen, *Verbintenissenrecht* (Leuven: Acco, 2015), 227.
458. Cass. 11 Dec. 1987, *Arr.Cass.* 1987-88, 481, *Arr.Cass.* 1988, 481 and *Pas.* 1988, 449.

application of the theory of appearance (*see* No. 32 *supra*) in the relationship between contracting parties and third parties. This means that the third party may, if he wishes to, consider the apparent situation the actual one, provided that he acted in good faith and believed in the apparent situation at the time of his own actions. However, he may also choose to call upon the actual, hidden contract because this contract corresponds to the will of the parties.[459]

III. Relativity of the Internal Effects of a Contract Towards Third Parties

A. *One May Not Lay a Burden on a Third Party*

306. As stated before, one may not lay a burden upon a third party. This rule is absolute and knows no exceptions. There are, however, techniques through which one may try to achieve a similar result, but these do not lay any obligations upon third parties.

307. A first example of such a technique is the clause of *sterkmaking/porte-fort.* According to Article 1120 OCC, one (contracting party A) may promise to another (contracting party B) that a third party C will take an obligation upon himself. Contracting party A takes an obligation to achieve upon himself: he obligates himself to obtain acceptance from the third party[460] or the execution of an obligation from the third party.[461] However, third party C is in not obligated in any way and retains the freedom to accept or not. The effects of *sterkmaking/porte-fort* depend upon the third party's reaction. If he accepts to bind himself, A provides the promised result and his obligation becomes extinguished. If he refuses, A did not achieve the promised result, and, according to Article 1120 OCC, he must pay damages to B.

308. A second example is the perpetual clause (*kettingbeding/stipulation en chaîne*), which is a clause in which a contracting party A promises to the other contracting party B that he will include a certain obligation in a contract he will conclude with third party C.[462] For instance, this may be done with a non-competition clause in case of sale of a commerce, where A, who takes over the commerce, not only binds himself not to compete against B but also to include a non-competition clause in the sale contract should he ever decide to sell the commerce to a third party. Such a clause is considered valid.[463] Third party C remains completely free to accept the clause or not. Only A is bound by an obligation to achieve. If C refuses

---

459. S. Stijns, *Leerboek Verbintenissenrecht 1* (Brugge: die Keure, 2016), 253; P. Wéry, *Droit des obligations, I, Théorie générale du contrat* (Brussels: Larcier, 2011), 878.
460. *Ibid.*, 254; *Ibid.*:, 914 et. seq.
461. Cass. 24 Mar. 2016, C.15.0324.N, *RW* 2016-17, 1219, note I. Samoy, *TBBR* 2017, 314, note D. Saonck, *TBO*, 550; N. Carette & V. Withofs, 'Gevolgen voor derden van de overeenkomst' in B. Weyts and T. Vansweevelt, *Handboek Verbintenissenrecht* (Mortsle, Intersentia, 2019), 635.
462. E. Dirix, B. Tilleman & S. Lierman (eds), *De Valks Juridisch woordenboek* (Antwerp-Oxford: Intersentia, 2018), 257.
463. S. Stijns, *Leerboek Verbintenissenrecht 1* (Brugge: die Keure, 2016), 255.

to accept the clause, A should abstain from concluding the planned contract with him. If he contracts with C without including the clause, A commits a breach of contract for which he is liable towards B.

309. A final example is the accession contract (*see* No. 294 *supra*). However, the joining party remains free to accept the contract (as a whole) or not; consequentially, no third parties are bound without their acceptance.

B. One May Contract for the Benefit of a Third Party

310. It is possible for contracting parties to grant rights to a third party if this possibility is explicitly granted by law. First, Articles 1121 and 1165 OCC allow the stipulation for the benefit of a third party. Second, in certain specific cases, the law grants the creditor of a contracting party a direct action.

1. Stipulation for the Benefit of a Third Party

311. The stipulation for the benefit of another (*beding ten behoeve van een derde/stipulation pour autrui*) is a contractual clause where one party A (the stipulator) makes the other party B (the promiser) promise to perform for the benefit of a third party C (the beneficiary).[464] C does not become a contracting party because A acts in his own name. However, C does become B's creditor for the performance. A classic example is life insurance, where insured person A makes the insurance company B promise that, in case of A's death, it will pay a certain sum of money to C.[465]

312. A valid stipulation for the benefit of a third party must meet the following requirements:[466] (1) there must be a valid contract between the stipulator and the promisor; (2) the stipulator must have a personal interest to stipulate for the benefit of the third party; (3) parties must have the intention to bestow a benefit on a third party and to grant him a new, personal right, must exist without any doubt; and (4) the beneficiary third party must be determined or at least determinable when the clause gains effect without, however, necessarily mentioning the name of the third party.[467] A contract can be made for the benefit of children as yet unborn.

---

464. E. Dirix, B. Tilleman & S. Lierman (eds), *De Valks Juridisch woordenboek* (Antwerp-Oxford: Intersentia, 2018), 42.
465. For example, Cass. 16 Jan. 2006, www.cass.be.
466. N. Carette & V. Withofs, 'Gevolgen voor derden van de overeenkomst' in B. Weyts and T. Vansweevelt, *Handboek Verbintenissenrecht* (Mortsle, Intersentia, 2019), 615; R. Kruithof e.a., 'Overzicht', *T.P.R.* (1994): No. 244; S. Stijns, *Leerboek Verbintenissenrecht 1* (Brugge: die Keure, 2016), 257; W. van Gerven en A. Van Oevelen, *Verbintenissenrecht* (Leuven: Acco, 2015), 235; P. Wéry, *Droit des obligations, I, Théorie générale du contrat* (Brussels: Larcier, 2011), 818–821.
467. Cass. 25 May 2018, C.17.0082.F, *J.L.M.B.* 2019, book 5, 208.

313. The beneficiary obtains a personal right from the contract between stipulator and promisor. The beneficiary has a direct action against the promisor,[468] even before he accepts the clause made for his benefit.[469] This right is created directly in the third party's patrimony. It never comes into the patrimony of the stipulator, thus remaining unattainable for his creditors. The stipulator can revoke the benefit conferred on the beneficiary as long as the third party has not accepted it. However, as soon as the third party has accepted the clause implicitly or explicitly, it can no longer be revoked (Article 1121 OCC). The personal right of the beneficiary depends on the contract between stipulator and promiser, as this contract is the source of the beneficiary's right. Thus, the promiser may invoke exceptions from the contract (e.g., extraneous cause) against the beneficiary, unless the contract stipulates otherwise.[470]

2. Direct Actions

314. The direct action (*rechtstreekse vordering/action directe*) is the right granted by law to a creditor (third party C) against the debtor (contracting party B) of his debtor (contracting party A).[471] Third party C thus acquires the independent and personal right to enforce performance of his contractual obligations from A. The direct action is certainly not applicable to any kind of contract: it only applies to cases explicitly specified by law.

315. A valid direct action must meet the following requirements.[472] First, there must be a valid, contractual or extracontractual, claim from third party C against contracting party A. Second, there must be a valid contract between debtor A and his contracting party B, such that A is creditor from a performance by B. Third, the law must grant a direct action to A towards the debtor of his debtor.

316. The main examples of laws granting a direct action are Article 1798 OCC and Article 29*bis* of the Law of 21 November 1989 on compulsory insurance of

468. Cass. 16 januari 2006, *Arr. Cass.* 2006, 153, *Pas*, 2006, 163 and *RW* 2008-09, 868; Cass. 4 Jan. 1988, *Arr.Cass.*1987-88, 556 and *Pas.* 1988, 524.
469. Cass. 16 januari 2006, *Arr. Cass.* 2006, 153, *Pas*, 2006, 163 and *RW* 2008-09, 868; Cass. 13 Jan. 1967, *Pas.* 1967, 571.
470. S. Stijns, *Leerboek Verbintenissenrecht 1* (Brugge: die Keure, 2016), 260; W. van Gerven en A. Van Oevelen, *Verbintenissenrecht* (Leuven: Acco, 2015), 237–238; P. Wéry, *Droit des obligations, I, Théorie générale du contrat* (Brussels: Larcier, 2011), 826.
471. E. Dirix, B. Tilleman & S. Lierman (eds), *De Valks Juridisch woordenboek* (Antwerp-Oxford: Intersentia, 2018), 382.
472. R. Dekkers & A. Verbeke, *Handboek Burgerlijk Recht*, III (Antwerp: Intersentia: 2007), 86; S. Stijns, *Leerboek Verbintenissenrecht 1* (Brugge: die Keure, 2016), 262; W. van Gerven en A. Van Oevelen, *Verbintenissenrecht* (Leuven: Acco, 2015), 238–239; P. Wéry, *Droit des obligations, I, Théorie générale du contrat* (Brussels: Larcier, 2011), 839.

motorised vehicles.[473] Article 1798 OCC provides that employees of a building contractor and his subcontractors who were not paid by their employer may claim payment from the person who has commissioned the building to the extent to which he is indebted to their employer. Article 29*bis* of the Law of 21 November 1989 on compulsory insurance of motorised vehicles[474] confers on a third party who was injured in a traffic accident the right to take direct action against the insurer of a motorised car who was involved in the accident, who is held to compensate all material and immaterial damages resulting from physical injury or death suffered by the victim or his legal successors. This right exists regardless of the existence or absence of guilt from the driver.

317. The treatment of exceptions existing in the contractual relation between A and B is somewhat different than stipulations for the benefit of a third party and depends on the type of direct action. The general rule is that exceptions which come into existence *after* the exercise of the direct action cannot be invoked against the third party who uses the direct action. On the other hand, exceptions that existed before the direct action was introduced can be opposed to him.[475] However, some specific laws grant more ample rights to the third party and provide that even exceptions anterior to the direct action cannot be opposed to him, e.g., Article 16 of the Law of 21 November 1989 on compulsory insurance of motorised cars[476] which stipulates that 'no nullity, defense or dissolution ensuing from the law or the insurance contract can be opposed to the prejudiced party by the insurer'.

3. Oblique Actions

318. Direct actions should not be confused with oblique actions (*zijdelingse vordering/action oblique*), which are governed by Article 1166 OCC. This article stipulates that, in case of inaction of their debtor, 'creditors may exercise all rights and claims from their debtor, except those which are strictly linked to his personality'. Thus, the creditor acts as an agent of the debtor and does not exercise a personal right nor becomes a contracting party in the relationship between the debtor and the debtor's debtors.[477] Claims are laid in the name of and on the debtor's expense.[478] As the gains obtained by the claim fall to the debtor and fall into his patrimony, this is no real exception to the relativity of contracts.

---

473. *Wet betreffende de verplichte aansprakelijkheidsverzekering inzake motorrijtuigen/Loi relative à l'assurance obligatoire de la responsabilité en matière de véhicules automoteurs, Belgian Official Gazette* 8 Dec. 1989.

474. *Ibid.*

475. Cass. 27 Feb. 2015, C.14.0344.N, *Arr.Cass.* 2015, 547, *TBBR* 2019, 103, *TBO* 2015, 208; S. Stijns, *Leerboek Verbintenissenrecht 1* (Brugge: die Keure, 2016), 265–266.

476. *Wet betreffende de verplichte aansprakelijkheidsverzekering inzake motorrijtuigen/Loi relative à l'assurance obligatoire de la responsabilité en matière de véhicules automoteurs, Belgian Official Gazette* 8 Dec. 1989.

477. S. Stijns, *Leerboek Verbintenissenrecht 1* (Brugge: die Keure, 2016), 265; W. van Gerven en A. Van Oevelen, *Verbintenissenrecht* (Leuven: Acco, 2015), 244.

478. L. Cornelis, *Algemene theorie van de verbintenis* (Antwerp: Intersentia, 2000), Nos 288–290; S. Stijns, W. van Gerven & P. Wéry, 'Chronique', *J.T.* 1996, No. 169.

§2. TRANSFER OF OBLIGATIONS

I. Transfer of Contractual Rights

319. Transfer of a specific right may take place through subrogation or through cession (*cessie* or *overdracht van schuldvordering/cession*). Subrogation will be discussed in Nos 357 ff. *infra*. Cession is a contract where the cedent (*cedent* or *overdrager/cédant*) transfers a right, towards one or several debtors to a cessionary (*cessionaris* or *overnemer/cessionaire*), so the cessionary takes up the cedent's place and becomes entitled to demand performance from the debtor.[479]

320. In principle, every right can be the subject of cession. There are a few exceptions. The first exception concerns rights which the law has declared to be non-transferable, e.g., the transfer of rights regarding the payment of wages is only partially possible.[480] The second regards debts about which the creditor and debtor have agreed that a cession should not be permitted. However, such agreement only binds the contracting parties and cannot affect the position of a bona fide cessionary. The third exception is debts which cannot be ceded due to their nature, e.g., a right which has been granted to the creditor by the debtor because of who the creditor was (*intuitu personae* contract).

The ceded right should be determined or determinable (*see* No. 230 *supra*). It is possible to cede future rights, provided they can be described with sufficient certainty, e.g., the right of a landlord regarding rent which has not yet fallen due.[481] Even contested rights, i.e., rights which are the object of a legal process, may be transferred.[482]

321. The general rules on cession are laid down in Articles 1689–1701 of the Civil Code. Although these articles are located in Chapter VIII, *Transfer of Legal Claims and Other Incorporeal Claims* of *Title VI, Sale*, a right may also be transferred through other contracts than a sale, e.g., a gift or a trade. These rules only apply to rights regarding debts which are not embodied in negotiable instruments. Rights which are embodied in negotiable instruments are subjected to other, specific rules.[483]

---

479. S. Stijns, *Leerboek Verbintenissenrecht 2* (Brugge: die Keure, 2020), 63.
480. Article 1409 §1 of the Judicial Code.
481. Cass. 9 Apr. 1959, *Arr.Cass.* 1959, 606 & *Pas.* 1959, 793; H. De Page, *Traité élémentaire de droit civil belge, IV* (Brussels: Bruylant, 1997), No. 510; S. Stijns, *Leerboek Verbintenissenrecht 2* (Brugge: die Keure, 2020), 65; W. van Gerven en A. Van Oevelen, *Verbintenissenrecht* (Leuven: Acco, 2015), 574.
482. Cass. 8 Feb. 1990, *Arr.Cass.* 1990-91, 755 & *Pas.* 1990, 678; Cass. 9 Sep. 1994, *Arr.Cass.* 1994, 711 & *Pas.* 1994, 697.
483. S. Stijns, *Leerboek Verbintenissenrecht 2* (Brugge: die Keure, 2020), 66; W. van Gerven en A. Van Oevelen, *Verbintenissenrecht* (Leuven: Acco, 2015), 574.

322. Cession is a consensual contract, i.e., a contract without any formal requirements for its validity between cedent and cessionary.[484] In practice, parties often draw up a written document as proof. As soon as there is a consensus, the right is validly transferred from the cedent's patrimony to the cessionary's patrimony. It should be noted that the acceptance of the debtor is not required.[485] However, as he needs to know to whom he must pay in order for the debt to be extinguished, he must be informed of the cession.[486]

323. As for the opposability to third parties, the general rule, as laid down in the first sentence of Article 1690 §1 OCC, is that the cession is opposable to them from the moment the cession contract is concluded. Consequentially, a situation of conflicting rights between cedent, cessionary and third parties is to be solved by reference to the moment of cession as agreed upon by the parties. This is called the anteriority-rule (*anterioriteitsregel/principe de l'antériorité*): anteriority is determined by the date of the cession.[487]

However, there are some exceptions to this rule, which aim to protect certain categories of third parties. The first concerns the ceded debtor, against whom the cession may only be invoked from the moment he is notified of it, or from the moment he recognises the cession contract (Article 1690 §1 OCC, second sentence). Notification implies that the debtor should be informed about the fact that his debt has been ceded and that he should pay to a new creditor.[488] Although this notification is not subject to formal requirements, it is necessary that it is written.[489] Both the cedent and the cessionary can do the notification. The cession may be recognised implicitly or explicitly. If the debtor claims not to have knowledge of the cession or not to have received any notification, it is up to the cessionary to prove that the debtor was notified.[490] According to Article 1691 OCC, the debtor who has paid in good faith before the cession was notified to him is freed of his debt. In this context, good faith means that the debtor did not know and did not have to know that there was a cession.[491] As soon as the debtor has been notified, he may only free himself of his debt by paying the cessionary. In that case, if he pays the cedent, he may have to pay a second time to the cessionary.[492]

---

484. L. Cornelis, *Algemene theorie van de verbintenis* (Antwerp: Intersentia, 2000), No. 329; S. Stijns, W. van Gerven & P. Wéry, 'Chronique', *J.T.* (1999): No. 33; S. Stijns, *Leerboek Verbintenissenrecht, vol. 2* (Brugge: die Keure, 2020), 67; W. van Gerven en A. Van Oevelen, *Verbintenissenrecht* (Leuven: Acco, 2015), 577.
485. L. Cornelis, *Algemene theorie van de verbintenis* (Antwerp: Intersentia, 2000), No. 330; S. Stijns, *Leerboek Verbintenissenrecht 2* (Brugge: die Keure, 2020), 68.
486. W. van Gerven en A. Van Oevelen, *Verbintenissenrecht* (Leuven: Acco, 2015), 573.
487. H. De Page & A. Meinertzhagen-Limpens, *Traité élémentaire de droit civil belge*, IV, 1997, 588–590; S. Stijns, W. van Gerven & P. Wéry, 'Chronique', *J.T.* (1999): No. 35.
488. Cass. 5 May 2008, AR C.06.0485.F, *Arr.Cass.* 2008, 1092.
489. R. Roodhooft (ed.), *Bestendig handbook verbintenissenrecht* (Antwerp: Kluwer Rechtswetenschappen, 1998–2018), No. 3221; S. Stijns, W. van Gerven & P. Wéry, 'Chronique', *J.T.* (1999): No. 35; S. Stijns, *Leerboek Verbintenissenrecht 2* (Brugge: die Keure, 2020), 69–70.
490. S. Stijns, W. van Gerven & P. Wéry, 'Chronique', *J.T.* 1999, No. 35.
491. S. Stijns, *Leerboek Verbintenissenrecht 2* (Brugge: die Keure, 2020), 71.
492. Cass. 15 Jun. 2007, C.06.0661.N, *Arr.Cass.* 2007, 1355.

The Civil Code also protects some other categories of third parties. According to the third sentence of Article 1690 §1 OCC, if the cedent cedes the same rights to different cessionaries, preference goes to the bona fide cessionary who was the first to notify the transfer to the debtor or to obtain the debtor's recognition of the transfer. The last sentence of Article 1690 §2 OCC states that a cession cannot be called upon against bona fide creditors of the cedent to whom the debtor has paid in good faith and before he was notified of the assignment. The bona fide requirement is the same as for the debtor: the protected third party must be unaware that there has been a cession.

324. The consequences of a cession are the following. Between cedent and cessionary, the ownership of the right is transferred with, as stated by Article 1692 OCC, all its accessories, such as cautions, privileges and mortgages. According to Article 1693 OCC, the cedent is responsible for the existence of the right at the time of the transfer. Article 1694 OCC further states that he is not responsible for the debtor's financial situation, unless he has stipulated otherwise, and even then he cannot be liable for more than the price he has received for the cession. When he has agreed to be responsible for the debtor's financial situation, that promise only counts for his situation at the time of the promise and not for the future, unless it has explicitly been stipulated (Article 1695 CC).

The cessionary replaces the cedent in his legal relation to the debtor, but the right itself remains unchanged.[493] Consequentially, the debtor may use all the exceptions and defences he had against the previous creditor against the new creditor.[494] This is explained by the maxim '*nemo plus iuris transferre potest quam ipse habet*': the cedent cannot transfer more rights than he owns. However, a distinction should be made between defences derived from the claim itself or its formation, which are opposable to the new creditor, and exceptions which are solely based on the person of the previous creditor, which are not opposable to the new one.[495] Furthermore, Article 1691 OCC, second sentence, makes a distinction between defences derived from juridical acts between the debtor and cedent and other defences. Defences which derive from legal acts between the cedent and the debtor, such as novation, respite of payment, compensation or modification of the contract terms, may only be invoked by the debtor if he acted in good faith. All other defences, such as defects of consent, illegality of object and cause and the *exceptio non adimpleti contractus* (*see* No. 448 *infra*), may be exercised without regard to the good faith of the debtor. It should however be noted that parties may deviate from these rules by contracting otherwise.

493. S. Stijns, *Leerboek Verbintenissenrecht 2* (Brugge: die Keure, 2020), 73.
494. Cass. 28 Jan. 2005, *Pas.* 2005, 204; W. van Gerven en A. Van Oevelen, *Verbintenissenrecht* (Leuven: Acco, 2015), 583; A. Van Oevelen, 'Kroniek', *R.W.* (2004-05): No. 52.
495. S. Stijns, *Leerboek Verbintenissenrecht 2* (Brugge: die Keure, 2020), 73; W. van Gerven en A. Van Oevelen, *Verbintenissenrecht* (Leuven: Acco, 2015), 583; A. Van Oevelen, 'Kroniek', *R.W.* (2004-05): No. 52.

II. Transfer of Contractual Debts

A. Concept

325. Transfer of debts (*schuldoverdracht or overname van een schuld/ transmission or cession or reprise de dettes*) takes place when a debtor's position is transferred to a third party, and a new debtor replaced the previous debtor without altering the obligation.[496] It is not treated in the Civil Code. The *Court of Cassation* stated that 'according to the principles of civil law, rights can be transferred, but debts cannot' and that 'the debtor must perform his obligation and may not force his creditor to accept another debtor instead of him'.[497] Thus, the transfer of debts necessitates the assent of the creditor.[498] Besides this assent, a complete transfer of debt also requires for the original debtor to be removed from the legal relationship, but for the legal relationship to be otherwise unaltered.[499] Such a complete transfer is called a complete transfer of debt (*voltooide schuldoverdracht/transmission de dette parfaite*). However, Belgian law also recognises two forms of 'transfer' where the original debtor is not freed: incomplete transfer of debts (*onvoltooide schuldoverdracht/transmission de dette imparfaite*) and delegation (*delegatie/ délégation*).

B. Complete Transfer of Debt

326. As stated above, transfer of debt is considered *complete* when the original debtor is freed and the new debtor becomes bound towards the creditor in the same way as the previous debtor used to be.[500] This requires the assent of the creditor.[501] The complete transfer of debts can be achieved by a three-party contract involving the original debtor, the new debtor and the creditor, or in two steps, namely a contract between the original debtor and the new one (also called an 'internal' contract), followed by the notification of this contract to the creditor who gives his approval. If these requirements are met, the debt is truly transferred to the new debtor. It is, in other words, the same debt, only the debtor changes.

C. Incomplete Transfer of Debt

327. When the creditor does not approve of the (internal) transfer, it is *incomplete*. The creditor is not a party to the transfer and thus the agreement to transfer

496. H. De Page, *Traité élémentaire de droit civil belge*, III, 1967, 373.
497. Cass. 26 Sep. 2003, *Pas*. 2003, 1487.
498. S. Stijns, *Leerboek Verbintenissenrecht 2* (Brugge: die Keure, 2020), 76.
499. W. van Gerven en A. Van Oevelen, *Verbintenissenrecht* (Leuven: Acco, 2015), 582.
500. S. Stijns, *Leerboek Verbintenissenrecht 2* (Brugge: die Keure, 2020), 76.
501. L. Cornelis, *Algemene theorie van de verbintenis* (Antwerp: Intersentia, 2000), No. 324; S. Stijns, *Leerboek Verbintenissenrecht, vol. 2* (Brugge: die Keure, 2020), 76; W. van Gerven en A. Van Oevelen, *Verbintenissenrecht* (Leuven: Acco, 2015), 590.

the debt will only bind the person who transfers the debt and the person it is transferred to. The creditor keeps his right against the original debtor. Such an incomplete or 'internal' transfer of debt is valid, as the payment of a debt by another than the debtor is allowed by Article 1236 OCC (*see* No. 341 *infra*). Thus, the debtor may agree with a third party that the debt will be paid by this third party. However, as this contract does not bind the creditor, he may still demand payment by the original debtor,[502] and cannot demand payment from the third party. However, if the original debtor pays the creditor, he will be able to recover from the person whom he transferred the debt to. There are some techniques to grant the creditor a right against the third party: the third party may make a unilateral binding promise to pay towards the creditor, or a clause to the benefit of the creditor (*see* No. 310 *supra*) may be stipulated in the contract between the transferrer and the person the debt is transferred to.

D. Delegation of Debt

328. Another possibility to 'transfer' a debt without freeing the original debtor is delegation. Delegation is a three-party contract where a debtor/creditor B charges his debtor C to bind himself towards his (the creditor's) creditor A, who agrees with this.[503] This requires the assent of all three parties. The original debtor/creditor B is not freed, and the debt is not transferred. Instead, a new obligation is created between A and C, which exists besides the original debt. Creditor A thus obtains two debtors instead of one.[504] Considering that the old obligation and the new one are two distinct obligations, there are some differences between them. Indeed, the new obligation is abstracted from the original legal relation which gave birth to it.[505] Consequentially, exceptions arisen from the original legal relationships (either between B and C or between A and B) cannot be invoked by the new debtor C (*see* No. 324 *supra*). Both B and C are bound *in solidum*, so that payment by one of them frees the other (*see* No. 300 *supra*). Another consequence of delegation is that B may no longer claim payment of the initial debt between him and C from C.[506]

502. S. Stijns, *Leerboek Verbintenissenrecht, vol. 2* (Brugge: die Keure, 2020), 78; W. van Gerven en A. Van Oevelen, *Verbintenissenrecht* (Leuven: Acco, 2015), 590.
503. E. Dirix, B. Tilleman & S. Lierman (eds), *De Valks Juridisch woordenboek* (Antwerp-Oxford: Intersentia, 2018), 118. *See* in more detail in I. Samoy & S. Van Loock, « La délégation en droit belge » in P. Jourdain & P. Wéry (ed.), *La transmission des obligations en droit français et en droit belge* (Brussels: Larcier, 2019) (919–978).
504. S. Stijns, *Leerboek Verbintenissenrecht, vol. 2* (Brugge: die Keure, 2020), 80.
505. G. Van Malderen & N. Peeters, 'De overdracht van verbintenissen' in R. Roodhooft (ed.), *Bestendig handbook verbintenissenrecht* (Antwerp: Kluwer Rechtswetenschappen, 1998–2018), No. 3253; S. Stijns, *Leerboek Verbintenissenrecht 2* (Brugge: die Keure, 2020), 81; W. van Gerven en A. Van Oevelen, *Verbintenissenrecht* (Leuven: Acco, 2015), 590–591.
506. S. Stijns, *Leerboek Verbintenissenrecht 2* (Brugge: die Keure, 2020), 82.

III. Transfer of Reciprocal Contracts

329. There are no general rules for the transfer of a reciprocal contract in its entirety.[507] Consequentially, in order to transfer a contract, it seems that the legal techniques for the transfer of rights have to be combined with the techniques for the transfer of debts.[508] The separate transfer of multiple rights and debts in order to transfer a complete contract is a laborious process which has often been criticised by doctrine. It advocates the transfer of contracts as a separate legal concept[509] and bases this on the autonomy of will of parties. The doctrine thereby makes a distinction between complete and incomplete transfer of contract. Complete transfer of contract (*volkomen contractoverdracht/cession parfaite de contrat*) is a three-party contract which requires the assent of all the parties involved, and results in the transfer of all the legal rights and debts and the release of the transferring contracting party from the contract. The transfer of contract is incomplete (*onvolkomen contractoverdracht/cession imparfaite de contrat*) without the agreement of the other party. In that case, the transferring party remains bound by the contract, although he may claim reimbursement of what was claimed from him by his opposing party from the person he transferred the contract to.[510] The Court of Cassation recognised the validity of the incomplete transfer of a contract.[511]

§3. Subcontracting

330. In principle, Belgian law allows subcontracting. In order to perform his own contractual obligation, a party may use the services of third parties, with whom, in turn, he concludes a contract (e.g., subcontract of supply of services or subbailment). This possibility of subcontracting will in some cases be reduced or excluded by statutory law, or by express contract terms or by the nature of the promised performance (e.g., an *intuitu personae* contract). The subcontract is considered an independent contract between the 'main debtor' (the main contractor) and the 'sub-debtor' (the subcontractor), which is distinct from the main contract.

---

507. There are, however, rules concerning some specific kinds of contracts, e.g., the transfer of a rent (Art. 1717 OCC), the transfer of insurance portfolio's (Arts 74–76 of the Law of 9 Jul. 1975 on the control on insurance companies) and the transfer of contracts regarding credit to consumers (Arts 25–27 of the Law of 12 Jun. 1991 on credit to consumers).

508. G. Van Malderen & N. Peeters, 'De overdracht van verbintenissen' in R. Roodhooft (ed.), *Bestendig handbook verbintenissenrecht* (Antwerp: Kluwer Rechtswetenschappen, 1998–2018), No. 3262; S. Stijns, *Leerboek Verbintenissenrecht 2* (Brugge: die Keure, 2020), 84; W. van Gerven en A. Van Oevelen, *Verbintenissenrecht* (Leuven: Acco, 2015), 592–593.

509. S. Stijns, W. van Gerven & P. Wéry, 'Chronique', *J.T.* (1999): No. 40; S. Stijns, *Leerboek Verbintenissenrecht 2* (Brugge: die Keure, 2020), 84; W. van Gerven en A. Van Oevelen, *Verbintenissenrecht* (Leuven: Acco, 2015), 593.

510. G. Van Malderen & N. Peeters, 'De overdracht van verbintenissen' in R. Roodhooft (ed.), *Bestendig handbook verbintenissenrecht* (Antwerp: Kluwer Rechtswetenschappen, 1998–2018), No. 3263.

511. Cass. 26 Jun. 2017, *JT* 2018, 587, note C. Biquet-Mathieu, *TBBR* 2018, 362, note V. Withofs.

I. Liability of the Main Contractor for the Defective Performance of the Subcontractor

331. If the main contract is not performed due to a fault of the subcontractor, the (main) creditor is entitled to the same contractual remedies against the main debtor as he would have had if no subcontracting had occurred (*see* Nos 415 ff. *infra*).

II. The Employer: Subcontractor Relationship: Quasi-Immunity of the Subcontractor

332. Due to the rule of privity of contract (*see* Nos 287 ff. *infra*), no contractual relation comes into existence between the principal (i.e., the contracting partner of the main creditor) and the subcontractor. The subcontract is a *res inter alios acta*. Consequentially, the principal cannot hold the subcontractor liable *contractually*, and vice versa. However, the question arises whether he may claim damages *extra-contractually*, for tort. According to the *Court of Cassation*, auxiliaries are not considered real third parties towards the principal.[512] Consequentially, a principal can only sue the auxiliary for tort in the cases where concurrence between tortious and contractual liability is allowed (*see* Nos 80 ff. *supra*). This is called the *quasi-immunity* of auxiliaries. Is considered to be an auxiliary 'a natural person or a legal entity entrusted by the a natural or legal person by the debtor of a contractual obligation to execute that obligation, either in whole or in part, regardless of whether he is executing it on his own behalf and in his own name, or on behalf of and in the name of the debtor'.[513] This quasi-immunity applies also to organs of legal persons[514] and to mandataries.

333. The quasi-immunity of auxiliaries is reinforced when the auxiliary is also a subordinate (whether legally or factually) of the main contractor. Article 18 of the Law on Labour Contracts[515] stipulates that employees who cause damages to their employer or to third parties to his labour contract are only liable in case of deceit, grave fault or slight fault which is rather usual than accidental to him. In other words, they are not liable for accidental, slight faults. This immunity also extends to recovery claims by employers who were considered liable contractually due to a fault made by their employee.

334. For the sake of completeness, it should be mentioned that, in some specific cases, the law makes an exception to this rule by granting a direct (contractual)

512. Cass. 7 Dec. 1973, *Arr.Cass.* 1974, 395 & *Pas.* 1974, 376.
513. Cass. 12 Mar. 2020, *RGAR* 2020, 15720, note C. Helas; *RW* 2020-21, 817; *TBBR* 2020, 438; *TBH* 2020, 402. Translation by the author. Original text: 'Een hulppersoon is een natuurlijke persoon of een rechtspersoon die door de schuldenaar van een contractuele verbintenis belast wordt met de gehele of gedeeltelijke uitvoering van deze verbintenis, ongeacht of hij deze verbintenis uitvoert voor eigen rekening en in eigen naam, dan wel voor rekening en in naam van de schuldenaar.'
514. Cass. 7 Nov. 1997, *Arr.Cass.* 1997, 1093 & *Pas.* 1997, 1146.
515. Law of 3 Jul. 1978 on Labour Contracts (*Arbeidsovereenkomstenwet/Loi relative aux contrats de travail*), *Belgian Official Gazette* 22 Aug. 1978.

action to the subcontractor against the principal of his contracting partner. For example, Article 1798 OCC states that masons, carpenters, workers and craftsmen who have been employed in the construction of a building or other works made in an undertaking have an action against him for whom the works were done only up to the amount for which he is debtor towards the contractor at the time when action is brought.

Chapter 5. The End of the Contract

§1. Performance and Breach

I. Performance

335. Article 1234 OCC stipulates that obligations are extinguished by payment (*see* Nos 336 ff. *infra*), novation (*see* Nos 370 ff. *infra*), discharge by agreement (*see* Nos 380 ff. *infra*), compensation (*see* Nos 373 ff. *infra*), confusion (*see* No. 379 *infra*), the destruction of the thing, nullity (*see* Nos 235 ff. *supra*), the operation of a resolutive condition (*see* Nos 275 ff. *supra*), prescription (*see* Nos 382 ff. *infra*) and termination (*see* No. 388 *infra*). Doctrine and jurisprudence add dissolution (*see* No. 233 *supra*) to this illustrative list.

A. *Payment*

1. Introductory Concepts

336. The normal method to extinguish an obligation is its performance. This is expressed in the Civil Code by the word 'payment' (*betaling/paiement*).[516] In this context, the meaning of the word 'payment' is broader than the delivery of a sum of money. The 'payment' of an obligation is its performance, which may be to do something, to abstain from doing something or to give something (*see* No. 36 *supra*).

337. A distinction is made between a simple payment (*eenvoudige betaling/paiement pur et simple*) and a payment with subrogation (*betaling met subrogatie/paiement avec subrogation*). While a simple payment extinguishes an obligation, a payment with subrogation does not, as the rights of the creditor towards the debtor will merely be transferred to another person.

338. Payment is an unilateral juridical act.[517] The debtor (or third person who paid for him, *see* No. 341 *infra*) who pays has the intention to create legal consequences, namely his release from the obligation and the settling of his debt.[518] Consequentially, it is submitted to the evidential requirements applicable to unilateral juridical acts (*see* No. 185 *supra*).

516. *See* Arts 1235 et seq. OCC.
517. Cass. 27 Apr. 2020, C.19.0468.N, *TBO* 2020, 354; Cass. 26 Oct. 2006, C.05.0167.F, *Arr.Cass.* 2125, *JT* 2007, nr. 6252, 51, *RW* 2009-10, 625; R. Dekkers & A. Verbeke, *Handboek Burgerlijk Recht*, III (Antwerp: Intersentia: 2007), 312; S. Stijns, *Leerboek Verbintenissenrecht, vol. 2* (Brugge: die Keure, 2020), 89 and W. van Gerven en A. Van Oevelen, *Verbintenissenrecht* (Leuven: Acco, 2015), 611; P. Van Ommeslaghe, *Les obligations vol. 3* in *Traité de droit civil, tome II* (Brussels: Bruylant, 2013), 2005. *Contra*: L. Cornelis, *Algemene theorie van de verbintenis* (Antwerp: Intersentia, 2000), No. 382 et al.
518. S. Stijns, *Leerboek Verbintenissenrecht, vol. 2* (Brugge: die Keure, 2009), 85.

339. Payment is called 'voluntary' (*vrijwillig/volontaire*) when the debtor voluntarily settles his debt. If he does not, the performance may be enforced by several means, which are treated in Chapter 6.

2. Simple Payment

a. Conditions for a Valid Payment

i Who Can Pay?

340. The debtor is both obligated and entitled to settle his debt. He must possess the capacity to commit juridical acts at the moment of the payment. In principle, payment by an agent or auxiliary of the debtor counts as payment by the debtor himself.[519] However, this should be nuanced in the case of *intuitu personae* contracts,[520] where the debtor cannot be replaced by an agent.

341. In principle, payment by a third person is also valid. Article 1236 OCC makes a distinction between those who have an interest in the payment and those who do not. If a third person who has an interest in the payment of the debt (Article 1236 cites co-debtors and securities as examples) fulfils it, there is subrogation for the rights of the creditor to the benefit of the third person. According to Article 1251,3° OCC, the rights of the creditor will be transferred to him by means of subrogation.[521] If the third person has no personal interest in the payment, a distinction must be made depending on whether he pays on behalf of the debtor (e.g., in case of agency or *negotiorum gestio)* or on his own behalf. In the last case, according to Article 1236, paragraph 2 OCC, he will not be subrogated to the rights of the creditor. This however does not exclude the possibility for the creditor to grant him subrogation by contract, in accordance with Article 1250 OCC.[522]

---

519. L. Cornelis, *Algemene theorie van de verbintenis* (Antwerp: Intersentia, 2000), No. 384; H. De Page, *Traité élémentaire de droit civil belge, III* (Brussels: Bruylant, 1967), No. 401; C. Vanackere, K. Swerts & K. Vanhalle, 'De gewone uitdovingsgrond: de vrijwillige betaling' in R. Roodhooft, ed., *Bestendig handboek verbintenissenrecht* (Antwerp: Kluwer rechtswetenschappen, 1998–2020), No. 4005; R. Steennot, 'v°, Tenietgaan van verbintenissen: algemeen' in *Bijzondere overeenkomsten, Artikelsgewijze commentaar* (Kluwer: 2003), No. 15; S. Stijns, *Leerboek Verbintenissenrecht, vol. 2* (Brugge: die Keure, 2020), 98; S. Stijns, W. van Gerven & P. Wéry, 'Chronique', *J.T.* 1996, No. 43.
520. A contract is called *intuitu personae* when the identity or qualities of one party was determining for the other party's will to contract (e.g., a lawyer or an architect). It is called *intuitu pecuniae* when the economic advantage was determining for a party's will to contract, and the other party's identity was less important.
521. Subrogation is the process by which a person or thing replaces another person or thing in a legal situation (E. Dirix, B. Tilleman & S. Lierman (eds), *De Valks Juridisch woordenboek* (Antwerp-Oxford: Intersentia, 2018), 433).
522. Cass. 21 Jan. 2008, *Pas.* 2008, 152, concl. Adv. Gen. J. Genicot, *R.W.* 2008-09, 1258, note J. De Coninck and *JLMB* 2008, 1780.

342. There are two exceptions to the rule that a third person may pay instead of the debtor. First, according to Article 1237 OCC, an obligation may not be discharged by a third person against the wishes of the creditor when the latter requires that it be fulfilled by the debtor himself. The legislator originally established this rule with *intuitu personae* contracts in mind. However, the *Court of Cassation* extended this to any case where the creditor has a legal interest to demand payment by the debtor himself or refuse payment by a specific third person.[523] Second, as Article 1236 OCC is a suppletive law,[524] parties may agree to exclude payment by any or specific third parties in the contract.[525]

ii Whom Should One Pay?

343. According to Article 1239, paragraph 1 OCC, payment must be made to the creditor, or to a person who was given a mandate to receive payment by the creditor, by law or by the courts.[526] In this regard, the creditor is either the original owner of the right to be paid or the person this right was transferred to by means of succession, transfer of contractual rights or subrogation. If the debtor pays someone who is nor the creditor, nor a person who was given aforementioned mandate, the creditor is entitled to demand a second payment. This should however be nuanced by the fact that the debtor can reclaim what he erroneously paid to someone else than the creditor by means of the doctrine of undue payment.

344. However, Article 1239, paragraph 2 OCC states that payment to one who does not have power to receive for the creditor is valid if the latter ratifies it either explicitly or implicitly.[527] The creditor is considered to recognise the existence of a mandate by confirming the validity of a payment to a third person. This mandate is

523. Cass. 28 Sep. 1973, *Arr.Cass.* 1974, 101, *Pas.* 1974, 91 and *R.W.* 1973-74, 1158. In this case, an insurance company had a legal interest to refuse payment of the insurance premium from an insurance agent instead of from the insured persons. The insurance agent had committed several irregularities in the past, and the insurance company wanted to avoid to appear to trust the agent by allowing the payments to be done via him. *Contra:* L. Cornelis, *Algemene theorie van de verbintenis* (Antwerp: Intersentia, 2000), No. 385.

524. Belgian law makes a distinction between laws of public order (public order/*ordre public)*, which intend to protect the public interest, imperative laws (*dwingende wetten/lois imperatives*), which protect the interests of individuals, and permissive laws (*aanvullende wetten/lois supplétives*). While breaches of the first two categories are forbidden and sanctioned with nullity, parties are free to deviate from permissive laws, which only apply in case the contract does not stipulate otherwise. Permissive laws (*aanvullende wetten/lois supplétives*) constitute the main body OCC.

525. H. De Page, *Traité élémentaire de droit civil belge*, III (Brussels: Bruylant, 1967), No. 406; S. Stijns, W. van Gerven & P. Wéry, 'Chronique', *J.T.* 1996, No. 43; S. Stijns, *Leerboek Verbintenissenrecht, vol. 2* (Brugge: die Keure, 2020), 85.

526. For example, Art. 221 OCC: in case of marriage, if one of the spouses fails to satisfy his obligation to contribute, the other spouse may, without prejudice to the rights of third parties, be authorised by the justice of the peace to receive to the exclusion of the defaulting spouse, all sums due to him or her from third parties.

527. L. Cornelis, *Algemene theorie van de verbintenis* (Antwerp: Intersentia, 2000), No. 393; H. De Page, *Traité élémentaire de droit civil belge, III* (Brussels: Bruylant, 1967), No. 429; C. Vanackere, K. Swerts & K. Vanhalle, 'De gewone uitdovingsgrond: de vrijwillige betaling' in R. Roodhooft, ed., *Bestendig handboek verbintenissenrecht* (Antwerp: Kluwer rechtswetenschappen, 1998–2020),

retroactively considered to have existed at the time of payment. A particular application of this rule is the *derdenbeslag/saisie-arrêt*, a form of enforcement where a creditor may directly seize claims of his debtor against third parties. This means of execution may be based on any money claim, whether or not due or liquidated.[528] This is also the case when a debtor is informed of a mandate given to someone to receive payment instead of the creditor by a judicial decision. Article 1242 OCC stipulates explicitly that any payment by a debtor to his creditor despite a seizure (*beslag/saisie*) or protest (*verzet/opposition*) is not valid towards the creditors of the creditor who put the seizure or filed the protest, and that they can claim a second payment from the debtor, after which he can reclaim reimbursement by his creditor.

345. The creditor must have the capacity to receive payment. According to Article 1241 OCC, payment made to an incapable creditor is not valid, unless the debtor proves that the creditor has obtained an advantage from the payment. Whether such advantage was obtained or not is a matter of fact. Some authors claim that the advantage should be patrimonial,[529] while others state that it should not even necessarily be permanent.[530]

346. There are two exceptions to the rule that payment must be done to the creditor or someone who has a mandate to receive payment in order to extinguish the debtor's obligation. First, according to Article 1239 OCC, a payment done to a third person is valid if the creditor benefitted from the payment. This benefit must be patrimonial.[531] This is, for instance, the case if payment was made to a creditor of the creditor, who imputed the payment to his debtor. Second, according to Article 1240 OCC, a debtor who made a payment in good faith to one who was in possession of the right is valid, even if the possessor was subsequently dispossessed. The legislator intended to regulate the situation where the payment was done to someone who appeared to be the creditor, yet turned out not to be the real owner of the claim, e.g., when the transfer of a claim is later undone. In that case, the real creditor can no longer demand payment from the debtor, although he can recoup the damage from the apparent creditor. The doctrine is divided on the question of whether or not this is an application of the doctrine of appearance (*vertrouwensleer/*

No. 4017; R. Steennot, 'v°, Tenietgaan van verbintenissen: algemeen' in *Bijzondere overeenkomsten, Artikelsgewijze commentaar* (Kluwer: 2003), No. 15; S. Stijns, *Leerboek Verbintenissenrecht, vol. 2* (Brugge: die Keure, 2020), 101.

528. *See* Arts 1539–1544 *Gerechtelijk wetboek/Code judiciaire* of 10 Oct. 1967, *Belgian Official Gazette* 10 Oct. 1967.

529. L. Cornelis, *Algemene theorie van de verbintenis* (Antwerp: Intersentia, 2000), No. 392; R. Steennot, 'v°, Tenietgaan van verbintenissen: algemeen' in *Bijzondere overeenkomsten, Artikelsgewijze commentaar* (Kluwer: 2003), No. 10.

530. W. van Gerven en A. Van Oevelen, *Verbintenissenrecht* (Leuven: Acco, 2015), 613.

531. L. Cornelis, *Algemene theorie van de verbintenis* (Antwerp: Intersentia, 2000), No. 394; H. De Page, *Traité élémentaire de droit civil belge, III* (Brussels: Bruylant, 1967), No. 430; R. Steennot, 'v°, Tenietgaan van verbintenissen: algemeen' in *Bijzondere overeenkomsten, Artikelsgewijze commentaar*, Kluwer, 2003, No. 16; S. Stijns, *Leerboek Verbintenissenrecht, vol. 2* (Brugge: die Keure, 20209), 102.

théorie de l'apparence).[532] According to this doctrine, an apparent situation can have legal consequences towards third parties if they could reasonably believe that the apparent situation corresponded to reality (*see* No. 32 *supra*).[533] Although jurisprudence has not specified whether this doctrine can be applied against whoever creates an apparent situation, it is steadily accepted in case of apparent mandate (*leer van het schijnmandaat/théorie de l'apparence*).[534] This doctrine protects the third party who has acted with an apparently authorised agent. According to the doctrine, a principal can be considered to be bound on account of an apparent agency, not only when he made this appearance possible by his negligence but also when, without negligence on the part of the principal, third parties could reasonably believe in the power of agency of the apparent agent.[535] If so, according to most authors, a debt erroneously paid to an apparent creditor would only be extinguished on the condition that the real creditor can be accounted for the appearance.[536]

iii What Must Be Paid?

347. The general rules applicable to all payments are governed by two principles. First, according to Article 1243 OCC, a creditor may not be forced to receive anything other than what is due to him, even though the value of the thing offered is equal to or even greater than the amount due. Consequentially, in case the debt is monetary, it can only be paid in money in the physical form of currency and the debtor cannot *force* the creditor to accept a check, a bank deposit or any other giro,[537] unless the creditor allows it tacitly or explicitly,[538] or if parties are both businesses.[539]

---

532. L. Cornelis, *Algemene theorie van de verbintenis* (Antwerp: Intersentia, 2000), No. 394; H. De Page, *Traité élémentaire de droit civil belge, III* (Brussels: Bruylant, 1967), No. 430; R. Steennot, 'v°, Tenietgaan van verbintenissen: algemeen' in *Bijzondere overeenkomsten, Artikelsgewijze commentaar*, Kluwer, 2003, No. 16; S. Stijns, *Leerboek Verbintenissenrecht, vol. 2* (Brugge: die Keure, 20209), 103.
533. E. Dirix, B. Tilleman & S. Lierman (eds), *De Valks Juridisch woordenboek* (Antwerp-Oxford: Intersentia, 2018), 481.
534. Cass. 20 Jun. 1988, *Arr.Cass.* 1987-88, 1365, *Pas.* 1988, 1258, *R.W.* 1989-90, 1425 with note by A. Van Oevelen, *J.T.* 1989, 547 with note by P.A. Foriers, *R.C.J.B.* 1991, 45 with note by R. Kruithof, *T.R.V.* 1989, 540 with note by P. Callens & S. Stijns.
535. For more on this subject, *see* I. Samoy, 'Unauthorised Agency in Belgian Law' in *The Unauthorised Agent*, ed. D. Busch & L.J. Macgregor (Cambridge: University Press, 2009), 3.
536. Following authors expressed the opinion that Art. 1240 is an application of the doctrine of appearance: R. Dekkers-A.Verbeke, *Handboek burgerlijk recht, III* (Antwerp: Intersentia, 2007), No. 562; W. van Gerven en A. Van Oevelen, *Verbintenissenrecht* (Leuven: Acco, 2015), 615. *Contra*: L. Cornelis, *Algemene theorie van de verbintenis* (Antwerp: Intersentia, 2000), No. 394.
537. Cass. 1 Nov. 1975, *Arr.Cass.* 1976, 370 and *Pas.* 1976, 366; L. Cornelis, *Algemene theorie van de verbintenis* (Antwerp: Intersentia, 2000), No. 387; H. De Page, *Traité élémentaire de droit civil belge, III* (Brussels: Bruylant, 1967), Nos 455 et al.; C. Vanackere, K. Swerts & K. Vanhalle, 'De gewone uitdovingsgrond: de vrijwillige betaling' in R. Roodhooft, ed., *Bestendig handboek verbintenissenrecht* (Antwerp: Kluwer rechtswetenschappen, 1998–2020), No. 4026; R. Steennot, 'v°, Tenietgaan van verbintenissen: algemeen' in *Bijzondere overeenkomsten, Artikelsgewijze commentaar (*Kluwer: 2003), No. 18; S. Stijns, W. van Gerven & P. Wéry, 'Chronique', *J.T.* (1999): No.

This however does not exclude the possibility for creditor and debtor to contract that the debtor will perform something else than what was contracted originally. This figure, called *inbetalinggeving/dation de paiement*, is merely a contract about the modalities of payment where the creditor does not intend to give up his original obligation.[540] It allows the old obligation to continue to exist with all its securities and exceptions so that it can still be claimed if the debtor fails to perform according to the contract of *inbetalinggeving/dation de paiement.*[541]

348. Second, according to Article 1244 OCC, a debtor may not force a creditor to receive payment of even a divisible debt in part. This rule concerns the case of a single debtor. In principle, when there are several debtors, the debt is divided among them, except in the case of indivisibility (*ondeelbaarheid/indivisibilité*) and/or solidarity (*hoofdelijkheid/solidarité*). Furthermore, it is possible for the law or the contract to deviate from the general rule of Article 1244 OCC, e.g., when legal compensation results in the partial payment of a debt, when the debts are unequal. Also, Article 1244 OCC provides that courts may grant limited delays for payment after considering the situation of the parties, albeit they should practice the greatest caution and take the delays the debtor already received into account when exercising this competence.

349. Articles 1245–1246 OCC provide some specific rules about liability for the delivery of specific goods and unascertained goods. According to Article 1245 OCC, the debt concerning the delivery of specific goods is extinguished by their delivery in their condition at the time of delivery, provided that any deterioration which occurred was not the result of an act or fault of the debtor, nor that of persons for whom he is responsible, and that he was put in delay (*see* Nos 411 ff. *infra*) prior to such deterioration. Consequentially, the risk of destruction or deterioration between contract and delivery lies with the creditor. Article 1246 OCC states that

45; S. Stijns, *Leerboek Verbintenissenrecht, vol. 2* (Brugge: die Keure, 2020), 103; P. Van Ommeslaghe, 'Examen', *R.C.J.B.* (1988): No. 199; W. van Gerven en A. Van Oevelen, *Verbintenissenrecht* (Leuven: Acco, 2015), 620.

538. For example, the acceptance by the creditor of payment by bank deposit is often deduced from the mention of his bank account number on his invoice. The law also makes several exceptions to the rule that a creditor cannot be forced to accept a giro payment, for instance, the duty of merchants to accept payments from EUR 247,89 by check or deposit from each other (Art. 3 of the Koninklijk Besluit nr. 56 of 10 Nov. 1967 *tot bevordering van het gebruik van giraal geld*).

539. Cass. 21 Nov. 1975, *A. C.* 1976, 370 and *Pas.* 1986, I. 1066.

540. H. De Page, *Traité élémentaire de droit civil belge, III* (Brussels: Bruylant, 1967), No. 511; S. Stijns, *Leerboek Verbintenissenrecht, vol. 2* (Brugge: die Keure, 2020), 104; P. Van Ommeslaghe, 'Examen', *R.C.J.B.* (1988): No. 202.

541. L. Cornelis, *Algemene theorie van de verbintenis* (Antwerp: Intersentia, 2000), No. 388; R. Dekkers & A.Verbeke, *Handboek burgerlijk recht, III* (Antwerp: Intersentia, 2007), Nos 565 and 595; H. De Page, *Traité élémentaire de droit civil belge, III* (Brussels: Bruylant, 1967), No. 511; J. Ghestin, 'Traité de droit civil, Le obligations, Le régime des créances et des dettes', *L.G.D.J.* (2005): No. 963; R. Steennot, 'v°, Tenietgaan van verbintenissen: algemeen' in *Bijzondere overeenkomsten, Artikelsgewijze commentaar* (Kluwer: 2003), No. 20; S. Stijns, W. van Gerven & P. Wéry, 'Chronique', *J.T.* (1996): No. 73; S. Stijns, *Leerboek Verbintenissenrecht, vol. 2* (Brugge: die Keure, 2020), 104; W. van Gerven en A. Van Oevelen, *Verbintenissenrecht* (Leuven: Acco, 2015), 615.

where unascertained goods are concerned, the debtor is not obliged to render it in its best form in order to be released, although he is also forbidden to offer it in its worst form. This means that, notwithstanding other terms in the contract, he must deliver normal, average quality goods.[542] In the case of payment by the delivery of unascertained goods, the risk of destruction or deterioration lies with the debtor, as even in this case, it remains possible to acquire similar unascertained goods (*'genera non pereunt'*). In accordance with Article 1248 OCC, expenses linked to the payment must be carried by the debtor. The reason for this is that the creditor is entitled to obtain payment of the exact object of the obligation.[543]

iv Location and Time of the Payment

350. The place of payment determines which court is competent *ratione loci* should a dispute arise.[544] According to Article 1247 OCC, parties may designate the place of the payment. This may be done either explicitly or tacitly while taking the type of contract, habits of the parties and customs into account.[545] Article 1247 OCC further stipulates that, in case no such designation occurred, the payment of a specific good is considered to be done where the specific good was at the moment of the contract. In all other cases, the payment is done at the residence of the debtor. As for the time of the payment, obligations are, generally speaking, immediately executable, safe where parties have provided otherwise or where a judge has granted a grace period (*respijttermijn/délai de grâce*[546]).[547]

b. Some Special Rules Concerning Payment

i Specific Rules for Payment of Monetary Debts

351. When the performance is the payment of a monetary debt, a distinction is made between a 'debt of sum' (*geldschuld/dette de sommes*) and a 'debt of value'

---

542. L. Cornelis, *Algemene theorie van de verbintenis* (Antwerp: Intersentia, 2000), No. 390; R. Dekkers-A.Verbeke, *Handboek burgerlijk recht, III* (Antwerp: Intersentia, 2007), No. 567; H. De Page, Traité *élémentaire de droit civil belge, III* (Brussels: Bruylant, 1967), No. 452; R. Steennot, 'v°, Tenietgaan van verbintenissen: algemeen' in *Bijzondere overeenkomsten, Artikelsgewijze commentaar* (Kluwer: 2003), Nos 21 and 23; S. Stijns, *Leerboek Verbintenissenrecht, vol. 2* (Brugge: die Keure, 2020), 105; W. van Gerven en A. Van Oevelen, *Verbintenissenrecht* (Leuven: Acco, 2015), 617.
543. C. Vanackere, K. Swerts & K. Vanhalle, 'De gewone uitdovingsgrond: de vrijwillige betaling' in R. Roodhooft, ed., *Bestendig handboek verbintenissenrecht* (Antwerp: Kluwer rechtswetenschappen, 1998–2020), No. 4066 et seq., S. Stijns, *Leerboek Verbintenissenrecht 2* (Brugge: die Keure, 2020), 105.
544. S. Stijns, W. van Gerven & P. Wéry, 'Chronique', *J.T.* (1999): No. 47; S. Stijns, *Leerboek Verbintenissenrecht 2* (Brugge: die Keure, 2020), 106.
545. S. Stijns, *Leerboek Verbintenissenrecht 2* (Brugge: die Keure, 2020), 106; P. Van Ommeslaghe, 'Examen', *R.C.J.B.* (1988): No. 201; W. van Gerven en A. Van Oevelen, *Verbintenissenrecht* (Leuven: Acco, 2015), 621.
546. E. Dirix, B. Tilleman & S. Lierman (eds), *De Valks Juridisch woordenboek* (Antwerp-Oxford: Intersentia, 2018), 396.
547. S. Stijns, *Leerboek Verbintenissenrecht 2* (Brugge: die Keure, 2020), 106.

(*waardeschuld/dette de valeur*). A debt is a debt of sum either when its object is a certain sum of money from the beginning or when its nominal value was determined by law or contract beforehand (e.g., house rent). It is a debt of value when its sum must be determined by a judge on the day of his judgment (e.g., liability claims, both contractual and tortious), or by parties in a common agreement (e.g., a settlement). In the case of a liability claim, for instance, the debt itself comes into existence at the moment the damage is caused, but only becomes enforceable when the court (or the parties) determines the amount of money due. Debts of sum generate moratory interests (*moratoires interesten/intérêts moratoires*), to which the legal interest rate applies and which start at the moment the debtor is put into delay (Article 1153 OCC), while debts of value generate compensatory interests (*compensatoire interesten/intérêts compensatoires*), whose rate can be chosen freely by the judge and which start at the moment the damages are caused.[548]

352. Physical currency is the sole recognised way of payment of monetary debts. The creditor can only be forced to accept other forms of payment in the cases stated by law or when the contract makes this possible. Parties are however free to contract in which currency a monetary debt must be paid. A distinction is made between the contractual currency (*verbintenismunt/monnaie de compte*), which is the currency in which the obligation to pay a sum of money is expressed, and the payment currency (*betaalmunt/monnaie de paiement*), which is the currency in which the debt will effectively be paid.[549] In practice, some legal exceptions notwithstanding, parties can choose the currency freely and in most cases, contractual and payment currency are the same. However, it is possible for both to differ, e.g., when an unwilling debtor is condemned to pay by a foreign court which is forbidden by national law to condemn anyone in another currency than the local one. In this case, the contractual currency must be converted into payment currency according to either a contractual stipulation or, by default, the law applicable to the contract.[550] In Belgium, official and administrative acts may use either euro or any currency from a Member State of the Organisation for Economic Co-operation and Development (OECD).[551]

548. T. Vansweevelt & B. Weyts, 'Nakoming van verbintenissen of betaling' in T. Vansweevelt and B. Weyts, *Handboek Verbintenissenrecht* (Antwerpen: Instersentia, 2019), 809.

549. C. Vanackere, K. Swerts & K. Vanhalle, 'De gewone uitdovingsgrond: de vrijwillige betaling' in R. Roodhooft, ed., *Bestendig handboek verbintenissenrecht* (Antwerp: Kluwer rechtswetenschappen, 1998–2020), No. 4036; R. Steennot, 'v°, Tenietgaan van verbintenissen: algemeen' in *Bijzondere overeenkomsten, Artikelsgewijze commentaar* (Kluwer: 2003), No. 25; P. Van Ommeslaghe, 'Le paiement: rapport introductif', *Rev. Dr. U.L.B.*, 1993, No. 27, pp. 50–51; T. Vansweevelt & B. Weyts, 'Nakoming van verbintenissen of betaling' in T. Vansweevelt and B. Weyts, *Handboek Verbintenissenrecht* (Antwerpen: Instersentia, 2019), 807.

550. C. Vanackere, K. Swerts & K. Vanhalle, 'De gewone uitdovingsgrond: de vrijwillige betaling' in R. Roodhooft, ed., *Bestendig handboek verbintenissenrecht* (Antwerp: Kluwer rechtswetenschappen, 1998–2020), No. 4036; R. Steennot, 'v°, Tenietgaan van verbintenissen: algemeen' in *Bijzondere overeenkomsten, Artikelsgewijze commentaar* (Kluwer: 2003), No. 25; T. Vansweevelt & B. Weyts, 'Nakoming van verbintenissen of betaling' in T. Vansweevelt and B. Weyts, *Handboek Verbintenissenrecht* (Antwerpen: Instersentia, 2019), 807.

551. Article 3 of the Law of 30 Dec. 1885, *Belgian Official Gazette* 31 Dec. 1885, as adapted by Law of 12 Jul. 1991 (*Belgian Official Gazette* 9 Aug. 1991) and Koninklijk Besluit of 20 Jul. 2000 (*Belgian Official Gazette* 30 Aug. 2000).

353. The debtor is freed of his debt after payment of the nominal amount of the debt fixed in the contract.[552] Consequentially, the risk of a devaluation of the contractual currency lies with the creditor. This principle is called monetary nominalism (*monetair nominalisme/nominalisme monétaire*).[553] It is based on Article 1895 OCC, which states that the debt incurred from a loan is always determined by the numerical sum of money mentioned in the contract. Although this article concerns loans, it is also applied to other money debts by jurisprudence and doctrine.[554] However, monetary nominalism does not apply to *waardeschulden/dettes de valeur* because the exact due amount of money is determined at the time of the judgment or settlement when it is possible to take the devaluation into account.[555] It does not apply when the obligation is expressed in foreign currency either.[556] As Article 1895 is suppletive law, parties can exclude its application in their contract. This can, for instance, be done by including gold clauses, foreign currency clauses, commodity clauses or clauses incorporating indices of prices. Although such clauses are considered valid, they are in certain cases submitted to legal limitations. For example, the rent prices for immovables can be submitted to the evolution of Belgian consumer price index, but only within some strict limits (*see* Article 1728*bis* OCC).

ii Imputation of Payments

354. The issue of imputation of payment arises when a debtor has to perform several obligations of the same nature (e.g., a payment of money) or when a debt generates interests, adding those to the principal, and the debtor makes a performance which does not suffice to extinguish all of his obligations. As detailed in No. 352 *supra*, this situation can only occur when the creditor has agreed to partial payment or when a judge has allowed this. The Civil Code contains a number of rules

552. Cass. 26 May 1931, *Pas.* 1931, 180; Cass. 9 Mar. 1933, *Pas.* 1933, 159; Cass. 29 Jan. 1953, *Pas.* 1953, 408; Brussels 12 Mar. 2002, *R.W.* 2005-06, 189.

553. T. Vansweevelt & B. Weyts, 'Nakoming van verbintenissen of betaling' in T. Vansweevelt and B. Weyts, *Handboek Verbintenissenrecht* (Antwerpen: Instersentia, 2019), 807.

554. L. Cornelis, *Algemene theorie van de verbintenis* (Antwerp: Intersentia, 2000), No. 401; H. De Page, *Traité élémentaire de droit civil belge, III* (Brussels: Bruylant, 1967), No. 465; C. Vanackere, K. Swerts & K. Vanhalle, 'De gewone uitdovingsgrond: de vrijwillige betaling' in R. Roodhooft, ed., *Bestendig handboek verbintenissenrecht* (Antwerp: Kluwer rechtswetenschappen, 1998–2020), Nos 4044–4047; R. Steennot, 'v°, Tenietgaan van verbintenissen: algemeen' in *Bijzondere overeenkomsten, Artikelsgewijze commentaar,* Kluwer, 2003, No. 26; W. van Gerven en A. Van Oevelen, *Verbintenissenrecht* (Leuven: Acco, 2015), 619; T. Vansweevelt & B. Weyts, 'Nakoming van verbintenissen of betaling' in T. Vansweevelt and B. Weyts, *Handboek Verbintenissenrecht* (Antwerpen: Instersentia, 2019), 807.

555. C. Biquet-Mathieu & C. Delforge, 'Le régime juridique des intérêts- essai de synthèse' in *Rechtskroniek voor de vrede- en politierechters 2008* (Brugge: die Keure, 2008), 257; C. Vanackere, K. Swerts & K. Vanhalle, 'De gewone uitdovingsgrond: de vrijwillige betaling' in R. Roodhooft, ed., *Bestendig handboek verbintenissenrecht* (Antwerp: Kluwer rechtswetenschappen, 1998–2020), No. 4046; R. Steennot, 'v°, Tenietgaan van verbintenissen: algemeen' in *Bijzondere overeenkomsten, Artikelsgewijze commentaar* (Kluwer: 2003), No. 26; W. van Gerven en A. Van Oevelen, *Verbintenissenrecht* (Leuven: Acco, 2015), 619; T. Vansweevelt & B. Weyts, 'Nakoming van verbintenissen of betaling' in T. Vansweevelt and B. Weyts, *Handboek Verbintenissenrecht* (Antwerpen: Instersentia, 2019), 808.

556. Cass. 4 Sep. 1975, *Arr.Cass.* 1976, 20.

relating to the imputation of payments. As those are suppletive law, they are only applicable when the parties do not decide otherwise, which they may do in the contract or afterwards, by explicit or tacit agreement.[557]

355. Following rules apply if there is no other arrangement between parties. First, according to Article 1253 OCC, the debtor may at the time of performance decide to which obligation the performance is to be imputed. However, according to Article 1254 OCC, payment is first imputed on any outstanding interest in full and then to the principal amount of the debt. This article however does not apply on *waardeschulden/dettes de valeur* caused by tortious liability. Also, as follows from Article 1244 OCC (*see* No. 348 *supra*), if the debtor pays an amount corresponding to the smaller debt, he cannot impute it on the greater one without the creditor's agreement.

Second, by virtue of Article 1255 OCC, if the debtor does not use his right to choose on which obligation to impute the payment, the creditor may impute the performance to one of the obligations, by giving the debtor a receipt (*kwijtschrift/ quittance*) on which is notified on which obligation the payment is imputed. This receipt can only be disputed by the debtor in case of fraud or deceit.

Third, Article 1256 OCC is applicable in the absence of an effective imputation by either party. In this case, the performance is imputed to that obligation which satisfies one of the following criteria in the sequence indicated: (1) the obligation which is due or is the first to fall due; (2) the obligation which is the most burdensome for the debtor and which he has the most interest to fulfil (e.g., because the interest or the sureties on this debt are highest); (3) the obligation that has arisen first; (4) if none of the preceding criteria applies, the performance is imputed proportionally to all the obligations.

iii Offer to Pay and Consignation

356. Certain problems are raised when a creditor refuses the payment offered. To address the issue, Articles 1257–1264 OCC provide for the debt to be paid by a system of formal offers of payment made on the debtor's behalf by a bailiff or notary (*aanbod van gerede betaling/offre réelle de paiement*) followed by the deposit of the payment in an indicated place (*consignatie/consignation*). Due to its complexity, this system is rarely used.[558] In practice, parties often agree to other solutions; e.g., one will pay into the bank account of one of the attorneys or into a common account

557. W. van Gerven en A. Van Oevelen, *Verbintenissenrecht* (Leuven: Acco, 2015), 622.

558. L. Cornelis, *Algemene theorie van de verbintenis* (Antwerp: Intersentia, 2000), No. 398; R. Steennot, 'v°, Tenietgaan van verbintenissen: algemeen' in *Bijzondere overeenkomsten, Artikelsgewijze commentaar* (Kluwer: 2003), No. 53; T. Vansweevelt & B. Weyts, 'Nakoming van verbintenissen of betaling' in T. Vansweevelt and B. Weyts, *Handboek Verbintenissenrecht* (Antwerpen: Instersentia, 2019), 833. For more on Arts 1257–1264 OCC: L. Cornelis, *Algemene theorie van de verbintenis* (Antwerp: Intersentia, 2000), No. 398; R. Steennot, 'v°, Tenietgaan van verbintenissen: algemeen' in *Bijzondere overeenkomsten, Artikelsgewijze commentaar* (Kluwer: 2003), Nos 50–53; S. Stijns, W. van Gerven & P. Wéry, 'Chronique', *J.T.* 1999, No. 50; W. van Gerven en A. Van Oevelen, *Verbintenissenrecht* (Leuven: Acco, 2015), 623.

until the judgment or settlement. In this case, however, Articles 1257 and following do not apply.[559] Consequentially, such payment does not extinguish the debt.

3. Payment with Subrogation

a. Concept

357. Subrogation (*subrogatie* or *indeplaatsstelling/subrogation*) is the process by which a person or thing acquires the legal position which was formerly occupied by another person or thing.[560] A distinction is made between personal and real subrogation.

358. Real subrogation or subrogation '*in rem*' (*zakelijke subrogatie* or *zaakvervanging/subrogation réelle*) is a legal concept which allows a thing that is replacing another to assume the legal function of the first thing in the patrimony of the person entitled.[561] Thus, it assumes the same legal function as the replaced thing.[562] Although there are no general rules on subrogation '*in rem*' in the Civil Code, it is applied to some specific cases, e.g., Article 10 of the Law on Mortgages,[563] according to which in case of damage or destruction of an insured thing, the compensation owed by third parties (e.g., the insurer against fire) replaces the destroyed thing for the benefit of the mortgage-holding creditors of the owner, on the condition that this compensation is not used to repair the damaged thing.

359. Personal subrogation or subrogation '*in personam*' (*persoonlijke subrogatie/subrogation personelle*) is the acquisition of the legal position of a creditor by a third party who pays the original creditor, and thus replaces the original creditor towards the debtor.[564] It is governed by Articles 1249 et seq. OCC, under the title 'payment with subrogation'. This title illustrates the dual nature of this type

---

559. Cass. 17 Feb. 1978, *Arr.Cass.* 1978, p. 725.
560. E. Dirix, B. Tilleman & S. Lierman (eds), *De Valks Juridisch woordenboek* (Antwerp-Oxford: Intersentia, 2018), 433.
561. *Ibid.* For more on real subrogation, *see*: V. Sagaert, *Zakelijke Subrogatie* (Antwerp-Intersentia, 2003), 793.
562. L. Cornelis, *Algemene theorie van de verbintenis* (Antwerp: Intersentia, 2000), No. 344; H. De Page, *Traité élémentaire de droit civil belge*, III, 1967, No. 513; E. Dirix, Zakelijke subrogatie, *R.W.* (1993-94): No. 1; C. Vanackere, K. Swerts & K. Vanhalle, 'De gewone uitdovingsgrond: de vrijwillige betaling' in R. Roodhooft, ed., *Bestendig handboek verbintenissenrecht* (Antwerp: Kluwer rechtswetenschappen, 1998–2020), No. 4089; S. Stijns, *Leerboek Verbintenissenrecht 2* (Brugge: die Keure, 2020), 107; R. Vandeputte, *De overeenkomst. Haar ontstaan, haar uitvoering en verdwijning, haar bewijs* (Brussels: Larcier, 1977), 227; W. van Gerven en A. Van Oevelen, *Verbintenissenrecht* (Leuven: Acco, 2015), 625.
563. Article 10 *Hypotheekwet/Loi hypothecaire*, *Belgian Official Gazette* 22 Dec. 1851.
564. E. Dirix, B. Tilleman & S. Lierman (eds), *De Valks Juridisch woordenboek* (Antwerp-Oxford: Intersentia, 2018), 433–434.

of subrogation:[565] first, it requires payment of a debt by a third party and, second, subrogation or replacement of that third party in the position of the paid creditor. This combination of figures is required to keep the obligation in existence. Indeed, a payment without subrogation would extinguish the obligation. Payment with subrogation is only possible in cases agreed upon by the parties or provided for by the Civil Code (Article 1249 OCC).

b. Conditions

i General Conditions Common to All Kinds of Subrogation

360. The following three conditions are applicable to all types of subrogation, regardless of their source:[566] First, there must be a valid debt. Second, an effective and valid payment must be made before the subrogation takes place (a simple promise is not enough[567] – the payment must be made to someone with the capacity to receive payment[568]).[569] Third, the payment must be made by a third party, who is not paying his own debt, but someone else's debt.[570]

361. The last condition has been the object of many disputes in the past because the third party who paid the debt was paying his own debt and could, consequentially, not benefit from subrogation. An example was the insurer of the liability of a person who caused a car accident. The payment of the victim by the insurer was not only the payment of a debt of the insured person who caused the damage but also the payment of an own debt of the insurer. Consequentially, the insurer could not claim to be subrogated in the position of the victim against his employer, who had the legal obligation to pay certain sums if the accident occurred on the way to or from the work.[571] This was also the case for an employer who paid contractual compensations to an employee who was the victim of an accident. As this was a debt of

565. H. De Page, *Traité élémentaire de droit civil belge*, III, 1967, No. 514; S. Stijns, W. van Gerven & P. Wéry, 'Chronique', *J.T.* (1999), No. 51; S. Stijns, *Leerboek Verbintenissenrecht 2* (Brugge: die Keure, 2020), 108; W. van Gerven en A. Van Oevelen, *Verbintenissenrecht* (Leuven: Acco, 2015), 626.
566. L. Cornelis, *Algemene theorie van de verbintenis* (Antwerp: Intersentia, 2000), No. 346; H. De Page, *Traité élémentaire de droit civil belge*, III, 1967, No. 517; C. Vanackere, K. Swerts & K. Vanhalle, 'De gewone uitdovingsgrond: de vrijwillige betaling' in R. Roodhooft, ed., *Bestendig handboek verbintenissenrecht* (Antwerp: Kluwer rechtswetenschappen, 1998–2020), No. 4100; S. Stijns, *Leerboek Verbintenissenrecht 2* (Brugge: die Keure, 2020), 111; R. Vandeputte, *De overeenkomst. Haar ontstaan, haar uitvoering en verdwijning, haar bewijs* (Brussels: Larcier, 1977), 227; W. van Gerven en A. Van Oevelen, *Verbintenissenrecht* (Leuven: Acco, 2015), 627; P. Van Ommeslaghe, *Les obligations vol. 3* in *Traité de droit civil, tome II* (Brussels: Bruylant, 2013), 2121–2123.
567. Cass. 22 May 1969, *Arr.Cass.* 1969, 932 & *Pas.* 1969, 869; Cass. 12 Mar. 1970, *Pas.* 1970, 618.
568. Cass. 8 Oct. 1971, *Pas.* 1972, 141; S. Stijns, W. van Gerven & P. Wéry, 'Chronique', *J.T.* (1999): No. 52.
569. Cass. 31 Oct. 1991, *Arr.Cass.* 1991-92, 203 & *Pas.* 1992, 167.
570. Cass. 11 Oct. 1989, *Arr.Cass.* 1989-90, 192 & *Pas.* 1982, 1221; Cass. 17 Jun. 1982, *Arr. Cass.* 1981-1982, 1306, *Pas.* 1982, 1221 and *RCJB* note L. Cornelis; Cass. 12 Nov. 1970, *Arr.Cass.* 1971, 236 & *Pas.* 1971, 224.
571. S. Stijns, *Leerboek Verbintenissenrecht vol.2* (Brugge: die Keure, 2020), 112.

the employer, he could not be subrogated in the employee's position against the person who caused the accident.[572] In order to remediate this, the legislator allowed an exception to this rule for certain specific cases. Since, in these cases, the requirements for subrogation are not all met, they are called 'quasi-subrogations' (*quasi-subrogaties/quasi-subrogations*). Most of these cases, which must always be specified by law, concern social and insurance matters. An example can be found in Article 95 of the Insurance Law,[573] which states that the insurer of the liability for damages who has granted compensation to the insured person is subrogated in his rights against the persons liable for the accident.

ii Specific Conditions

362. Some specific requirements are added to the general requirements, depending on the type of subrogation: contractual or legal.

363. Contractual subrogation (*conventionele subrogatie/subrogation conventionelle*) is subrogation which was agreed upon by the parties.[574] It may be initiated by the creditor or by the debtor (Article 1250 OCC). Different requirements apply depending on who took the initiative for subrogation.

364. An example of subrogation on the initiative of the creditor is the financing of the purchase of a vehicle: the creditor (salesman) receives payment from the financing company, who stipulates that the payment will only be made if she can immediately replace him in his rights against the debtor (buyer), who will pay his debt to the financing company. According to Article 1250, 1° OCC, when the creditor who receives payment from a third party lets the third party replace him regarding his rights, claims, privileges or mortgages against the debtor, the agreement of the creditor about the subrogation must be explicit (whether oral or in writing) and the subrogation must be simultaneous with the payment. The approval of the debtor is not required, nor is the fulfilment of the formalities of Article 1690 OCC (which are required for an assignment). It is, however, prudent to notify the debtor in order to prevent him from paying the original creditor.[575]

365. Subrogation on the initiative of the debtor may happen, for instance, if the debtor finds a third party who is prepared to take over the claim under conditions which are more favourable to him (for instance, a lower interest rate, or the dispensation of sureties). This type of subrogation always takes the form of a loan.[576] According to Article 1250, °2 OCC, the following requirements must be met for the

572. Cass. 27 Feb. 1964, *Pas.* 1964, 682.
573. *Wet betreffende de verzekeringen/Loi relative aux assurances* of 4 Apr. 2014, *Belgian Official Gazette* 30 Apr. 2014.
574. E. Dirix, B. Tilleman & S. Lierman (eds), *De Valks Juridisch woordenboek* (Antwerp-Oxford: Intersentia, 2018), 434.
575. S. Stijns, *Leerboek Verbintenissenrecht* 2 (Brugge: die Keure, 2020), 115.
576. H. De Page, Traité élémentaire de droit civil belge, III, 1967, 529; C. Vanackere, K. Swerts & K. Vanhalle, 'De gewone uitdovingsgrond: de vrijwillige betaling' in R. Roodhooft, ed., *Bestendig*

subrogation to be valid: first, the instrument of loan and the receipt must be signed before a notary (*see* Nos 143 ff. *supra*). Second, it must be declared in the instrument of loan that the money was borrowed in order to make the payment. Third, it must be declared in the receipt that the payment has been made from funds furnished for this purpose by the new creditor.

366. Article 1251 OCC sums up the four situations where legal subrogation (*wettelijke subrogation/subrogation légale*) occurs. It takes place for the benefit of one who, being himself a creditor, pays another creditor who is preferred over him by reason of priorities or mortgages (for instance, in order to prevent the sale of mortgaged land at an inopportune moment); of the buyer of immovables who uses the purchase price to pay creditors to whom such immovable was mortgaged; of one who, being obligated with others for the payment of the debt, had an interest in discharging it (e.g., a surety or a co-debtor); and of an heir under benefit of inventory[577] who paid debts of the succession from his own funds.

In all these cases, an interested third party pays another person's debt and strengthens his recovery position, thanks to the subrogation. Legal subrogation takes place automatically as soon as the requirements are met.[578] One has to add the special statutory cases of quasi-subrogation, as mentioned above, to the four cases mentioned in Article 1251 OCC.

c. Consequences of a Payment with Subrogation

367. The dual nature of payment with subrogation is very clear when it comes to its consequences. A distinction is made between the consequences linked to the aspect 'transfer of rights' and those linked with the payment.

368. Similarly to a transfer of rights, the original creditor's claim is transferred to the third party who paid him, with inclusion of all its accessories (*see* Nos 319 ff. *supra*). In other words, the third party replaces the creditor towards the debtor.[579] However, as is the case with simple transfer of rights (*see* Nos 319 ff. *supra*), subrogation may not put the debtor in a less favourable position than he used to be with the original creditor. Consequentially, the debtor may use all the exceptions and

---

handboek verbintenissenrecht (Antwerp: Kluwer rechtswetenschappen, 1998–2020), No. 4114; S. Stijns, *Leerboek Verbintenissenrecht 2* (Brugge: die Keure, 2020), 115.

577. In Belgium, an inheritance may be refused, or be accepted either 'simply' (*zuivere aanvaarding/acceptation pure et simple*) or under benefit of inventory (*aanvaarding onder voorbehoud van boedelbeschrijving/acceptation sous bénéfice d'inventaire*) (Arts 774–775 OCC). While simple acceptance implies that the heir immediately becomes liable for the debts of the succession, even if those exceed the assets, acceptance under benefit of inventory means that first an inventory of assets and debts will be made, after which the heir will still have the choice to either accept or refuse the inheritance.

578. S. Stijns, *Leerboek Verbintenissenrecht 2* (Brugge: die Keure, 2020), 116.

579. Cass. 6 Jun. 1994, *Arr.Cass.* 1994, 577; Cass. 9 Mar. 1995, *Arr.Cass.* 1995, 287 & *Pas.* 1995, 297; H. De Page, *Traité élémentaire de droit civil belge*, III, 1967, 551; S. Stijns, W. van Gerven & P. Wéry, 'Chronique', *J.T.* (1999): No. 58.

defences he had against the previous creditor against the new creditor.[580] However, exceptions which arise after the payment which caused the subrogation may not be invoked by the debtor against the new creditor.[581]

369. Similarly to a payment, the debt of the debtor towards the original creditor is diminished with the paid amount.[582] As soon as the original creditor is paid by the third party, he may no longer demand payment of that sum from the debtor.[583] Problems may arise in the case of partial payment, as in that case, both the original creditor and the subrogating creditor will be able to make a claim against the debtor. Article 1252 OCC answers the question of what must happen if the debtor is unable to pay both: the subrogation may not prejudice the creditor to whom only a part of the debt has been paid. In this case, he may exercise his rights concerning what is owed to him with preference above the person from whom he only received a partial payment. It is contested whether this rule only applies to legal and contractual subrogation, or also to quasi-subrogation.[584]

B. Novation

1. Concept

370. Novation (*schuldvernieuwing or novatie/novation*) is the substitution of an existing obligation by a new one. As a result, the existing obligation is extinguished and a new one is created.[585] According to Article 1271 OCC, the new obligation will have a new object (a new debt), a new creditor, or a new debtor. A combination of several of these new elements is also possible.[586] Novation is not presumed: the intent to make it (*animus novandi*) must be clear (Article 1273 OCC).

---

580. Cass. 22 Jun. 1988, *Arr.Cass.* 1987-88, 1381 & *Pas.* 1988, 1275; C. Vanackere, K. Swerts & K. Vanhalle, 'De gewone uitdovingsgrond: de vrijwillige betaling' in R. Roodhooft, ed., *Bestendig handboek verbintenissenrecht* (Antwerp: Kluwer rechtswetenschappen, 1998–2020), No. 4135; S. Stijns, W. van Gerven & P. Wéry, 'Chronique', *J.T.* (1999): No. 59; S. Stijns, *Leerboek Verbintenissenrecht 2* (Brugge: die Keure, 2020), 117; W. van Gerven en A. Van Oevelen, *Verbintenissenrecht* (Leuven: Acco, 2015), 633.
581. Cass. 22 Jun. 1988, *Arr.Cass.* 1987-88, 1381 & *Pas.* 1988, 1275.
582. Cass. 5 Dec. 1949, *Pas.* 1950, 223.
583. L. Cornelis, *Algemene theorie van de verbintenis* (Antwerp: Intersentia, 2000), No. 348; R. Kruithof, H. Bocken, F. De Ly en B. de Temmerman, 'Overzicht van rechtspraak. Verbintenissenrecht (1981-1982)', *T.P.R.* (1994): No. 383; S. Stijns, W. van Gerven & P. Wéry, 'Chronique', *J.T.* (1999), No. 60; S. Stijns, *Leerboek Verbintenissenrecht 2* (Brugge: die Keure, 2020), 117.
584. S. Stijns, *Leerboek Verbintenissenrecht 2* (Brugge: die Keure, 2020), 118.
585. E. Dirix, B. Tilleman & S. Lierman (eds), *De Valks Juridisch woordenboek* (Antwerp-Oxford: Intersentia, 2018), 415.
586. L. Cornelis, *Algemene theorie van de verbintenis* (Antwerp: Intersentia, 2000), No. 658; H. De Page, *Traité élémentaire de droit civil belge*, III, 1967, 584; S. Stijns, *Leerboek Verbintenissenrecht 2* (Brugge: die Keure, 2020), 122.

2. Conditions

371. Following requirements must be met in order for the compensation to be valid.[587] First, there must be a valid existing obligation. The novation will not be valid if the existing obligation is absolutely void. However, it is possible for a relatively void obligation to be the object of a novation, as the will to call a new obligation into existence may be considered a confirmation (*see* No. 236 *supra*),[588] provided that both parties were aware of the voidability of the old obligation.[589] For the same reason, the will to recognise a natural obligation or to renunciate the right to invoke prescription may be deduced from the will to novate.[590] Second, there must be an *animus novandi*: both parties must have the intention to novate. This is not presumed and must be proven (Article 1273 OCC).[591] Third, the parties must hold the capacity to conclude contracts (Article 1272 OCC). Fourth, there must be a 'new' obligation, which requires a new element: a new object, a new debtor, a new creditor or a combination of these elements. This requirement distinguishes novation from delegation (*see* Nos 328 ff. *supra*), transfer of rights (*see* Nos 319 *supra*) and subrogation (*see* Nos 357 *supra*). Indeed, while novation creates a new legal bond, the other three figures leave the legal bond itself unaltered.[592] The requirement of a *new object* necessitates an alteration of essential or substantial elements,[593] e.g., the price of a good or the wages of an employee.[594] An alteration of inessential elements (e.g., the deletion of a penalty clause)[595] does not suffice. According to Article 1271,2° OCC, when the new element is a *new debtor*, the old debtor must be relieved from his obligation. This differs from delegation, where the old debtor remains held to perform (*see* Nos 328 ff. *supra*). Article 1271,3° OCC stipulates that when the new element is a *new creditor*, the debtor must be relieved from the old obligation and he must bind himself towards the new creditor. In other words, the assent of all parties involved is required (as opposed to transfer of rights, where this is not the case, *see* Nos 319 ff. *supra*).[596]

---

587. R. Dekkers & A. Verbeke, *Handboek Burgerlijk Recht*, III (Antwerp: Intersentia: 2007), 350.
588. R. Roodhooft, 'Schuldvernieuwing' in R. Roodhooft (ed.), *Bestendig handboek verbintenissenrecht* (Antwerp: Kluwer Rechtswetenschappen, 1998–2020), No. 4311; W. van Gerven en A. Van Oevelen, *Verbintenissenrecht* (Leuven: Acco, 2015), 636.
589. H. De Page, *Traité élémentaire de droit civil belge*, III, 1967, 584; R. Roodhooft, 'Schuldvernieuwing' in R. Roodhooft (ed.), *Bestendig handboek verbintenissenrecht* (Antwerp: Kluwer Rechtswetenschappen, 1998–2020), No. 4311; S. Stijns, *Leerboek Verbintenissenrecht 2* (Brugge: die Keure, 2020), 123.
590. R. Roodhooft, 'Schuldvernieuwing' in R. Roodhooft (ed.), *Bestendig handboek verbintenissenrecht* (Antwerp: Kluwer Rechtswetenschappen, 1998–2020), No. 4313; W. van Gerven en A. Van Oevelen, *Verbintenissenrecht* (Leuven: Acco, 2015), 636.
591. Cass. 16 Mar. 2018, AR. C.17.0403.F, *JLMB* 2019, nr. 5, 204; Cass. 23 Mar. 2009, AR. C.08.0098.F, www.judidat.be; Cass. 26 Sep. 2003, *Arr. Cass.*, 2003, 1760 and *Pas.* 2003, 1487.
592. S. Stijns, *Leerboek Verbintenissenrecht 2* (Brugge: die Keure, 2020), 124.
593. Cass. 5 Dec. 2002, *Pas.* 2002, 2346.
594. Cass. 28 May 1979, *Arr.Cass.* 1978-79, 1137 & *Pas.* 1979, 1116.
595. S. Stijns, *Leerboek Verbintenissenrecht 2* (Brugge: die Keure, 2020), 124.
596. H. De Page, *Traité élémentaire de droit civil belge*, III, 1967, 581; R. Roodhooft, 'Schuldvernieuwing' in R. Roodhooft (ed.), *Bestendig handboek verbintenissenrecht* (Antwerp: Kluwer Rechtswetenschappen, 1998–2020), No. 4304; S. Stijns, *Leerboek Verbintenissenrecht 2* (Brugge: die Keure, 2020), 125.

3. Consequences

372. The consequences of novation, which only affect the future,[597] are the following. First, the existing obligation disappears. Consequentially, all priorities, mortgages and sureties disappear (Articles 1278–1279 OCC) as well as the eventual co-debtors (Article 1281 OCC). The creditor can explicitly reserve the priorities and mortgages, but not the ones given by third parties (Article 1280 OCC). Exceptions linked to the old obligation can no longer be invoked by the debtor.[598] Second, a new obligation is created. Parties may determine its contents. For example, they might agree that priorities and mortgages which were applicable to the old obligation will apply to the new one as well (Article 1278 OCC).

C. Compensation or Set-off

1. Concept and Types

373. Compensation (*compensatie* or *schuldvergelijking/compensation*) is the extinction of debts between parties who are each other's debtors.[599] Only the common (and thus lowest) sum is extinguished, so that only the surplus of the highest debt must still be paid.[600] There are three types of compensation: legal compensation, judicial compensation and contractual compensation.

2. Legal Compensation

374. Legal compensation (*wettelijke schuldvergelijking/compensation légale*) happens automatically, even without the knowledge of the debtor. Both debts cancel each other from the moment they both exist, for their mutual sum (Article 1290 OCC), accessories included.[601] Accessories do however continue to exist for the remaining obligation.[602] Legal compensation is not of public order, so that parties may deviate from these rules by agreement[603] or renounce the right to invoke legal compensation – safe for the prohibition to provide contractually that a consumer renounces to his right of compensation (Article VI.83, 16° CEL).[604]

---

597. L. Cornelis, *Algemene theorie van de verbintenis* (Antwerp: Intersentia, 2000), No. 657.
598. S. Stijns, *Leerboek Verbintenissenrecht 2* (Brugge: die Keure, 2020), 126.
599. E. Dirix, B. Tilleman & S. Lierman (eds), *De Valks Juridisch woordenboek* (Antwerp-Oxford: Intersentia, 2018), 414.
600. S. Stijns, *Leerboek Verbintenissenrecht 2* (Brugge: die Keure, 2020), 127.
601. H. De Page, *Traité élémentaire de droit civil belge*, III, 1967, 618; R. Roodhooft, 'Schuldvergelijking' in R. Roodhooft (ed.), *Bestendig handboek verbintenissenrecht* (Antwerp: Kluwer Rechtswetenschappen, 1998–2020), No. 4360; S. Stijns, *Leerboek Verbintenissenrecht 2* (Brugge: die Keure, 2020), 128; W. van Gerven en A. Van Oevelen, *Verbintenissenrecht* (Leuven: Acco, 2015), 639–640.
602. L. Cornelis, *Algemene theorie van de verbintenis* (Antwerp: Intersentia, 2000), No. 678.
603. Cass. 19 Feb. 1979, *Arr.Cass.* 1978-79, 722 & *Pas.* 1979, 722.
604. Cass. 20 Oct. 2005, *Pas.* 2005, 1994.

375. Legal compensation takes place automatically under the following requirements: first, there must be two debts between the same persons[605] who must have obligated themselves in their own name and in the same capacity in both obligations. Second, the object of the obligations must be the payment of a sum of money or a certain quantity of replaceable things of the same kind (Article 1291 OCC). Third, both debts must be liquid (*effen/liquide*) (Article 1291 OCC), which means that they must exist and be certain. Thus, they may not be disputed, and their amount must be determined or easy to determine through calculation.[606] Fourth, both debts must be due immediately (*opeisbaar/exigible*) (Article 1291 OCC).

376. There are several exceptions to the applicability of legal compensation. First, Article 1293 OCC sums up three situations where the compensation does not take place: 1° a restitution claim regarding a thing that was taken away from the owner illegally, 2° a restitution claim regarding something that was given as storage or loan, 3° a debt regarding sustenance which was declared not to be seizable. Second, Article 1298 OCC states that compensation may not harm the rights of third parties. Thus, according to Article 1298 OCC, compensation does not take place when the credit balance of a party has been seized by a third party prior to the same event (Article 1298 OCC), or, by extension, when a party has become bankrupt prior to the concourse of debit and credit.[607] An exception to this anteriority requirement is made when contracts are considered connected (*samenhangende contracten/ contrats connexes*).[608] However, the courts determine sovereignly whether or not there is a connection, whereby it is not easy to predict what the result will be, for lack of clear criterion and because this concept is still evolving (currently towards a broader interpretation).[609] Finally, some specific laws contain exceptions to automatical legal compensation; e.g., Article 23 of the Law on the protection of wages limits the boundaries within which an employer may withhold salary because of claims he has against the employee.[610]

3. Judicial Compensation

377. Judicial compensation (*gerechtelijke schuldvergelijking/compensation judiciaire*) is compensation that is pronounced by a court in a judgment.[611] The requirements are the same as for legal compensation, except for the fact that the debts must

605. Cass. 17 Dec. 2010, *Arr. Cass.* 2010, 3054, *Pas.* 2010, 3269 and *RW* 2011-12, 181, note R. Houben; Cass. 29 Jun. 2006, *R.W.* 2006-07, 403.
606. Cass. 6 Jun. 2017, AR P.16.0715.N; Cass. 11 Apr. 1986, *Arr.Cass.* 1985-86, 1093 & *Pas.* 1986, 98.
607. Cass. 2 Sep. 1982, *Arr.Cass.* 1982-83, 3 & *Pas.* 1983, 3.
608. Cass. 4 Feb. 2011, *Pas.* 2011, 438 and *RW* 2011-12, 488; Cass. 24 Jun. 2010, C.09.0365.N & Cass. 24 Jun. 2010, C.09.0085.N, www.cass.be.
609. S. Stijns, *Leerboek Verbintenissenrecht*, vol. 2 (Brugge: die Keure, 2020), 132.
610. *Loonbeschermingswet/Loi concernant la protection de la rénumération des travailleurs* of 12 Apr. 1965, *Belgian Official Gazette* 20 Apr. 1965.
611. S. Stijns, *Leerboek Verbintenissenrecht*, vol. 2 (Brugge: die Keure, 2020), 133.

not be liquid, as they are the object of the dispute. Also, while legal compensation starts as soon as both debts exist, judicial compensation can only take place from the judgment.

4. Contractual Compensation

378. Contractual compensation (*conventionele schuldvergelijking/compensation conventionelle*) is compensation which was agreed on by parties in their contract. This type of compensation is also limited by Article 1298 OCC, which states that compensation should not prejudice third parties (*see* No. 376 *supra*). However, this principle has been eroded by a recent law on *netting*, i.e., a form of contractual compensation where parties agree to constantly settle claims against each other, in order to only have to pay the net-surplus. This law made netting contracts and their consequences almost entirely opposable to third parties.[612] Examples of compensation clauses can often be found in contracts with banks, e.g., clauses which allow a bank to compensate between the balances of several separate bank accounts, or even more drastic, clauses installing a 'unity of accounts'.[613]

D. Confusion

379. Confusion (*schuldvermenging/confusion de dettes*) is the joining in one person of the qualities of creditor or debtor, which means that the obligation necessarily disappears (Article 1300 OCC).[614] Most situations of confusion happen when two patrimonies merge, e.g., in the case of inheritance or fusion of companies.

E. Discharge by Agreement

380. Discharge by agreement (*kwijtschelding van schuld/remise de dette*) is a contract between creditor and debtor (*see* Article 1285 OCC) where a creditor voluntarily renunciates to the payment or performance, and the debtor accepts that renunciation.[615] As a consequence of the discharge, the debt is extinguished along with all its accessories, such as securities (Articles 1285–1287 OCC). The discharge of one *in solidum* debtor releases all the other debtors as well, unless the creditor made an explicit reservation regarding his rights towards them. Even then,

---

612. *See* Arts 14 & 15 of the Law of 12 Dec. 2004 *betreffende de financiële zekerheden/concernant les sûretés financiers*, *Belgian Official Gazette* 1 Feb. 2005.
613. S. Stijns, *Leerboek Verbintenissenrecht*, vol. 2 (Brugge: die Keure, 2020), 135.
614. E. Dirix, B. Tilleman & S. Lierman (eds), *De Valks Juridisch woordenboek* (Antwerp-Oxford: Intersentia, 2018), 415.
615. R. Dekkers & A. Verbeke, *Handboek Burgerlijk Recht*, III (Antwerp: Intersentia: 2007), 366; S. Stijns, *Leerboek Verbintenissenrecht*, vol. 2 (Brugge: die Keure, 2020), 139.

the part of the person whom he discharged must be subtracted from the amount he may claim from the remaining debtors (Article 1285 OCC).

381. Proof of the discharge must be given in accordance with the general rules regarding proof of contracts (*see* Nos 149 ff. *supra*). However, the Civil Code simplifies this proof with a presumption of discharge. There is a refutable presumption that the debtor is released if the creditor voluntarily gives him the written act which proved the claim or the executory copy (*grosse/expedition*) of a notarial deed (Article 8.27 OCC).[616]

F. Extinctive Prescription (Period of Limitation)

382. The general rules regarding prescription are laid down in Articles 2219–2280 OCC. Article 2219 OCC states: 'Prescription (*verjaring/prescription*) is a means of acquiring or of being discharged by a certain lapse of time, and under conditions determined by law.' Thus, the passing of a certain lapse of time may lead to acquisition ('acquisitive prescription'), or discharge ('extinctive prescription'). It is the latter we will discuss hereinafter. Although prescription is mentioned in Article 1234 OCC as one of the causes for extinction of an obligation (*see* No. 335 *supra*), it does not, strictly speaking, extinguish it. According to the *Court of Cassation*, it does not alter the existence of a debt, but only the possibility to claim it.[617]

383. Prescription is considered to concern public order, which means that the parties may not stipulate that a right is not subject to prescription, that they may not agree among themselves to waive the right to plead prescription (Article 2220 OCC), and that they may not validly agree to extend the statutory prescription periods before the prescription starts to run. But the *defence* of prescription and the right to invoke it, once this right comes into existence, only affect private interests.[618] It follows from the foregoing that the courts may not apply prescription ex officio (Article 2223 OCC), except where matters of public policy are involved. Furthermore, the parties may validly waive a prescription which has already been acquired or agree that a prescription period which has already commenced shall remain suspended.[619] The parties may also reduce the statutory prescription periods.[620]

384. The most important prescription periods for contract law are the following. Claims based on 'personal rights' (i.e., rights in personam, except for tort, *see* No. 27 *supra*) are subject to a prescription period of ten years (Article 2262*bis* §1 OCC).

---

616. S. Stijns, *Leerboek Verbintenissenrecht*, vol. 2 (Brugge: die Keure, 2020), 141.
617. Cass. 13 Jun. 2014, *Arr. Cass.* 2014, 1476; Cass. 22 Sep. 1986, *Arr.Cass.* 1986-87, 88 & Pas. 1987, 82.
618. H. De Page & A. Meinertzhagen-Limpens, *Traité élémentaire de droit civil belge*, IV (Brussels: Bruylant, 1997), 1134; S. Stijns, *Leerboek Verbintenissenrecht 2* (Brugge: die Keure, 2020), 142; W. van Gerven en A. Van Oevelen, *Verbintenissenrecht* (Leuven: Acco, 2015), 655.
619. Cass. 23 Oct. 1986, *Arr.Cass.* 1986-87, 268 & *Pas.* 1987, 250.
620. S. Stijns, *Leerboek Verbintenissenrecht 2* (Brugge: die Keure, 2020), 142.

Claims based on tort have a prescription period of five years after the victim gains knowledge of the damages, or their augmentation, and of the identity of the liable person, with a maximum of twenty years from the day after the day when the facts that caused the damages took place (Article 2262*bis* §1–2 OCC). Claims based on 'real rights' (i.e., rights in rem*)* are subject to a prescription period of thirty years (Article 2262 OCC). The Civil Code contains several shorter terms of prescription as well (e.g., Article 2271 OCC, which states that the claim of employees regarding their wages is prescribed after six months).[621]

385. These periods may be interrupted or suspended (*see* Articles 2242–2259 OCC). In the case of interruption (*stuiting/interruption*) of the prescription period, the part of the prescription period which has already elapsed is undone, whereafter a new prescription period starts. For example, prescription may be interrupted by a summons to appear before a court or orders for payment notified to those whom one seeks to prevent from acquiring prescription (Article 1244 OCC). Prescription periods may also be interrupted by virtue of the debtor recognising the right of the party against whom the prescription can be invoked (Article 2248 OCC). In case of suspension, the prescription ceases to run temporarily for the benefit of certain persons (e.g., minors), between certain persons (e.g., spouses) or because of certain reasons determined by law, whereafter the prescription period is lengthened with the period of suspension. For example, prescription shall not apply to minors and persons under judicial disability (Article 2252 OCC) or between spouses (Article 2253 OCC).

G. Renunciation and 'Rechtsverwerking'

386. Renunciation to a right (*afstand van recht/renonciation à un droit*) is a unilateral juridical act where the creditor renounces a right granted to him by an obligation.[622] As a consequence, the obligation is cancelled and the debtor is freed. Given the radical nature of these consequences, renunciation is not presumed and interpreted restrictively (*see* No. 266 *supra*).[623] It may be done explicitly or silently, but the latter case requires a circumstantial silence, i.e., the circumstances and actions of the creditor may not allow any other interpretation than the will to renounce his right.[624]

---

621. *See* I. Claeys, M. De Ruysscher & L. Wermoes, *Verjaringsbepalingen in het Belgisch recht* (Antwerp: Kluwer, 2010), 774. This book provides an overview of the 1007 prescription periods in Belgian law. *See also* B. Weyts & T. Vansweevelt, 'De bevrijdende verjaring', in B. Weyts and T. Vansweevelt, *Handboek Verbintenissenrecht* (Mortsle, Intersentia, 2019), 944 et seq.
622. R. Dekkers & A. Verbeke, *Handboek Burgerlijk Recht*, III (Antwerp: Intersentia: 2007), 375; S. Stijns, *Leerboek Verbintenissenrecht*, vol. 2 (Brugge: die Keure, 2020), 144; W. van Gerven en A. Van Oevelen, *Verbintenissenrecht* (Leuven: Acco, 2015), 650. However, a part of the doctrine judges that renunciation may also take the form of a contract (*See*: L. Cornelis, *Algemene theorie van de verbintenis* (Antwerp: Intersentia, 2000), Nos 296 & 298).
623. Cass. 9 Nov. 2015, S.13.0042.N, *JTT* 2016, 1236, 26; Cass. 24 Sep. 1981, *Arr.Cass.* 1981-82, 140; Cass. 13 Sep. 2004, *Pas.* 2004, 1306.
624. Cass. 28 Sep. 2017, *RW* 2017-18, 1543 and *NJW* 2018, 23, note F. De Leo.Cass. 23 Jan. 2006, *J.T.T.* 2006, 178 & *RABG* 2006, 981.

387. The theory of *rechtsverwerking* deprives the holder of a right from the possibility to invoke this right if he adopts a behaviour which is objectively incompatible with the exercise of that right and, due to that conduct, the other party could and in fact did, in reliance on such conduct, legitimately expect that he would not exercise his right.[625] However, the *Court of Cassation* judged that *rechtsverwerking* is not a general principle nor an autonomous legal concept.[626] Nevertheless, the jurisprudence continued to apply it as an application of the moderating function of good faith (*see* No. 103 *supra*).[627] This means that it is possible to apply *rechtsverwerking* on the condition that there is abuse of rights (*see* No. 104 *supra*).

H. Termination

388. Termination (*opzegging/résiliation*) is a manner to end a contract where the parties terminate a contract they concluded, unilaterally or by mutual agreement, and where the contract ceases to exist *ex nunc*.[628] This termination is independent from the parties' (non-) performance of the contract, and should not be confused with termination in case of breach of reciprocal contracts (*ontbinding/résolution*) (*see* Nos 433 ff. *infra*). Although the same term, i.e., 'termination', is used for both *opzegging/résiliation* and *ontbinding/résolution* in this contribution (by lack of English equivalents for the Belgian notions), these are fundamentally different concepts with different consequences. Termination only affects the future. It has no retroactive effect.

Article 1134, paragraph 2 OCC provides that contracts can only be terminated by mutual assent of the parties or in cases where it is authorised by the law. It follows that there are two methods of termination: either contractually, which requires the mutual assent of all the parties involved ('*mutuus dissensus*'), or unilaterally, albeit only in certain specific cases where the law allows it.[629]

389. In principle, any contract may be ended by *mutuus dissensus*. Like any contract, termination by mutual assent requires an offer and an acceptance by all the parties.[630] It is, in principle, consensual, and may be explicit or silent.[631]

625. S. Stijns, *Leerboek Verbintenissenrecht 2* (Brugge: die Keure, 2020), 145.
626. Cass. 17 May 1990, *Arr.Cass.* 1989-90, 1188 & *Pas.* 1990, 1061.
627. Cass. 1 Oct. 2010, *Arr. Cass* 2010, 2385; *Pas.* 2010, 2470; *RW* 2011-12, 142, note S. Jansen and S. Stijns; *TBBR* 2012, 387, note P. Bazier; *TBH* 2011, 77. *See* further S. Stijns, *Leerboek Verbintenissenrecht*, vol 2 (Brugge: die Keure, 2020), 146.
628. E. Dirix, B. Tilleman & S. Lierman (eds), *De Valks Juridisch woordenboek* (Antwerp-Oxford: Intersentia, 2018), 330–331.
629. F. Vermander, '(Eenzijdige) opzegging', in B. Weyts and T. Vansweevelt, *Handboek Verbintenissenrecht* (Mortsel, Intersentia, 2019), 563; P. Wéry, *Droit des obligations, I, Théorie générale du contrat* (Brussels: Larcier, 2011), 901.
630. P. Wéry, *Droit des obligations, I, Théorie générale du contrat* (Brussels: Larcier, 2011), 901.
631. Even if the initial contract was solemn, this does not necessarily mean that the termination contract must be solemn as well. In such case, the formalities necessary for the conclusion of the initial solemn contract will only be required for the termination contract if their goal is relevant for the termination contract as well.

390. Unilateral termination (*opzegging/résiliation*) is a juridical act by unilateral declaration of will by one party, which terminates a contract concluded between parties for the future, independently of the intention to sanction. There are four grounds of unilateral termination.[632] First, there are certain specific cases where the law explicitly grants the competence to terminate the contract unilaterally to one or several parties. For instance, Articles 2004 OCC and 2007 OCC on agency grant the right to terminate unilaterally to the principal and the agent, while Article 1794 OCC on hire of work only confers this right to the principal. Second, contracts with an indefinite duration can be terminated unilaterally at all times. This right to terminate is considered grounded on the autonomy of will, which implies that one cannot obligate himself indefinitely without the possibility to free himself from his obligations.[633] However, recent doctrine nuances this and states that this right is based on fundamental values, such as individual freedom, freedom of commerce and freedom of competition. Third, parties can include a termination clause in their contract. A termination clause allows for a party to terminate a contract prematurely and unilaterally, often against the payment of a fixed sum to the other party (*see* No. 255 *supra*).[634] Fourth, in some cases, the right to terminate unilaterally is granted by custom or usages. For example, the contract between a lawyer and his client can be ended unilaterally by the lawyer (provided that this is not untimely and that the client can still consult another counsel), or by the client (provided that he pays for the provided services). Unilateral termination requires the notification of the other party, but, in principle, it must not be motivated. In principle, unilateral termination is definitive and irrevocable.[635]

II. Breach of Contract

391. As stated before, Belgian law defines a contract as a juridical act where one or several parties obligate themselves towards one or several other parties to give something, do something or not do something.[636] When at least one of the parties to a valid contract fails to perform his obligations, this will lead to his contractual liability if this failure was caused by his own fault, that of a person he is responsible for or that of a thing he uses for the performance of his contractual obligations. Such *'accountable'* non-performance (*toerekenbare niet-nakoming/*

632. *See*: F. Vermander, '(Eenzijdige) opzegging', in B. Weyts and T. Vansweevelt, *Handboek Verbintenissenrecht* (Mortsel, Intersentia, 2019), 560; P. Wéry, *Droit des obligations, I, Théorie générale du contrat* (Brussels: Larcier, 2011), 904.

633. W. van Gerven en A. Van Oevelen, *Verbintenissenrecht* (Leuven: Acco, 2015), 257.

634. S. Stijns, *Leerboek Verbintenissenrecht 1* (Brugge: die Keure, 2016), 195; F. Vermander, '(Eenzijdige) opzegging', in B. Weyts and T. Vansweevelt, *Handboek Verbintenissenrecht* (Mortsle, Intersentia, 2019), 563; P. Wéry, *Droit des obligations, I, Théorie générale du contrat* (Brussels: Larcier, 2011), 917.

635. *See* among others L. Cornelis, *Algemene theorie van de verbintenis* (Antwerp: Intersentia, 2000); F. Vermander, '(Eenzijdige) opzegging', in B. Weyts and T. Vansweevelt, *Handboek Verbintenissenrecht* (Mortsle, Intersentia, 2019), 567; P. Wéry, *Droit des obligations, I, Théorie générale du contrat* (Brussels: Larcier, 2011), 914.

636. E. Dirix, B. Tilleman & S. Lierman (eds), *De Valks Juridisch woordenboek* (Antwerp-Oxford: Intersentia, 2018), 105.

inexécution fautive) is considered a breach of contract.[637] Consequentially, the existence of a breach of contract depends on which obligations the debtor took upon himself in a valid contract. A breach of contract may concern any kind of failure to achieve the object of the obligation: it may be a total lack of performance, an incomplete performance, a lacking performance, a late performance, or a combination of several of these.

A. *Faulty Behaviour of the Debtor*

1. Personal Faulty Behaviour of the Debtor

392. First and foremost, the debtor is responsible for his own faults. He has to be accountable (*toerekenbaar/imputable*) for a faulty behaviour in order for the non-performance to be considered a breach of contract. If, on the contrary, the non-performance is the result of an extraneous cause (*vreemde oorzaak/cause étrangère*), this accountability is lacking, and there will be no contractual liability (*see* Nos 400 ff. *infra*). Even the slightest faulty behaviour can induce contractual liability.[638] The criterion used to determine whether a behaviour is faulty or not is called the '*prudence criterion*' (*zorvuldigheidscriterium/critère général de prudence*).[639,640] According to it, everyone must always behave like a *bonus pater familias (goede huisvader/bon père de famille)*, which is a normal, prudent and careful person in the same circumstances. Behaviour is faulty if it fails to meet this requirement.[641]

393. '*Normal*' indicates a normal person, with normal limits and weaknesses.[642] '*Prudent*' means that one tries to anticipate the reasonable consequences of one's actions. Damages are considered foreseeable as soon as one could foresee that damage would result from his behaviour. In other words, only the existence of damages must be foreseeable, not its scope.[643] '*Careful*' means that one has to take the necessary measures to avoid the foreseeable harmful consequences of his behaviour. A behaviour can only be considered faulty when the damage ensuing could be avoided. In other words, the duty to act like a *bonus pater familias* is a duty of best efforts (*see* No. 398 *infra*), which imposes upon one the duty to make all necessary

---

637. S. Stijns, *Leerboek Verbintenissenrecht 1* (Brugge: die Keure, 2016), 152; W. van Gerven en A. Van Oevelen, *Verbintenissenrecht* (Leuven: Acco, 2015), 166.
638. S. Stijns, *Leerboek Verbintenissenrecht 1* (Brugge: die Keure, 2016), 154; W. van Gerven en A. Van Oevelen, *Verbintenissenrecht* (Leuven: Acco, 2015), 167; P. Wéry, *Droit des obligations, I, Théorie générale du contrat* (Brussels: Larcier, 2011), 513.
639. *Ibid.*
640. This should not be confused with due diligence in the English legal system, which, according to the *Oxford Dictionary of Law*, 6th ed. (Oxford: University Press, 2006), 181, is 'the legal obligation of states to exercise all reasonable efforts to protect aliens and their property in the host state'.
641. The same criterion is used for contractual and extracontractual liability.
642. S. Stijns & I. Samoy, *Leerboek Verbintenissenrecht 1bis* (Brugge: die Keure, 2020), 55, nr. 12.
643. Cass. 5 May 1971, *Arr.Cass.* 1971, 869; Cass. 17 Apr. 1975, *Arr.Cass.*1975, 308; S. Stijns & I. Samoy, *Leerboek Verbintenissenrecht 1bis* (Brugge: die Keure, 2020), 55, nr. 12.

efforts which can be expected from a *bonus pater familias* to avoid harmful consequences to others.[644] The criterion of the normal, prudent and careful person is abstract, as personal characteristics are not taken into account. Nevertheless, when applying this abstract criterion, judges must also consider the *concrete circumstances*.[645] Consequentially, it is possible to take some so-called *'external'* circumstances into account, such as the place, time and climate, but also one's education and professional experience.[646] *'Internal'* circumstances, i.e., individual characteristics such as age, sex, intelligence or personality, however, may not be taken into consideration.[647]

394. The distinction between a duty to achieve (*resultaatsverbintenis/obligation de résultat*) and a duty of best efforts (*inspanningsverbintenis/obligations de moyens*) is important to determine whether a debtor's behaviour may induce contractual liability. A duty to achieve is an obligation which obligates the debtor to achieve a certain result.[648] When the debtor fails to produce the promised result, the faulty behaviour of the debtor is assumed as soon as the creditor can prove both the existence of the obligation and the lack of result. The debtor can only escape liability by proving that his failure has an extraneous cause (*see* Nos 35–36 *infra*). Examples of a duty to achieve are the obligation of a lawyer to respect procedural deadlines or that of a mechanic to repair or clean a car. Conversely, a duty of best efforts only obligates the debtor to take the measures a reasonable person would take to achieve the purpose of the contract, without promising that he will actually achieve it.[649] For the debtor to be liable, the creditor must prove not only the existence of the obligation and the lack of result but also the fact that the debtor has not taken the measures that could be expected from a reasonable person (*see* Nos 35–36 *supra*). In other terms, unlike in the case of a duty to achieve a certain result, the fault of the debtor is not assumed, but must be proven by the creditor.[650] Examples are: the duty of a doctor to cure his patient or that of a lawyer to advise, negotiate or plead a case.

2. Persons and Objects for which the Debtor Is Responsible

395. The debtor is not only responsible for his own faults. He is also responsible for contractual faults made by auxiliaries (*hulppersonen/auxilliaires*), i.e., persons who help him to perform his obligations. Both persons appointed by the debtor

644. S. Stijns & I Samoy, *Leerboek Verbintenissenrecht 1bis* (Brugge: die Keure, 2020), 56, nr. 13.
645. S. Stijns, *Leerboek Verbintenissenrecht 1* (Brugge: die Keure, 2016), 154; S. Stijns & I. Samoy, *Leerboek Verbintenissenrecht 1bis* (Brugge: die Keure, 2020), 56, nr. 14.
646. For example, Cass. 25 Oct. 1974, *Arr.Cass.* 1975, 263 and *Pas.* 1975, 241, where the criterion is the 'normally careful garage man'.
647. S. Stijns & I. Samoy, *Leerboek Verbintenissenrecht 1bis* (Brugge: die Keure, 2020), 58, nr. 15; W. van Gerven en A. Van Oevelen, *Verbintenissenrecht* (Leuven: Acco, 2015), 167; P. Wéry, *Droit des obligations, I, Théorie générale du contrat* (Brussels: Larcier, 2011), 514.
648. E. Dirix, B. Tilleman & S. Lierman (eds), *De Valks Juridisch woordenboek* (Antwerp-Oxford: Intersentia, 2018), 396.
649. *Ibid.*, 233.
650. S. Stijns, *Leerboek Verbintenissenrecht 1* (Brugge: die Keure, 2016), 153.

(i.e., persons he employs) and independent agents fall within this category.[651] If such person commits a faulty behaviour in regard to the performance obliged by the contract, his fault is considered to be a fault of the debtor himself, which makes him personally liable for the breach, regardless of his own behaviour. Although the *Court of Cassation* has recognised and recently confirmed this principle,[652] its exact ground is unclear.[653] Auxiliaries benefit from an ample immunity against claims from the creditor. As they are no contract party to the contract between creditor and debtor, they cannot incur contractual liability for a breach of this contract. Moreover, as they are no real third parties to this contract either, no extracontractual claim can be laid upon them by the creditor to the extent that they acted under the terms of the contract.[654] They are only liable extracontractually if the requirements for concurrence of contractual and extracontractual liability are met (*see* Nos 84 *supra*).[655]

396. The debtor is also held liable for objects used either by himself or by his auxiliaries; e.g., a hospital is liable for the use of a contaminated needle by its nurses. This liability is incurred regardless of the question of whether the breach is caused by a faulty use of the object by the debtor or his auxiliaries, or by a flaw of the object itself.[656]

3. Proof of the Fault

397. The burden of proof regarding a breach of contract lies with the creditor (*see* No. 162 *supra*). This proof is easier to provide for a duty to achieve (*resultaatsverbintenis/obligation de résultat*) than for a duty of best efforts (*inspanningsverbintenis/obligations de moyens*) (*see* Nos 35–36 *supra*). Besides the

651. *Ibid.*, 155; W. van Gerven en A. Van Oevelen, *Verbintenissenrecht* (Leuven: Acco, 2015), 167; P. Wéry, *Droit des obligations, I, Théorie générale du contrat* (Brussels: Larcier, 2011), 529; *see also* B. Weyts & T. Vansweevelt, 'Contractuele aansprakelijkheid', in B. Weyts and T. Vansweevelt, *Handboek Verbintenissenrecht* (Mortsle, Intersentia, 2019), 532.

652. Cass. 24 Mar. 2016, *Arr. Cass.* 2016, 716; *TBH* 2017, 200, note R. Steennot; Cass. 25 Mai 2012, *Pas.* 2012, 1196, *RW* 2013-14, 338, note B. Van den Bergh and *JLMB* 2012, 1346; Cass. 4 Feb. 2010, *Pas.* 2010, 376, *TBH* 2010, 498 en *TBO* 2011, 25; Cass 29 Sep. 2006, *Pas.* 2006, 1991, *NJW* 2006, 946, note I. Boone, *RW* 2006-2007, 1717, note A. Van Oevelen, *TBO* 2007, 66, note K. Vanhove, *RAGB* 2007, 1256, *TBBR* 2008, 557; Cass. 27 Feb. 2003, AR. C010457F, *Arr.Cass.* 2003, 51, *Pas.* 2003, 422; Cass. 5 Oct. 1990, *Arr.Cass.* 1990-91, 125 and *Pas.* 1991; Cass. 21 Jun. 1979, *Arr.Cass.* 178-79, 1268 and *Pas.* 1979, 1226.

653. According to the following authors, this is an *algemeen rechtsbeginsel/principe général du droit*: S. Stijns, W. van Gerven & P. Wéry, 'Chronique', *J.T.* (1996): No. 105; S. Stijns, *Leerboek Verbintenissenrecht, vol. 1* (Brugge: die Keure, 2016), 155.

654. As recognised in the judgment of Cass. 7 Dec. 1973, *Arr.Cass.* 1974, 395, note J. Herbots and confirmed in Cass. 8 Apr. 1983, *R.W.* 1983-84, 163, note J. Herbots; Cass. 1 Jun. 2001, *R.W.* 2001-02, 379; Cass. 17 Mar. 2017, RW 2018-19, 382, note, TBH 2017, 952 note P. Gillaerts; Cass. 12 Mar. 2020, C.19.0408.N, *TBBR* 2020, 438.

655. S. Stijns & I. Samoy, *Leerboek Verbintenissenrecht 1bis* (Brugge: die Keure, 2020), 186, nr. 152.

656. S. Stijns, *Leerboek Verbintenissenrecht 1* (Brugge: die Keure, 2016), 157; W. van Gerven en A. Van Oevelen, *Verbintenissenrecht* (Leuven: Acco, 2015), 168; P. Wéry, *Droit des obligations, I, Théorie générale du contrat* (Brussels: Larcier, 2011), 531.

breach, the creditor must also prove the resulting damage and the causal link between breach and damage.[657] However, not all remedies require these three elements. If a fault by the debtor is proven, the creditor may pursue performance *in kind* (*see* Nos 415 ff. *infra*) or, in case of synallagmatic contracts, termination (*see* Nos 431 ff. *infra*), without having to prove that the fault caused damage. If however the creditor claims damages, he has to prove fault, damage and a causal link between them (*see* Nos 421 ff. *infra*).

398. As the rules regarding proof are suppletive, parties may agree to apply different rules in their contract.[658]

B. Defence of Non-performance by the Debtor

399. There are several ways for the debtor to defend himself against a contractual liability claim. First, he may dispute the scope of the contractual obligations, which will incite the judge to determine the scope of the obligation through interpretation, completion and moderation (*see* Nos 101–104 and 264–270 *supra*). If the contract contains exemption clauses, he may invoke them to escape liability (*see* Nos 246–253 *supra*). Second, he may claim that the cause of the non-performance was not his faulty behaviour but an extraneous cause (*see* Nos 400 *infra*). Third, in the case of synallagmatic contracts, he may call upon the *exceptio non adimpleti contractus*, according to which a contract party may suspend his own obligation to perform until the other party performs (*see* Nos 448–450 *infra*).

§2. Impossibility, Frustration and Hardship

I. Impossibility

A. Concept

400. According to Articles 1147 and 1148 OCC, a debtor does not incur liability for breach in case the non-performance was caused by extraneous cause (*vreemde oorzaak/cause étrangère libératoire*), irresistible force (*overmacht/force majeure*) or fortuitous event (*toeval/cas fortuit*). These three terms are usually used as synonyms.[659] Irresistible force indicates events which happen independently of assignable human behaviour, such as natural causes (acts of God[660]), e.g., flood, earthquake, storms on land or sea, snow, ice, hail, lightning, fire, illness, death, war

657. S. Stijns, *Leerboek Verbintenissenrecht, vol. 1* (Brugge: die Keure, 2016), 157.
658. Cass. 20 Jun. 1957, *Arr.Cass.* 1957, 885 and *Pas.* 1957, I, 1256; Cass. 20 Apr. 1978, *Arr.Cass.*1977-78, 958.
659. S. Stijns, *Leerboek Verbintenissenrecht, vol. 1* (Brugge: die Keure, 2016), 161; P. Wéry, *Droit des obligations, I, Théorie générale du contrat* (Brussels: Larcier, 2011), 538 et seq.
660. J. Law & E. Martin, *Oxford Dictionary of Law*, 6th ed. (Oxford: University Press, 2006), 11.

or uprising.[661] Extraneous cause includes these as well, but also contains acts of independent third parties for whose behaviour the creditor is not responsible,[662] e.g., decisions by the authorities (called '*fait du prince*'), strikes, theft, or actions of the creditor which make performance by the debtor impossible. Indeed, in this context, any person the debtor is not responsible for is considered a third person, creditor included.[663] The *Court of Cassation* defines extraneous cause as an insurmountable impediment for the performance of the obligation which is not caused by a faulty behaviour of the debtor.[664]

401. The rules regarding extraneous cause are suppletive, except in some special cases specified by law (e.g., Article VI.83, 12° CEL which forbids terms that require the consumer to pay damages in order to terminate the contract in case of irresistible force). Consequentially, it is possible for parties to include clauses on irresistible force (*overmachtsclausules/clauses de force majeure*) in their contracts. These terms may define, exclude or limit the application of extraneous cause and the circumstances that will (or will not) be considered as such, thus extending (or limiting) the obligation and the scope of liability.

B. Conditions

402. In order to have consequences, extraneous cause must meet the requirements of 'the doctrine of the non-imputable impossibility' (*leer van de ontoerekenbare onmogelijkheid/doctrine de l'impossibilité d'exécution non imputable au débiteur*). According to this doctrine, two conditions must be met for the application of extraneous cause. First, the impediment may not be imputable to the party invoking extraneous cause. This means that the occurrence should have been unforeseeable at the moment the contract came into existence, that the debtor was not able to avoid or prevent it, and that the debtor was not yet put in delay at the moment it occurred (Article 1302 OCC).[665] Second, it must make the performance impossible either temporarily or permanently. Although initially, this requirement was absolute,[666] and is still understood as such by a part of the jurisprudence,[667] doctrine pleads for a more practical or humane interpretation.[668]

---

661. S. Stijns, *Leerboek Verbintenissenrecht 1* (Brugge: die Keure, 2016), 161.
662. Cass. 21 Sep. 1990, *Arr.Cass.* 1990-91, 66 and *Pas.* 1991, 62; H. De Page, *Traité élémentaire de droit civil belge, III* (Brussels: Bruylant, 1967), No. 598.
663. S. Stijns, *Leerboek Verbintenissenrecht 1* (Brugge: die Keure, 2016), 161.
664. Cass. 18 Nov. 1996, *Arr.Cass.* 1996, 1051 and *Pas.* 1996, 1121; Cass. 9 Dec. 1976, *Arr.Cass.* 1977, 404 and *Pas.* 1977, 408; Cass. 23 Feb. 1967, *Arr.Cass.* 1967, 797 and *Pas.* 1967, 782; Cass. 15 Feb. 1951, *Arr.Cass.* 1951, 327 and *Pas.* 1951, 388; Cass. 12 juni 1947, *Arr. Verbr.* 1947, 202 and *Pas.* 1947, 264.
665. H. De Page, *Traité élémentaire de droit civil belge, II* (Brussels: Bruylant, 1967), No. 602; S. Stijns, *Leerboek Verbintenissenrecht 1* (Brugge: die Keure, 2016), 162; W. van Gerven en A. Van Oevelen, *Verbintenissenrecht* (Leuven: Acco, 2015), 171; P. Wéry, *Droit des obligations, I, Théorie générale du contrat* (Brussels: Larcier, 2011), 540.
666. Cass. 23 Feb. 1967, *Arr.Cass.* 1967, 797 and *Pas.* 1967, 782.

C. Consequences of Extraneous Cause and Contractual Risk

403. If the impossibility to perform is temporary, the obligation is suspended from the start of the occurrence which constitutes irresistible force, until the performance becomes possible again, unless the performance has become useless.[669] If it is permanent, the debt is extinguished.[670] Thus the risk of loss because of an extraneous cause lies with the creditor (*'res perit creditori'*). However, according to Article 1302 OCC, if the debtor has received a default notice (*see* Nos 411 ff. *infra*) prior to the situation of extraneous cause, the risk comes back to him, and he will not be able to invoke extraneous cause unless he can prove that the impossibility would also have arisen if the obligation had already been performed.

404. In the case of reciprocal contracts,[671] when one party cannot perform due to extraneous cause, the obligations of the other party are extinguished (or suspended, in case of a temporary impossibility)[672] too and the reciprocal contract is automatically terminated.[673] Consequentially, in this case, the risk lies with the debtor, as he does not obtain payment and carries the economic loss (*'res perit debitori'*). According to Article 1138 OCC, if the object of a reciprocal contract is a specific good, ownership and risks are both transferred at the moment the contract is concluded, even if the delivery does not happen at the same time.[674] Thus, if the good is destroyed by extraneous cause, the debtor is freed of his duty of delivery,

---

667. S. Stijns, *Leerboek Verbintenissenrecht 1* (Brugge: die Keure, 2016), 163; T. Vansweevelt & B. Weyts, 'De contractuele aansprakelijkheid', in T. Vansweevelt & B. Weyts, *Handboek Verbintenissenrecht* (Antwerpen: Intersentia, 2019), 367; P. Wéry, *Droit des obligations, I, Théorie générale du contrat* (Brussels: Larcier, 2011), 540.
668. H. De Page, *Traité élémentaire de droit civil belge, II* (Brussels: Bruylant, 1967), No. 599/B; S. Stijns, *Leerboek Verbintenissenrecht 1* (Brugge: die Keure, 2016), 163; W. van Gerven en A. Van Oevelen, *Verbintenissenrecht* (Leuven: Acco, 2015), T. Vansweevelt & B. Weyts, 'De contractuele aansprakelijkheid', in T. Vansweevelt and B. Weyts, *Handboek Verbintenissenrecht* (Antwerpen: Intersentia, 2019), 367; 172.
669. Cass. 12 Jan. 1956, *Arr.Cass.* 1956 and *Pas.* 1956, 461; S. Stijns, *Leerboek Verbintenissenrecht 1* (Brugge: die Keure, 2016), 163; W. van Gerven en A. Van Oevelen, *Verbintenissenrecht* (Leuven: Acco, 2015), 173; T. Vansweevelt & B. Weyts, 'De contractuele aansprakelijkheid', in T. Vansweevelt and B. Weyts, *Handboek Verbintenissenrecht* (Antwerpen: Intersentia, 2019), 370; P. Wéry, *Droit des obligations, I, Théorie générale du contrat* (Brussels: Larcier, 2011), 543.
670. S. Stijns, *Leerboek Verbintenissenrecht 1* (Brugge: die Keure, 2016), 163.
671. For the concept of reciprocal, *see* No. 49 *supra*.
672. W. van Gerven en A. Van Oevelen, *Verbintenissenrecht* (Leuven: Acco, 2015), 173.
673. Cass. 27 Jun. 1946, *Arr.Cass.* 1946, 249 and *Pas.* 1946, 270; H. De Page, *Traité élémentaire de droit civil belge, II* (Brussels: Bruylant, 1967), Nos 774 and 841; S. Stijns, *Leerboek Verbintenissenrecht 1* (Brugge: die Keure, 2020), 164.
674. Within the category of the obligations to give, the object of the gift can be either a unascertained good or a specific one. In the case of a generic good, the first obligation is one to do, as the generic good must be separated from the others before being able to transfer its possession (to give). Usually, both the separation and the transfer will happen at the same time and take place simultaneously with the delivery of these goods, especially in the case of a commercial trade. In the case of a specific good, the transfer of property generally occurs at the same time as the meeting of minds (Art. 1138 OCC), after which only an obligation to do, i.e., the obligation to deliver, remains. The distinction between unascertained goods and specific ones is also important to determine when the transfer of the property occurs, as well as the resulting transfer of the risks. Barring clauses stating otherwise, property and risk of loss due to an extraneous cause are transferred at the same time.

while the creditor remains obligated to pay. In other words, the risk lies with the owner (‘*res perit domino*’). When the obligation is one for the delivery of a quantity of unascertained goods, the principle ‘*genera non pereunt*’ applies. There are exceptions to the rule that ownership and risk are transferred at the moment of the contract. First, parties may validly contract that the risk will be borne by the debtor. Second, as stated before, the obligation also subsists if the debtor was in default when the thing perished (*see* No. 414 *infra*).

II. Doctrine of Unforeseen Circumstances

A. Concept

405. The doctrine of unforeseen circumstances (*imprevisieleer/théorie de l'imprévision*) concerns the situation where unforeseen/unforeseeable and unaccountable circumstances (mostly economic or financial) arise after the conclusion of the contract which make performance much more difficult, although not impossible.[675] According to this doctrine, it should be possible for a judge to adapt or terminate a contract due to changed circumstances which thoroughly upset the balance between the contractual performances and due to which the performance of his obligations by one party becomes unreasonable.[676]

B. Rejection of the Doctrine of Unforeseen Circumstances

406. The traditional opinion of the Belgian courts is to reject the doctrine of unforeseen circumstances.[677] This stance is justified by the obligatory force of contracts, which does not allow for judges to alter the contents of a contract.[678] It is argued that deviating from this rule would endanger legal certainty.[679] The legislator, not the judge, should decide when relief should be given for changed or unforeseen circumstances (*see*, e.g., Article 301 §7 OCC allowing a judge to adapt the amount of alimony in case of change of circumstances). Moreover, relief can already be given through the application of Article 1244 OCC (*see* No. 348 *supra*)

For specific goods, this is the time of the meeting of minds, while for unascertained goods, it is the moment of the individualisation or separation, which usually is the moment of the physical transfer of the good.

675. S. Stijns, *Leerboek Verbintenissenrecht 1* (Brugge: die Keure, 2016), 165.
676. E. Dirix, B. Tilleman & S. Lierman (eds), *De Valks Juridisch woordenboek* (Antwerp-Oxford: Intersentia, 2018), 226.
677. Implicitly: Cass. 19 May 1921, *Pas.* 1921, 380; Cass. 30 Oct. 1924, *Pas.* 1924, 565. Explicitly: Cass. 7 Feb. 1994, *Arr.Cass.* 1994, 146 and *Pas.* 1994, 150; Cass. 14 Apr. 1994, *Arr.Cass.* 1994, 369 and *Pas.* 1994, 365; Cass. 20 Apr. 2006, *Arr.Cass*, 2006, 904 and *Pas*. 2006, 884.
678. S. Stijns, *Leerboek Verbintenissenrecht 1* (Brugge: die Keure, 2016), 166; T. Vansweevelt & B. Weyts, ‘De contractuele aansprakelijkheid’, in T. Vansweevelt and B. Weyts, *Handboek Verbintenissenrecht* (Antwerpen: Intersentia, 2019), 375.
679. H. De Page, *Traité élémentaire de droit civil belge, II* (Brussels: Bruylant, 1967), Nos 568–570.

which allows for the judge to grant respite to a debtor. Besides, if they wish for such circumstances to be taken into account, parties may include hardship clauses in their contract.

407. However, part of the recent doctrine is somewhat more nuanced in its view. It cautiously pleads that the judge could be allowed to alter the contract through the application of the doctrine of good faith (*see* Nos 101 ff. *supra*). Some authors ground this on the moderative function of good faith and the prohibition of abuse of rights (*see* Nos 102–104 *supra*).[680] This view was implicitly accepted by the *Court of Cassation*.[681] Some other authors grant good faith a new, distinct function, according to which the courts could adapt the contract to new circumstances.[682] This view was rejected by the *Court of Cassation* in two judgments of 1994.[683,684] This was very clear in the judgment of 14 April 1994, where it stated that: '*performance in good faith does not imply that the creditor could not demand payment of his claim when new and unforeseen circumstances hinder the performance of the contract by the debtor*'. However, the Court seems more nuanced in a judgment of 19 June 2009, where it recognises the right of a party who is confronted with a change in circumstances which deeply disturbs the contractual balance to demand re-negotiations about the contract.[685] This judgment concerns an international sale, which is why the *Court* takes the terms of the United Nations Convention on Contracts for the International Sale of Goods, 1980 (CISG) into account. Article 79 CISG recognises unforeseen circumstances as a ground to exclude liability. Article 7.2 CISG provides that questions left unanswered in the convention can be complemented by the general principles which laid its foundation. The *Court* states that this includes the International Institute for the Unification of Private Law (UNIDROIT) Principles of International Commercial Contracts. Article 6.2.3 of the UNIDROIT Principles grant the right to renegotiate to a party who is confronted with a change in circumstances which deeply disturbs the contractual balance. It is unlikely that this reasoning would already be adopted for a national contract.[686]

---

680. E. Dirix & A. Van Oevelen, 'Kroniek van het verbintenissenrecht (1985-1992)', *R.W.* 1992-93, 1249; P. Wéry, *Droit des obligations, I, Théorie générale du contrat* (Brussels: Larcier, 2011), 558.
681. Cass. 19 Sep. 1983, *R.C.J.B.* 1986, 283, which judged that demanding performance in case of a deeply upset contractual balance can constitute an abuse of rights. Cass. 14 Apr. 1994, *Arr.Cass.* 1994, 369 and *Pas.* 1994, 365, which rejected unforeseen circumstances as an autonomous ground for the judge to adapt a contract in case of changed circumstances, also made an explicit reserve for the application of abuse of rights. Cass. 14 oktober 2010, *Pas.* 2010, 2643.
682. M. Fontaine, 'Portée et limites du principe de la convention-loi' in *Les obligations contractuelles* (Brussels: Editions du Jeune Barreau, 1984), 190; D. Philippe, *Changement de circonstances et bouleversement de l'économie contractuelle* (Brussels: Bruylant: 1986), 651.
683. Cass. 7 Feb. 1994, *Pas.* 1994, 150.
684. Cass. 14 Apr. 1994, *Arr.Cass.* 1994, 369 and *Pas.* 1994, 365.
685. Cass. 19 Jun. 2009, *R.W.* 2009-10, 744.
686. *See* P. Wéry, *Droit des obligations, I, Théorie générale du contrat* (Brussels: Larcier, 2011), 557.

III. Contractual Allocation of Liability

408. In their contract, parties may deviate from the suppletive laws concerning contractual liability, and define when it will occur (or not), what the sanctions will be, which situations will be considered extraneous cause or unforeseen circumstances, etc. There is a great diversity in the possible clauses to this effect. Parties can uphold their rights regarding the performance of an obligation through the use of terms such as rescission clauses, suspension clauses, replacement clauses, clauses regarding default notices or penalty clauses, or terms which limit or complicate the application of sanctions, such as exemption clauses and clauses regarding irresistible force or unforeseen circumstances (*see* Nos 243 ff. *supra*).[687]

409. Although parties enjoy a vast freedom in defining the terms of the contract, the execution of those terms might be disputed by one of them. If the case is brought before a court, it will qualify and interpret the terms (*see* Nos 264 ff. *supra*), determine their validity, evaluate whether or not their enforcement is reasonable, and decide whether or not to nullify (*see* Nos 235 ff. *supra*), moderate or declare it without effect (*see* Nos 103–105 *supra*).

687. S. Stijns, *Leerboek Verbintenissenrecht, 1* (Brugge: die Keure, 2016), 170.

Chapter 6. Remedies

§1. General Provisions

410. In Belgian law, remedies are considered aspects of the effect of contracts or of obligations. A contract intends to create legal consequences, or, more specifically, obligations. The effect of an obligation is either that it is performed, whether voluntarily or under legal compulsion, or that a substitute for performance is provided by way of damages. The primary recourse in case of breach of contract is performance in kind (*uitvoering in natura/exécution en nature*), and possibly supplementary damages. Subsidiary to this is performance by equivalent (*uitvoering bij equivalent/exécution par équivalence*). These recourses are the object of paragraph 3. If a contract is reciprocal, the creditor has the right to choose between enforcing performance (*uitvoering/exécution*) or termination (*ontbinding/résolution*), plus possibly supplementary damages. In addition, he may call upon the *exceptio non adimpleti contractus*, which allows him to withhold his own performance as long as the other party fails to perform her obligation. These options are examined in paragraph 4. However, before discussing remedies, it is important to define the notion of putting the debtor in delay (*ingebrekestellen/mettre en demeure*), which is required to enable most kinds of enforcement. This is the object of paragraph 2.

§2. Formal Requisition of Putting the Debtor in Delay

I. Putting the Debtor in Delay: A General Principle of Law

411. In case of breach, the debtor must be 'put in delay' before the creditor may enforce his rights towards him.[688] This is done by the delivery of a default notice (*ingebrekestelling/mise en demeure*), which must clearly and unambiguously demand performance of his obligations by the debtor. This requirement has explicitly been recognised as a general principle of law by the *Court of Cassation*.[689] Consequentially, a debtor must be put in delay before judicial sanctions (such as enforcement or termination of a contract) can be demanded.[690] It is also necessary to put the debtor in delay before calling upon a clause which provides a sanction in case of breach and before applying private sanctions (*see* No. 444 *infra*).[691]

412. There are many exceptions to the principle of putting a debtor in delay. First, some are stated expressly or implicitly in the Civil Code and other laws. For

688. R. Dekkers & A. Verbeke, *Handboek Burgerlijk Recht*, III (Antwerp: Intersentia: 2007), 212; P. Van Ommeslaghe, *Les obligations vol. 3* in *Traité de droit civil, tome II* (Brussels: Bruylant, 2013), 2164.
689. Cass. 9 Apr. 1976, *Arr.Cass.* 1976, 921 and *Pas.* 1976, 887.
690. Cass. 28 May 2020, C.19.0128.N, *TBBR* 2020, 582.
691. S. Stijns, *Leerboek Verbintenissenrecht 1* (Brugge: die Keure, 2016), 181; W. van Gerven en A. Van Oevelen, *Verbintenissenrecht* (Leuven: Acco, 2015), 601–602; P. Wéry, *Droit des obligations, I, Théorie générale du contrat* (Brussels: Larcier, 2011), 451 et seq.

example, according to Article 5 of the Law on combating late payment in transactions between companies, if the debtor fails to pay within the contracted time period or, within the absence of such terms, within the period determined in Article 4, interests automatically start to run from the next day without default notice.[692] Second, a precise and unambiguous stipulation of the contract may relieve the creditor from the necessity of putting the debtor in delay. Such clause is submitted to a restrictive interpretation,[693] but is otherwise valid, unless a specific law forbids it. Third, the *Court of Cassation* ruled that putting the debtor in delay is not necessary when the nature of the contract, the intention of the parties or the circumstances of the case make it evident that performance has become impossible or has lost any usefulness for the creditor. This principle is, for instance, applicable when the obligation to abstain from something has been breached,[694] when the source of the obligation is delictual,[695] or when the debtor has announced that he has no intention to perform.[696]

II. Form and Contents

413. According to Article 1139 OCC, a default notice must have the form of 'a notice or other equivalent act'. According to the *Court of Cassation*, this amounts to '*any act containing an injunction due to which the debtor has necessarily understood that he was put in delay to perform his obligation*'.[697] Consequently, a letter, whether registered or not, or even a telegram or email may suffice.[698] As for its contents, it must convey the clear and unambiguous will of the creditor to obtain performance.[699] Yet, it must not be specified which remedies the creditor will rely on in case of non-execution.[700] No specific terms, such as 'default notice', are required. However, the notice must be sufficiently compelling to make it clear that performance is being *demanded*.[701]

---

692. Law of 2 Aug. 2002 on combating late payment in commercial transactions, *Belgian Official Gazette* 7 Aug. 2002.
693. A restrictive interpretation (*restrictieve interpretatie/interprétation restrictive*) means that the application of the clause is reduced to a minimum. On the other hand, a strict interpretation (*strikte interpretatie/interprétation stricte*) means that the clause does not get restricted nor extended. It is interpreted according to its exact wording.
694. Cass. 23 Sep. 1994, *Arr.Cass.* 1994, 777 and *Pas.* 1994, 759.
695. Cass. 26 Sep. 1996, *Arr.Cass.* 1996, 810 and *Pas.* 1996, 868.
696. Cass. 17 Jan. 1992, *Arr.Cass.* 1991-92, 436 and *Pas.* 1992, 421.
697. Cass. 28 Mar. 1994, *Arr.Cass.* 1994, 319 and *Pas.* 1994, 317.
698. W. van Gerven en A. Van Oevelen, *Verbintenissenrecht* (Leuven: Acco, 2015), 605–606.
699. Cass. 16 Sep. 1983, *Arr.Cass.* 1983-84, 45 and *Pas.* 1984, 48.
700. Cass. 28 May 2020, C.19.0128.N, *TBBR* 2020, 582.
701. S. Stijns, W. van Gerven & P. Wéry, 'Chronique', *J.T.* (1996): No. 88; S. Stijns, *Leerboek Verbintenissenrecht 1* (Brugge: die Keure, 2016), 183; W. van Gerven en A. Van Oevelen, *Verbintenissenrecht* (Leuven: Acco, 2015), 605–606; P. Wéry, *Droit des obligations, I, Théorie générale du contrat* (Brussels: Larcier, 2011), 437.

III. Consequences

414. A default notice has two important consequences in addition to the consequences listed in No. 411 *supra*. The first is that the default notice fixes the date from which damages for late performance (Article 1146 OCC) – or moratory interests, in the case of an obligation to pay a sum of money (Article 1153 OCC) – will run. The second consequence concerns the allocation of risks in case of sale of specific goods, whose ownership and risks are both transferred at the moment the contract is concluded, even if the delivery does not happen at the same time (*see* No. 404 *supra*).[702] However, if the seller (i.e., the debtor of the delivery) is put in delay, the risks will return to him. Nevertheless, according to Article 1302 OCC, even when the debtor is in default, the risks are left with the buyer if the debtor can prove that the thing would also have perished if it had been delivered.

§3. General Remedies in Case of Faulty Behaviour

I. Performance in Kind

A. Definition and Priority Rule

415. If the debtor fails to perform his obligations, the creditor may enforce specific performance. This specific performance may take two forms. 'Performance in kind' (*uitvoering in natura/exécution en nature*) is the execution of the specific performance the debtor obligated himself to perform in the contract. 'Performance by equivalent' (*uitvoering bij equivalent/execution par équivalence*), on the other hand, is the compensation of the damage caused by the breach of contract, either by means of a non-pecuniary equivalent (*herstel in natura/réparation en nature*) or by means of a pecuniary equivalent (*schadevergoeding/dommages*).[703]

416. Belgian law favours performance in kind, which is considered the normal means of enforced performance by the *Court of Cassation*.[704] Performance by equivalent is subsidiary to it: it must only be done when performance in kind is impossible[705] or would be an abuse of rights.[706] It is also possible for parties to

702. Article 1138 OCC.
703. *See* on this matter: S. De Rey, *Herstel in natura* (Brugge: die Keure, 2019) 927 p.; S. De Rey, 'Herstel in natura van contractuele en buitencontractuele schade: onbekend, onbemind?', *RW* 2019, 163.
704. Cass. 30 Jan. 1965, *Pas.* 1965, 538; Cass. 23 Dec. 1977, *Arr.Cass.* 1978? 505 and *Pas.* 1978, 477; Cass. 14 Apr. 1994, *Arr.Cass.* 1994, 374 and *Pas.* 1994, 370; Cass. 30 Jan. 2003, *T.B.B.R.* 2004, 405 and *J.L.M.B.* 2004, 672.
705. L. Cornelis, *Algemene theorie van de verbintenis* (Antwerp: Intersentia, 2000), No. 416; S. Stijns, *De gerechtelijke en de buitengerechtelijke ontbinding van overeenkomsten* (Antwerp: Maklu, 1994), No. 237; S. Stijns, *Leerboek Verbintenissenrecht 1* (Brugge: die Keure, 2016), 186; P. Wéry, *Droit des obligations, I, Théorie générale du contrat* (Brussels: Larcier, 2011), 486.
706. C. Henskens, 'Sancties bij contractbreuk', in T. Vansweevelt and B. Weyts, *Handboek Verbintenissenrecht* (Antwerpen: Intersentia, 2019), 403; S. Stijns, *Leerboek Verbintenissenrecht 1* (Brugge: die Keure, 2016), 186; W. van Gerven en A. Van Oevelen, *Verbintenissenrecht* (Leuven: Acco,

exclude performance in kind in their contract or for the creditor to renounce his right to obtain performance in kind. Performance in kind is a right held by both creditor and debtor:[707] if the debtor offers performance in kind to the creditor, the latter cannot refuse it unless it has become impossible or cannot grant him satisfaction (e.g., because the debtor turned out to be utterly incompetent and the creditor justifiably has lost faith in his professionalism). Performance in kind can be cumulated with supplementary damages, covering, e.g., the damages caused by the delay in performance in kind.

B. *Performance in Kind by the Debtor*

417. In order to enforce performance in kind by the debtor, the creditor must obtain a judgment that orders the debtor to perform, and be able to enforce that judgment towards an unwilling debtor. Of course, a creditor cannot take justice into his own hands and exert force upon the debtor. However, some compelling measures are allowed by law. First, a court may attach an order to a judgment which obliges the debtor to pay a specified sum for each day (or other fixed period, or per breach, etc.) that he fails to perform (*dwangsom*/astreinte). Furthermore, the creditor may ask the court to grant him the authorisation to replace the debtor if the latter remains idle, as outlined in Nos 417 ff. below.

C. *Performance in Kind by a Third Party*

1. Replacement of the Debtor by a Judge

418. According to Article 1144 OCC, if the debtor fails to perform, the creditor may ask the court to grant him the authorisation to perform the obligation himself or to appoint a third person. According to Article 1143 OCC, if the debtor's obligation was to abstain from something, the creditor may ask for an authorisation to undo what was done by breaching the contract. In both cases, the debtor has to pay for the expenses caused by his replacement. The replacement of the debtor by a judge is subsidiary to the performance by the debtor. Consequently, if the debtor offers to perform himself, and this performance can still be satisfactory to the creditor, the court cannot grant his replacement by a third person.[708]

2015), 183; P. Wéry, *Droit des obligations, I, Théorie générale du contrat* (Brussels: Larcier, 2011), 487. *Contra:* L. Cornelis, *Algemene theorie van de verbintenis* (Antwerp: Intersentia, 2000), No. 417.

707. R. Dekkers & A. Verbeke, *Handboek Burgerlijk Recht*, III (Antwerp: Intersentia: 2007), 221; S. Stijns, *Leerboek Verbintenissenrecht 1* (Brugge: die Keure, 2016), 186; W. van Gerven en A. Van Oevelen, *Verbintenissenrecht* (Leuven: Acco, 2015), 183; P. Van Ommeslaghe, *Les obligations vol. 1* in *Traité de droit civil, tome II* (Brussels: Bruylant, 2013), 838 et seq.

708. S. Stijns, *De gerechtelijke en de buitengerechtelijke ontbinding van overeenkomsten* (Antwerp: Maklu, 1994), No. 255; S. Stijns, *Leerboek Verbintenissenrecht 1* (Brugge: die Keure, 2016), 188; W. van Gerven en A. Van Oevelen, *Verbintenissenrecht* (Leuven: Acco, 2015), 183; P. Wéry, *Droit des obligations, I, Théorie générale du contrat* (Brussels: Larcier, 2011), 499.

2. Extrajudicial Replacement

419. Replacement of the debtor by a judge requires legal proceedings, which often results in unwanted delay. A possible solution to avoid a lawsuit is to include a replacement clause (*vervangingsclausule/clause de remplacement*) in the contract, by which the creditor is relieved from the duty to obtain an authorisation from a court to replace the debtor at the debtor's expense.[709] However, parties only rarely include such terms in their contract. Recent doctrine and jurisprudence recognise the possibility of extrajudicial replacement (*buitengerechtelijke vervanging/ remplacement unilateral*).[710] This grants the creditor the right to replace the debtor at the debtor's expense without prior authorisation of the court. The Court of Cassation recently confirmed the validity of extrajudicial replacements.[711] This is only valid in case of exceptional circumstances, such as urgency and only insofar as the performance is suitable for replacement. The judge retains an a posteriori control upon the extrajudicial replacement. If the judge comes to decide that the replacement was not justified by exceptional circumstances, the creditor will merely be allowed to recover his cost to the value of the original performance.

D. Enforced Performance Against the Government

420. Enforced performance against government authorities is more problematic due to the principle of continuity of public service (*algemeen beginsel van continuïteit van de openbare dienst/principe de la continuité du service public*), which forbids measures that endanger this continuity.[712] Initially, this principle was absolute and resulted in the impossibility to enforce performance against the assets of public authorities.[713]

However, the *Court of Cassation* gave this principle a more relative interpretation afterwards, by stating that it 'only aims to guarantee the constancy and activities of public institutions and doesn't necessarily mean that the courts have no injunction right whatsoever against the authorities'.[714] Thus, judges may examine whether or not there is an actual risk for the continuity of public services, and allow execution if there is no such risk. The *Court of Cassation* later explicitly confirmed the validity of this interpretation of the principle in case of replacement of the debtor by a judge.[715] However, the burden of proof concerning the fact that the continuity of the public services is not endangered lies with the creditor.[716]

709. S. Stijns, *Leerboek Verbintenissenrecht 1* (Brugge: die Keure, 2016), 188; P. Wéry, *Droit des obligations, I, Théorie générale du contrat* (Brussels: Larcier, 2011), 774.
710. S. Stijns, *De gerechtelijke en de buitengerechtelijke ontbinding van overeenkomsten* (Antwerp: Maklu, 1994), Nos 437–439; S. Stijns, *Leerboek Verbintenissenrecht 1* (Brugge: die Keure, 2016), 188.
711. Cass. 18 Jun. 2020, C.18.0357.N, *TBBR* 2020, 583, note S. De Rey.
712. S. Stijns, *Leerboek Verbintenissenrecht, 1* (Brugge: die Keure, 2016), 189.
713. Cass. 26 Jun. 1980, *Arr.Cass.* 1979-80, 1365 and *Pas.* 1980, 1341.
714. Cass. 30 Sep. 1993, *Arr.Cass.* 1993, 778 and *Pas.* 1993, 769.
715. Cass. 24 Apr. 1998, *Arr.Cass.* 1998, 462 and *Pas.* 1998, 488.
716. S. Stijns, *Leerboek Verbintenissenrecht, 1* (Brugge: die Keure, 2016), 191.

II. Performance by Equivalent: Damages

A. *Principle and Scope*

421. When performance in kind is either impossible or would constitute an abuse of rights, the creditor may demand performance by equivalent, which often comes down to the payment of damages by the debtor. In that case, the creditor is entitled to the integral payment of the loss he suffered (*integrale vergoeding van de schade/réparation intégrale du dommage*) in consequence of the breach. According to Article 1149 OCC, damages include both the loss which the creditor incurred (‘*damnum emergens*’) and the gain of which he was deprived (‘*lucrum cessans*’). Thus, damages are based on loss to the plaintiff and not on gain to the defendant. The aim of the damages is to put the creditor into the position in which he would have been if the contract had been properly performed (and not the position in which he would be, if there had been no contract). The relevant moment for the calculation of damages is that of the judgment.[717] In addition to damages intended to compensate the fact the contract was not performed, the creditor may claim compensation for any disadvantage caused by the non-performance, even non-pecuniary losses, or costs he made to avoid or limit more loss.[718]

422. There are two exceptions to the principle of integral payment. First, Article 1151 OCC states that the damage must be an immediate and direct effect of the non-performance of the contract. The jurisprudence interprets this as damage which is a necessary consequence (*noodzakelijk gevolg/suite nécessaire*) of the non-performance, i.e., damage that would not have happened without the non-performance.[719] This is, in fact, an application of the general rule that a causal link between breach and damages is necessary to cause liability (both contractual and tortuous). Second, according to Article 1150 OCC, the damages are limited to what was foreseen or foreseeable at the time of the contract, unless he willingly caused the non-performance. The requirement of foreseeability only concerns the cause of the damage, and not its extent.[720]

717. Cass. 28 Sep. 1995, *Arr.Cass.* 1995, 830 and *Pas.* 1995, 860; Cass. 4 Mar. 2010, *TBH* 2010, 685.
718. C. Henskens, ‘Sancties bij contractbreuk’, in T. Vansweevelt and B. Weyts, *Handboek Verbintenissenrecht* (Antwerpen: Intersentia, 2019), 411; S. Stijns, *Leerboek Verbintenissenrecht 1* (Brugge: die Keure, 2016), 191; W. van Gerven en A. Van Oevelen, *Verbintenissenrecht* (Leuven: Acco, 2015), 185.
719. Cass. 9 May 1986, *Arr.Cass.* 1985-86, 1223 and *Pas.* 1986, 1100; Cass. 14 Oct. 1985, *Arr.Cass.* 1986, 179 and *Pas.* 1986, 155; Cass. 24 Jun. 1977, *Arr.Cass.* 1977, 1101 and *Pas.* 1977, 1087.
720. Cass. 11 Apr. 1986, *Arr.Cass.* 1985-86, 1091 and *Pas.* 1986, 986; Cass. 23 Oct. 1987, *Arr.Cass.* 1987-88, 228 and *Pas.* 1988, 212; Cass. 4 Feb. 2010, *TBH* 2010, 498.

B. Payment of a Compensation in Case of a Late Payment of a Sum of Money

1. General Rules

423. When the contracted obligation is the payment of a sum of money, only performance in kind is possible, as performance by equivalent would be pointless.[721] According to Article 1153, paragraphs 1–4 OCC, damages caused by the delay in execution can only consist of interest at the legal rate, apart from exceptions established by law. These damages are due without the creditor having to prove any loss. The interest is due from the day of the demand for payment, i.e., the moment when the debtor is put in delay (*see* Nos 411 ff. *supra*) except where the law makes them run automatically. If the debtor willingly failed to perform, damages may exceed the legal interest.

424. As these rules are not mandatory, parties may deviate from them, e.g., by stipulating that the conventional interest – which usually has a higher rate than the legal interest – will continue to run after putting the debtor into delay. Such terms will be considered penalty clauses (*see* Nos 256–261 *supra*).[722] However, Article 1153, paragraph 5 OCC grants the courts the possibility to lower conventional interests that aim to compensate for damages caused by delays in execution if the stipulated interest is evidently higher than the damages caused by the delay. They however may not reduce the interest rate below the legal interest rate.

425. According to Article 1154 OCC, interest due on capital can produce interest, either by a judicial summons or by a specific contract, provided that the summons or the contract concerns interest due for at least an entire year. This rule aims to protect the debtor against surprisingly rapid increases of his debt as a consequence of the capitalisation of interest. This rule is mandatory so that the debtor cannot relinquish its application beforehand.[723]

426. Belgian law makes a complex distinction between several debts of sum and debts of value, which result in different kinds of interests (*see* Nos 351–353 *supra*). The rules laid down in Articles 1153 et seq. OCC only apply to debts of sum.

---

721. S. Stijns, *Leerboek Verbintenissenrecht 1* (Brugge: die Keure, 2016), 192; W. van Gerven en A. Van Oevelen, *Verbintenissenrecht* (Leuven: Acco, 2015), 192.
722. S. Stijns, *Leerboek Verbintenissenrecht 1* (Brugge: die Keure, 2016), 193.
723. Cass. 22 Dec. 1938, *Pas.* 1938, 405. There is discussion within the doctrine concerning the question of whether the rule of Art. 1154 is mandatory or of public order/*ordre public*. In any case, it is not permissive and thus, parties may not deviate from it. *See* C. Henskens, 'Sancties bij contractbreuk', in T. Vansweevelt and B. Weyts, *Handboek Verbintenissenrecht* (Antwerpen: Intersentia, 2019), 413.

2. Specific Rules Applicable to Contracts Between Enterprises

427. Specific rules apply to contracts between enterprises. Article 5 of the Law on combating late payment in commercial transactions, which implements the principles of Directive 2000/35/EC of the European Parliament and of the Council of 29 June 2000 on combating late payment in commercial transactions and the Directive of 2011/7/EU of the European Parliament and the Council of 16 February 2011 on combating late payment in commercial transactions into Belgian law, stipulates that if the debtor fails to pay within the contracted time period or, within the absence of such terms, within thirty days (*see* No. 74 *supra*), interests automatically start to run from the next day without default notice, at a referential interest rate augmented with 8% and rounded up to the nearest half percent.[724] This interest rate is substantially higher than the general legal interest rate, thus imposing a higher penalty for non-performance to enterprises than to consumers. For example, for the first part of 2021, this was 8%, while the general legal interest rate was only 1.75%.

428. Article 7 also grants the courts ampler appreciative powers for this type of contract. According to it, contractual terms which deviate from this law may be readjusted by a judge on demand from the creditor if they contain a clear unfairness towards the creditor, all circumstances taken into account, with inclusion of good market practices and the type of product or service. The court must thereby, among other things, verify whether or not the debtor had objective reasons to deviate from this law. However, the judge may not grant the creditor more rights than those which would have been granted to him by the application of Articles 4–7 of the same law. Article 7 is mandatory, as it states that 'any terms conflicting with this article will be considered null'. This article is complementary with the rules of the CC, thus resulting in the possibility for interests to be reduced as well as augmented.[725]

III. Penalty Clauses

429. *See* Nos 256–261 *supra.*

IV. Astreinte

430. An astreinte is an additional condemnation of a party to pay a sum of money in case this party does not comply with the main judgment.[726] The rules on

724. Law of 2 Aug. 2002 on combating late payment in commercial transactions, *Belgian Official Gazette* 7 Aug. 2002. *See* H. Vanhees, E. Dirix & R. Steennot, *Ondernemingsrecht in hoofdlijnen* (Antwerpen: Intersentia), 27.

725. I. Samoy &. M. Aguirre, 'De raakvlakken tussen de contractuele en de buitencontractuele aansprakelijkheid. Schadeherstel, schadevergoeding en interesten', in *De raakvlakken tussen de contractuele en de buitencontractuele aansprakelijkheid*, ed. S. Stijns & P. Wéry (Brugge: die Keure, 2010), 97 et seq.

726. E. Dirix, B. Tilleman S. Lierman (eds), *De Valks Juridisch woordenboek* (Antwerp-Oxford: Intersentia, 2018), 135. For more on this subject, *see* J. Van Compernolle & G. De Leval,

astreinte are laid down in Articles 1385*bis*–1385*octies* of the Judicial Code. The astreinte aims to exercise pressure on the debtor in case he does not willingly execute the main condemnation against him.[727] If the debtor fails to comply, the debtor must pay the astreinte to the creditor, even if its sum exceeds the prejudice suffered by the creditor.[728] It must be requested by the creditor (Article 1385*bis* Judicial Code). The judge is free to grant or refuse it and to determine its amount, which may be superior to the amount demanded by the creditor.[729]

§4. Additional Remedies in Synallagmatic Contracts

I. The Right to Choose

A. The Right to Choose Between Performance and Termination

431. According to Article 1184, paragraph 2 OCC, if a contract is reciprocal (*see* No. 59 *supra*), the creditor has the right to choose between enforcing performance (*exécution/uitvoering*), or termination (*ontbinding/résolution*), plus supplementary damages.

432. The right to make this choice is held only by the creditor who is a victim of non-performance, so that neither the debtor nor the courts may make it in his stead.[730] However, the exercise of the right to choose is submitted to the requirement of good faith and the prohibition of abuse of rights (*see* Nos 103–104 *supra*).[731] Thus, if the choice the creditor makes is an abuse of rights, courts may decide to choose the other option instead by applying the moderative function of good faith.[732] This doctrine is often applied in case of tenancy, when the landlord demands continuation of the rent even when termination and damages would be far more harmless to the tenant.[733]

L'astreinte (Brussels: Larcier, 2013), 102, K. Wagner, *Dwangsom* in *Algemene praktische rechtsverzameling* (Antwerp: Kluwer, 2003), E. Dirix, *Beslag* in *Algemene praktische rechtsverzameling* (Antwerpen: Kluwer, 2019).

727. P. Wéry, *Droit des obligations, I, Théorie générale du contrat* (Brussels: Larcier, 2011), 505.
728. *Ibid.*, 506.
729. *Ibid.*:, 508.
730. Cass. 5 Sep. 1980, *Arr.Cass.* 1980-81, 12 and *Pas.* 1981, 17; Cass. 22 May 1981, *Arr.Cass.* 1980-81, 1105 and *Pas.* 1981, 1267; Cass. 15 Apr. 1994, *Arr.Cass.* 1994, 378 and *Pas.* 1994, 373; Cass. 30 Jan. 2003, C.00.0632.F.
731. Cass. 16 Jan. 1986, *Arr.Cass.* 1985-86, 683 and *Pas.* 1986, 602.
732. S. Stijns, *Leerboek Verbintenissenrecht 1* (Brugge: die Keure, 2016), 201; F. Vermander, 'Ontbinding wegens wanprestatie' in T. Vansweevelt and B. Weyts, *Handboek Verbintenissenrecht* (Antwerpen: Intersentia, 2019), 521–522.
733. S. Stijns, *Leerboek Verbintenissenrecht 1* (Brugge: die Keure, 2016), 202.

B. Cumulation Prohibition and Change of Choice

433. The right to choose is also a duty to choose, as the creditor may not cumulate performance and termination.[734] Consequentially, the choice for termination excludes the possibility to demand performance (in kind or by equivalent). Thus, a penalty clause which grants damages in case of delay in performance cannot be called upon if the creditor chooses to terminate the contract.[735] It is, however, possible to demand one option principally and the other subsidiarily. The creditor retains the right to choose until there is a definitive judgment,[736] and can thus modify his choice until then. However, if he has renounced the other option (e.g., by calling upon an express resolutive clause), of which he has informed the debtor (*see* No. 440 *infra*), he may no longer change his choice.[737]

II. Termination

A. Three Ways to Terminate

434. Article 1184, paragraph 3 OCC states that termination must be demanded to a judge (and thus can only be granted by courts). However, parties may deviate from this rule, as it is merely suppletive, by including an express resolutive clause (*uitdrukkelijk ontbindend beding/clause résolutoire expresse*) in their contract, which allows them to terminate the contract without the intervention of a judge (*see* Nos 438 ff. *infra*). Also, recent doctrine and jurisprudence recognise the possibility to terminate a contract by unilateral notification of one party (*see* Nos 442 ff. *infra*). Thus, there are three ways to terminate a contract.

435. Three requirements are applicable to all types of termination, albeit with some nuances: there must be a valid reciprocal contract at the moment of the breach; there must be a breach of the contract which is accountable to the debtor; and the debtor must have been put into delay beforehand. The consequences are the same as well (*see* No. 411 and 414 *supra*). The main difference is the role of the judge.

B. Judicial Termination

436. If the three requirements cited here above are present, the creditor can demand the termination of the contract by a judge. The judge must then evaluate

734. H. De Page, *Traité élémentaire de droit civil belge, II* (Brussels: Bruylant, 1967), No. 885bis; S. Stijns, *Leerboek Verbintenissenrecht 1* (Brugge: die Keure, 2016), 204.
735. Cass. 16 Jun. 1955, *Arr.Cass.* 1955, 850; Cass. 26 Oct. 1956, *Arr.Cass.* 1957, 122.
736. S. Stijns, *De gerechtelijke en de buitengerechtelijke ontbinding van overeenkomsten* (Antwerp: Maklu, 1994), Nos 265–268.
737. *Ibid.*, No. 363; P. Wéry, *Droit des obligations, I, Théorie générale du contrat* (Brussels: Larcier, 2011), 633.

and decide whether or not there is a breach of contract that is severe enough to justify termination.[738,739] He can also choose how to sanction the breach. He may, of course, terminate the contract with or without the attribution of supplementary damages, but he may also grant the debtor a delay in order for him to perform in kind, pronounce a conditional termination (e.g., if the debtor fails to perform within a certain period), or reject the request for termination and, eventually, grant the creditor damages instead. If both parties committed sufficiently severe breaches simultaneously (or within the same period), the judicial termination may be pronounced against both.[740] In this case, each one's damage is compensated, and the granted compensation must be proportional to each one's failures to perform – it is of decisive importance how much each fault contributed to the loss.

437. The classic view on the role of the judge is that he can decide whether or not termination is opportune. According to modern authors, the role of the judge holds two distinct components. First, Article 1184, paragraph 3 OCC grants the judge the possibility to grant the debtor a delay. Second, the judge can evaluate the breach of contract in relation to the sanction of termination, a competence that is not granted by Article 1184 OCC, but which comes down to moderating the contract according to good faith and the prohibition of abuse of rights (*see* Nos 103–105 *supra*).[741]

C. Extrajudicial Termination due to an Express Resolutive Clause

438. In its broadest sense, an express resolutive clause (*uitdrukkelijk ontbindend beding/clause résolutoire expresse*) is a clause that declares judicial termination in case of breach of contract applicable or that modifies it.[742] For instance, they may declare judicial termination possible for a unilateral contract, or they may stipulate which breaches of contract are sufficient to justify judicial termination. However, express resolutive clauses most often aim to organise a possibility for extrajudicial termination, in order to avoid the delay and the uncertainty (*see* Nos 435–436 *supra*) that come with legal proceedings.[743] An express resolutive clause may even

738. Cass. 9 Jun. 1961, *Pas.* 1962, 1104; Cass. 28 May 1965, *Pas.* 1965, 1051; Cass. 9 Sep. 1965, *Pas.* 1966, 47; Cass. 12 Nov. 1976, *Arr.Cass.* 1977, 293 and *Pas.* 1977, 291; Cass. 31 Jan. 1991, *Arr-.Cass.* 1990-91, 584 and *Pas.* 1991, 520; Cass. 24 Sep. 2009, *RAGB* 2009, 131 and *TBH* 2010, 249.
739. R. Dekkers & A. Verbeke, *Handboek Burgerlijk Recht*, III (Antwerp: Intersentia: 2007), 105; H. De Page, *Traité élémentaire de droit civil belge, II* (Brussels: Bruylant, 1967), No. 889; S. Stijns, *Leerboek Verbintenissenrecht 1* (Brugge: die Keure, 2016), 206; P. Van Ommeslaghe, *Les obligations vol. 1* in *Traité de droit civil, tome II* (Brussels: Bruylant, 2013), 895.
740. Cass. 9 May 1986, *Arr.Cass.* 1985-86, 1223 and *Pas.* 1986, 1100.
741. S. Stijns, *De gerechtelijke en de buitengerechtelijke ontbinding van overeenkomsten* (Antwerp: Maklu, 1994), Nos 202, 129–146, 150–154, 159, 183, 202, 304–323; P. Wéry, *Droit des obligations, I, Théorie générale du contrat* (Brussels: Larcier, 2011), 632.
742. S. Stijns, *De gerechtelijke en de buitengerechtelijke ontbinding van overeenkomsten* (Antwerp: Maklu, 1994), No. 325.
743. *Ibid.*, Nos 325 and 344–346; S. Stijns, *Leerboek Verbintenissenrecht 1* (Brugge: die Keure, 2016), 210.

release the creditor from his duty to put the debtor in delay.[744] Express resolutive clauses aiming to organise extrajudicial termination always contain at least the two following components: (1) termination must depend on an imputable breach of contract by one party, and (2) the other party must be granted the possibility to terminate the contract unilaterally, without intervention of a judge.

439. As Article 1184 OCC is a suppletive rule, parties may validly deviate from it by means of an express resolutive clause, unless specific laws forbid it, e.g., Article 1762*bis* OCC which prohibits express resolutive clauses in tenancy contracts.

440. It is up to the creditor to decide whether or not he wants to call upon the clause, as his decision is always required,[745] given that the clause does not alter his right to choose.[746] The notification to the debtor is also required. Unless specified otherwise in the contract, the debtor must also be put in delay in advance.[747] Both may be done in one document, for instance, a registered letter that includes a summons to perform as well as the decision to terminate the contract should the debtor fail to perform.[748]

441. It is possible for the debtor against whom an express resolutive clause has been used to submit the case to a judge afterwards. However, contrary to judicial termination, the judge may only verify the formal validity (*formele legaliteit/régularité formelle*) of the extrajudicial termination, i.e., the qualification and validity of the clause, the presence of the necessary conditions and the effects of the clause.[749] The judge can no longer grant delays to the debtor (*see* No. 436 *supra*). He may only determine if there are breaches of the contract, not how severe these breaches were.[750] However, the greater part of the recent doctrine advocates that moderation is still possible, as the application of an express resolutive clause is a unilateral decision made by only one of the contract parties (*partijbeslissing/décision de partie*).[751] Such unilateral decisions are submitted to the requirement of

744. S. Stijns, *De gerechtelijke en de buitengerechtelijke ontbinding van overeenkomsten* (Antwerp: Maklu, 1994), No. 347; S. Stijns, *Leerboek Verbintenissenrecht 1* (Brugge: die Keure, 2016), 210.
745. Cass. 31 May 1956, Pas. 1956, 1051.
746. S. Stijns, *De gerechtelijke en de buitengerechtelijke ontbinding van overeenkomsten* (Antwerp: Maklu, 1994), Nos 349 and 361–365; S. Stijns, *Leerboek Verbintenissenrecht 1* (Brugge: die Keure, 2016), 231.
747. Cass. 24 Mar. 1995, *Arr.Cass.* 1995, 346 and Pas. 1995, 358.
748. S. Stijns, *Leerboek Verbintenissenrecht 1* (Brugge: die Keure, 2016), 213.
749. J. Ghestin, *Traité de droit civil, Les obligations: les effets du contrat* (Paris: L.G.D.J., 1992), Nos 441–442; S. Stijns, *De gerechtelijke en de buitengerechtelijke ontbinding van overeenkomsten* (Antwerp: Maklu, 1994), Nos 368–369.
750. *See* L. Cornelis, *Algemene theorie van de verbintenis* (Antwerp: Intersentia, 2000), No. 598.
751. S. Stijns, *Leerboek Verbintenissenrecht 1* (Brugge: die Keure, 2016), 215; W. van Gerven en A. Van Oevelen, *Verbintenissenrecht* (Leuven: Acco, 2015), 203.

good faith and the doctrine of abuse of rights (*see* Nos 103–105 *supra*).[752] Consequentially, a judge may find the decision to terminate an abuse of rights if the breach of contract was negligible or if he refused a reasonable offer by the debtor to solve the issue. The possibility for the courts to examine whether or not an application of an express resolutive clause is an abuse of rights has recently been confirmed by the *Court of Cassation*.[753]

D. Extrajudicial Termination upon Notification

442. The Court of Cassation has repeatedly accepted that a creditor can terminate the contract provided he notifies his debtor of his decision.[754] While prior to these decisions, the doctrine assumed that such an extrajudicial termination only was possible in exceptional circumstances, the Court has decided that such exceptional circumstances are no longer required to justify extrajudicial termination. This extrajudicial termination stands on equal footing with the other ways of termination.

443. Following cumulative conditions must be met in order to allow unilateral extrajudicial termination.[755] First, the debtor must have committed a breach of contract which was sufficient to justify a judicial termination. Second, the creditor must explicitly notify the debtor of his decision to terminate the contract and of the motives of this decision, i.e., the breach(es) of the contract.

E. Consequences of Termination and Partial Termination

444. In principle, termination is total: it counts for the future and the past (*ratione tempore*), concerns all terms of the contract (*ratione materiae*) and is effective towards all parties (*ratione personae*). *Ratione tempore* termination works retroactively, and returns matters to their state at the moment of the conclusion of the contract.[756] This means that the contracting parties must restitute the performances they already received.[757]

---

752. M. Coipel, *Eléments de théorie générale des contrats* (Diegem: Story-Scientia, 1999), Nos 237 and 258; S. Stijns, *De gerechtelijke en de buitengerechtelijke ontbinding van overeenkomsten* (Antwerp: Maklu, 1994), Nos 352 and 373–379; S. Stijns, *Leerboek Verbintenissenrecht 1* (Brugge: die Keure, 2016), 215. *Contra*: L. Cornelis, *Algemene theorie van de verbintenis* (Antwerp: Intersentia, 2000), No. 598.

753. Cass. 9 Mar. 2009, *J.T.* 2009, p. 392; Cass. 8 Feb. 2010, AR C.09.0416.F, *Arr.Cass.* 2010, 383.

754. Cass. 23 Mai 2019, *JT* 2020, 26, note S. Stijns and P. Wéry; *TBBR* 2019, 474, note S. Stijns and S. Jansen; *TBH* 2020, 497, note S. Van Loock; Cass. 11 Dec. 2020, *NJW* 2021, 540, note C. Lebon.

755. S. Stijns & S. Jansen, 'De buitengerechtelijke ontbinding eindelijk erkend: van het ontbonden beschouwen naar de ontbinding op kennisgeving', *TBBR* 2019, 488; S. Stijns & P. Wéry, 'La résolution par voie de notification, enfin admise par la Cour de cassation', *J.T.* 2020, nr. 2, 23.

756. Cass. 25 Feb. 1991, *Pas.* 1991, 616 and *Arr.Cass.* 1990-91, 693.

757. S. Stijns, *De gerechtelijke en de buitengerechtelijke ontbinding van overeenkomsten* (Antwerp: Maklu, 1994), Nos 211–217; S. Stijns, *Leerboek Verbintenissenrecht 1* (Brugge: die Keure, 2016), 220–221.

445. However, there is currently an evolution towards the acceptance of partial termination. Belgian law has recognised temporal partial termination for contracts with successive or continuous obligations for a long time. A classic example is the case of a tenancy contract, where restitution of the performance is impossible, and thus termination may only have effect for the future.[758] In that case, it is retroactive to the date of the start of the proceedings unless the performances that have been executed after this date cannot be returned.[759] It may also go back further in time, to the moment that the contract was no longer pursued and there was, consequentially, no reason for return.[760] In practice, determining when this moment was may be quite complex. The traditional criterion to determine whether temporal partial termination is allowed is the material impossibility of restitution of performances[761] and equivalence of the performances of both parties. This jurisprudence is criticised by several authors. The modern doctrine, hereby followed by a part of the jurisprudence, pleads for a new criterion, namely the (in)divisibility of the contract.[762] If the contract is indivisible, its breach will affect the whole contract and its termination will retroact until its conclusion. If, on the contrary, the contract is divisible, i.e., if performance is done in several instalments (i.e., a tenancy), the termination will not undo the performed instalments and will only start from the breach of the contract.[763] This is in fact a better criterion, as it allows to apply a partial temporal termination outside the scope of contracts with successive performances. It may be related to the type of contract or depend on the will of the parties.

446. Belgian law also shows indications of acceptance of material partial termination. As stated before, the general rule is that termination affects all the terms of the contract. However, some exceptions are made. First, termination does not affect the right of the creditor to claim damages. Second, several so-called post-contractual clauses, which aim to lay down rules for the termination of the contract, may remain applicable, e.g., a penalty clause, an exemption clause, or a confidentiality clause. Finally, within complex contracts, it is possible for the termination to affect only certain related obligations if these can be detached from the rest of the contract.[764] The criterion of (in)divisibility is instrumental here as well.

447. Last but not least, even personal partial termination seems possible in some circumstances. Here too, the rule is termination towards all parties. However, termination towards one party in a multiparty contract should be possible if only one

758. Cass. 24 Jan. 1980, *Arr.Cass.* 1979-80, 592 and *Pas.* 1980, 581; Cass. 31 Jan. 1991, *Arr.Cass.* 1990-91, 584 and *Pas.* 1991, 520; Cass. 25 Feb. 1991, *Pas.* 1991, 616 and *Arr.Cass.* 1990-91, 693.
759. Cass. 28 Jun. 1990, *Arr.Cass.* 1989-90, 1401 and *Pas.* 1990, 1242; Cass. 10 Apr. 1997, *Arr.Cass.* 1997, 426 and *Pas.* 1997, 443.
760. Cass. 14 Apr. 1994, *Arr.Cass.* 1994, 374 and Pas. 1994, 370.
761. Cass. 28 Jun. 1990, *A.C.* 1989-90, 1401 and *Pas.* 1990, 1242; Cass. 10 Apr. 1997, *A.C.* 1997, 426 and *Pas.* 1997, 443.
762. *See* for an overview: I. Samoy, 'La résolution judiciaire des contrats multipartites' in *Questions spéciales en droit des contrats*, ed. J.F. Germain (Brussels: Larcier, 2010), p. 208.
763. S. Stijns, *De gerechtelijke en de buitengerechtelijke ontbinding van overeenkomsten* (Antwerp: Maklu, 1994), Nos 218–221.
764. *See* I. Samoy, 'La résolution judiciaire des contrats multipartites' in *Questions spéciales en droit des contrats*, ed. J.F. Germain (Brussels: Larcier, 2010), p. 211.

party did not perform. Again, the relevant criterion is (in)divisibility.[765] This theory could be considered implicitly supported by the judgment of the *Court of Cassation* of 17 October 2008.[766]

III. Suspension

A. Exceptio Non Adimpleti Contractus

448. The plea of non-performance (*exceptie van niet-uitvoering/exception d'inexécution*) or *exceptio non adimpleti contractus* (below: ENAC) is a temporary defence which allows a party to a reciprocal contract not to perform as long as the other party fails to perform his own obligations.[767] This plea is always possible in reciprocal contracts, and does not require legal proceedings. It can be called upon against the creditor who claims performance or termination, and results in the suspension of the duty to perform of the person who invokes it.

449. The plea of non-performance is subject to the following conditions.[768] First, there must be a reciprocal contract or another reciprocal legal relationship.[769] Second, the party who invokes it must be creditor of a certain claim that is first due. He may not have the duty to perform first. Third, he must be able to prove an imputable breach of the contract by the other party. As this plea is a defence, putting the debtor into delay might seem unnecessary. However, if there might be confusion in the other party about who has to perform first or which breaches of contract he committed, a default notice might still be required by good faith.[770] Fourth, he must generally act in accordance with good faith when calling upon the plea. This means that the non-performance by the other party and the suspension of performance by the party calling upon the plea must be proportional to each other,[771] and that the non-performance by the other party may not have been caused by the party calling upon the plea.

765. *Ibid.*, p. 212.
766. Cass. 17 Oct. 2008, *R.W.* 2008-09, 1640 and *T.B.O.* 2008, p. 218.
767. R. Dekkers & A. Verbeke, *Handboek Burgerlijk Recht*, III (Antwerp: Intersentia: 2007), 96; H. De Page, *Traité élémentaire de droit civil belge, II* (Brussels: Bruylant, 1967), No. 859; J. De Weghelheire, T. Vansweevelt & B. Weyts 'Schorsing van verbintenissen' in T. Vansweevelt and B. Weyts, *Handboek Verbintenissenrecht* (Antwerpen: Intersentia, 2019), 441; S. Stijns, *Leerboek Verbintenissenrecht 1* (Brugge: die Keure, 2016), 223; W. van Gerven en A. Van Oevelen, *Verbintenissenrecht* (Leuven: Acco, 2015), 210.
768. Cass. 24 Oct. 2019, C.19.0132.N, *TBO* 2020, 42; S. Stijns, *Leerboek Verbintenissenrecht 1* (Brugge: die Keure, 2016), 224.
769. P. Van Ommeslaghe, *Les obligations vol. 1* in *Traité de droit civil, tome II* (Brussels: Bruylant, 2013), 876.
770. S. Stijns, *Leerboek Verbintenissenrecht, vol. 1* (Brugge: die Keure, 2016), 224; W. van Gerven en A. Van Oevelen, *Verbintenissenrecht* (Leuven: Acco, 2015), 212. Different opinion: J. Herbots, 'L'exception d'inexécution et la mesure à garder dans le contrat de bail', *R.C.J.B.* (1990): 563, No. 26.
771. J. Herbots, 'L'exception d'inexécution et la mesure à garder dans le contrat de bail', *R.C.J.B.* (1990): 563, No. 24; S. Stijns, *Leerboek Verbintenissenrecht 1* (Brugge: die Keure, 2016), 224.

450. The effect of the plea is the suspension of the performance of the obligations of the person who called upon it. It is no means of termination. As the rules regarding this plea are suppletive, it is possible to exclude or alter them in the contract, unless a specific law prohibits it.

B. Suspension of the Duty to Perform in Case of Irresistible Force

451. As described in No. 51 *supra*, the debt is suspended from the start of an occurrence which constitutes an irresistible force for as long as it is impossible to perform.

Selected Bibliography

§1. Handbooks

Claeys, I. & Tanghe, T., *Algemeen contractenrecht*. Antwerp: Intersentia, 2021.

Coipel, M., *Eléments de théorie générale des contrats*. Brussels: Story-Scientia, 1999.

Cornelis, L., *Algemene theorie van de verbintenis*. Antwerp: Intersentia, 2000.

De Boeck, A., S. Stijns & R. Van Ransbeeck (eds), *Het vermogensrechtelijk bewijsrecht vandaag en morgen*. Brugge: die Keure, 2008.

Dekkers, R. & E. Dirix, *Handboek van Burgerlijk Recht, II*. Antwerp: Intersentia, 2005.

Dekkers, R. & A. Verbeke, *Handboek Burgerlijk Recht, III*. Antwerp: Intersentia: 2007.

De Man, M., *De verbintenisrechtelijke tijdsbepaling*. Brugge: die Keure, 2013.

De Page, H., *Traité élémentaire de droit civil belge, 10 volumes*. Brussels: Bruylant, 1949–1975.

De Page, H. & A. Meinertzhagen-Limpens, *Traité élémentaire de droit civil belge*, IV, *Les principaux contrats*. Brussel, Bruylant, 1997.

De Rey, S., *Herstel in natura*. Brugge: die Keure, 2019.

Dieux, X. et al., *Les obligations contractuelles*. Brussels: Ed. Jeune Barreau de Bruxelles, 2000.

Fontaine, M. & J. Ghestin (eds), *Les effets du contrat à l'égard des tiers. Comparaisons franco-belges*. Paris: L.G.D.J., 1992.

Fontaine, M. & G. Viney (eds), *Les sanctions de l'inexécution des obligations contractuelles*. Brussels: Bruylant, 2001.

Foriers, P.A., *La caducité des obligations contractuelles par disparition d'un élément essentiel à leur formation*. Brussels: Bruylant, 1998.

Kluyskens, A., *Beginselen van burgerlijk recht, I, De Verbintenissen*. Antwerp: Standaard, 1938.

Lambrecht, D. & V. Sagaert (eds), *Actuele ontwikkelingen inzake verbintenissenrecht, Vlaams pleitgenootschap Brussel*. Antwerpen: Intersentia, 2009.

Peeraer, F., *Nietigheid en aanverwante rechtsfiguren in het vermogensrecht*. Antwerpen: Intersentia, 2019.

Renard, C., E. Vieujean & Y. Hannequart, *Théorie générale des obligations* in *Les Novelles, Droit Civil*, IV/2, 1958.

Roodhooft, J. (ed.), *Bestendig handboek verbintenissenrecht*. Antwerp: Kluwer Rechtswetenschappen, 1998.

Selected Bibliography

Samoy, I. (ed.), *De evolutie van de basisbeginselen van het contractenrecht*, in *Ius Commune Europaeum*. Antwerp-Oxford: Intersentia, 2010.

Smits, J. & S. Stijns (eds), *Inhoud en werking van de overeenkomst naar Belgisch en Nederlands recht*. Antwerp-Groningen: Intersentia, 2005.

Stijns, S., *De gerechtelijke en buitengerechtelijke ontbinding van overeenkomsten*. Antwerp: Maklu, 1994.

Stijns, S., *Leerboek Verbintenissenrecht 1*. Brugge: die Keure, 2016.

Stijns, S., *Leerboek Verbintenissenrecht 2*. Brugge: die Keure, 2020.

Stijns, S. (ed.), *Verbintenissenrecht. Themis Cahier*. Brugge: die Keure, 2004.

Stijns, S. (ed.), *Verbintenissenrecht. Themis Cahier 41*. Brugge: die Keure, 2007.

Stijns, S. (ed.), *Verbintenissenrecht. Themis Cahier 75*. Brugge: die Keure, 2012.

Stijns, S. (ed.), *Verbintenissenrecht. Themis Cahier 95*. Brugge: die Keure, 2015.

Stijns, S. (ed.), *Verbintenissenrecht. Themis Cahier 108*. Brugge: die Keure, 2019.

Stijns, S., I. Samoy & A. De Boeck (eds), *Verbintenissenrecht, Themis Cahier 56*. Brugge: die Keure, 2009–2010.

Stijns, S. & I. Samoy, *Leerboek Verbintenissenrecht 1bis*. Brugge: die Keure, 2020.

Stijns, S. & H. Vandenberghe (eds), *Verbintenissenrecht. Themis Cahier 5*. Brugge: die Keure, 2001.

Stijns, S. & K. Vanderschot (eds), *Contractuele clausules rond de (niet-)uitvoering en de beëindiging van contracten*. Antwerp: Intersentia, 2006.

Stijns, S. & P. Wéry (eds), *De bronnen van niet-contractuele verbintenissen – Les sources d'obligations extracontractuelles*. Brugge: die Keure, 2007.

Stijns, S. & P. Wéry (eds), *De raakvlakken tussen de contractuele en de buitencontractuele aansprakelijkheid – Les rapports entre les responsabilités contractuelle et extracontractuelle*. Brugge: die Keure, 2010.

Stijns, S. & P. Wéry (eds), *Le juge et le contrat – De rol van de rechter in het contract*. Brugge: die Keure, 2014.

Vandenbogaerde, M., *Pluraliteit van schuldenaars bij verbintenissen*. Brugge: die Keure, 2015.

Vandeputte, R., *De overeenkomst. Haar ontstaan, haar uitvoering en verdwijning, haar bewijs*. Brussels: Larcier, 1977.

van Gerven, W., *Algemeen deel*. In *Beginselen van Belgisch privaatrecht* ed. R. Dillemans & W. van Gerven. Antwerp: Standaard Uitgeverij, 1973.

van Gerven, W. & A. Van Oevelen, *Verbintenissenrecht*. Leuven: Acco, 2015.

Van Ommeslaghe, P., *Les obligations vol. 1 and 3* in *Traité de droit civil, tome II*. Brussels: Bruylant, 2013.

Van Ransbeeck, R., S. Stijns & A. De Boeck (eds), *Schorsing van verbintenissen en overeenkomsten*. Brugge: die Keure, 2010.

Vansweevelt, T. & B. Weyts, *Handboek Verbintenissenrecht*. Antwerpen: Intersentia, 2019.

Verkempinck, B., *Schadevergoeding wegens wanprestatie in Europees perspectief*. Brugge: die Keure, 2017.

Vermander, F., *De opzegging van overeenkomsten*, Antwerpen: Intersentia, 2014.

Waelkens, J., *Interpretatie van overeenkomsten en eenzijdige rechtshandelingen deel I &II*. Antwerpen: Intersentia, 2016.

Wéry, P., *Droit des obligations, I, Théorie générale des contrats*. Brussels: Larcier, 2021.

Wéry, P. (ed.), *La fin du contrat, volume 51 de la Commission Université-Palais.* Liège: CUP, 2001.
Wéry, P. (ed.), *La théorie générale des obligations.* Liège: Formation permanente CUP, 2002.
Wéry, P. (ed.), *Le droit des obligations contractuelles et le Bicentenaire du Code civil.* Brugge: die Keure, 2004.
Withofs, V., *Contractsoverdracht.* Brugge: die Keure, 2015.
X, *Bijzondere overeenkomsten. Artikelsgewijze commentaar met overzicht van rechtspraak en rechtsleer.* Mechelen: Kluwer, 9 volumes, looseleaf.
X, *Obligations, commentaire pratique.* Brussels: Kluwer, 2005, 2 volumes.
X, *La volonté unilatérale dans le contrat.* Brussels: Ed. du Jeune Barreau de Bruxelles, 2008.

§2. Overviews of Jurisprudence

Allemeersch, B., I. Samoy & W. Vandenbussche. Overzicht van rechtspraak – Het urgerlijk bewijsrecht. *TPR* 2015, 597–962.
Claeys, I., F. Coryn & L. Van Valckenborgh. *Overzicht van rechtspraak verbintenissenrecht (1992-2017). Bronnen van verbintenissen (Deel I). Zaakwaarneming, onverschuldigde betaling en ongerechtvaardigde verrijking. TPR* 2017, 1395–1501.
Dirix, E. & A. Van Oevelen, 'Kroniek van het verbintenissenrecht (1978-1979 en 1979-1980)'. *R.W.* (1980–1981): 2367–2396 and 2435–2478.
Dirix, E. & A. Van Oevelen, 'Kroniek van het verbintenissenrecht (1985-1992)'. *R.W.* (1992–1993): 1209–1237 and 1249–1265.
Kruithof, R., H. Moons & C. Paulus, 'Overzicht van rechtspraak (1965-1973). Verbintenissen'. *T.P.R.* (1975): 439–542 and 715–784.
Kruithof, R., 'Overzicht van rechtspraak (1974-1980). Verbintenissen'. *T.P.R.* (1983): 495–717.
Kruithof, R. et al. 'Overzicht van rechtspraak (1981-1992). Verbintenissen'. *T.P.R.* (1994): 171–721.
Matthys, J. & G. Baeteman, 'Overzicht van rechtspraak (1961-1964).Verbintenissen'. *T.P.R.* (1966): 67–136 and 225–299.
Limpens, J. & J. Van Damme, 'Examen de jurisprudence (1953-1955). Les obligations'. *R.C.J.B.* (1956): 199–239.
Stijns, S., D. van Gerven & P. Wéry, 'Chronique de jurisprudence (1985-1995). Les obligations: les sources'. *J.T.* (1996): 689–752.
Stijns, S., D. van Gerven & P. Wéry, 'Chronique de jurisprudence (1985-1995). Les obligations: le régime général de l'obligation'. *J.T.* (1999): 821–853.
Van Oevelen, A., 'Kroniek van het verbintenissenrecht (1993-2004)'. *R.W.* (2004–2005): 1641–1670.
Van Oevelen, A., 'Kroniek van het verbintenissenrecht (1975-1976)'. *R.W.* (1976–1977): 2385–2414.
Van Oevelen, A. & E. Dirix, 'Kroniek van het verbintenissenrecht (1976-1977)'. *R.W.* (1977–1978): 2289–2304.
Van Oevelen, A., 'Kroniek van het verbintenissenrecht (1977-1978)'. *R.W.* (1979–1980): 153–182.

Van Oevelen, A. & E. Dirix, 'Kroniek van het verbintenissenrecht (1981-1984)'. *R.W.* (1985–1986): 1–28, 81–108 and 145–176.
Van Ommeslaghe, P., 'Examen de jurisprudence (1974-1982). Les obligations'. *R.C.J.B.* (1986): 33–259 and *R.C.J.B.* (1988): 33–199.
Van Ommeslaghe, P., 'Examen de jurisprudence (1968-1973). Les obligations'. *R.C.J.B.* (1975): 423–538 and 597–736.

§3. Books, Articles and Notes on Specific Topics

The reader can find references on specific topics in the footnotes of the relevant paragraph. The main publications are gathered in the first footnotes of each chapter.

Index

The numbers refer to the paragraph numbers.

Abuse of rights (doctrine of), 37, 50, 103–105, 107, 230, 253, 260–261, 387, 407, 416, 421, 432, 437, 441
Acceptance (of an offer), 121–123
Acte de disposition, 203, 279
Administrative contract, 23
Advance payments, 56
Agency, 51, 61, 292, 341, 346, 390
Agreement, 23, 31, 38, 40, 42, 54, 66, 69, 71, 111, 114, 115, 117, 124, 125, 130, 137, 144, 229, 244, 287, 294, 320, 327, 329, 335, 351, 354, 355, 364, 374, 380–381, 388
Aleatory contracts, 63–64
Annuity (life), 64
Apparent agency, 292, 346
Arbitration, 10, 262
Arbitration court, 10
Assignment, 323, 364
Astreinte, 37, 430
Autonomy of the will, 43–45, 51–53, 55, 68, 138, 153, 230, 329, 390
Auxiliary performer, 85

Bad faith, 213
Bankruptcy, 376
Bank, 140, 164, 266, 272, 347, 356, 378
Beginning of written proof, 174, 177, 187, 192
Benefit of a third party (contract for the), 310–318
Bill of exchange, 144
Bonus pater familias, 90, 133, 392, 393
Breach of contract, 78, 81, 83, 86, 252, 299, 300, 308, 391–399, 410, 415, 436–438, 441, 443
Building contractors, 290, 316
Burden of proof, 35, 151, 162–166, 179, 397, 420
Business, 347

Capacity, 145, 146, 148, 193–206, 340, 345, 360, 371, 375
Catalogue, 110
Child (*see also* Minor), 14, 164, 312
Collateral contract, 243
Collective bargaining, 14
Commercial law, 74
Company, 22, 259, 311, 364, 379, 412(*see also* Corporation)
Compensation (set-off), 373–378 (*see also* Set-off)
Compensation, 137–138, 373–378, 423–428
Condition, 193–242, 271–286, 296–297, 360–366, 371, 402
Conduct, 146, 387
Consensual contract, 58, 140, 141, 322
Consideration, 52, 102, 124–128, 134, 287, 393
Construction, 126, 334
Consumer, 56, 74–75, 106, 123, 135, 140, 151, 164, 250, 259, 269, 374, 401, 427
Contractual intention, 115, 213, 266 (*see also* Intention to create legal relations)
Corporation, 14 (*see also* Company)
Counter-offer, 121
Crime, 79, 81
Criminal penalty, 49, 119, 254–261, 408, 424, 427, 433, 446
Cumul, 80
Custom, 120, 158, 350, 390

Damages, 242, 421–428
Date (of a signed instrument), 173

Index

Death, 126, 173, 250, 293, 311, 316, 400
Deceit, 210, 213–215, 217, 238, 333, 355
Deed, 139, 219, 381
Default, 352, 403, 404, 408, 411–414, 427, 449
Defects of consent, 210–221, 324
Defect, 210, 211, 216, 217, 219, 235–242
Delay (in the execution), 411–414
delays for payment, 348
putting in delay, 411–414, 424, 449 (*see also* Default)
Delivery, 34, 58, 143, 336, 349, 404, 411, 414
Deposit, 58, 347, 356
Direct action, 288, 310, 313–318
Discharge by agreement, 335, 380–381)
Disproportion, 104, 219, 220
Distributors, 71
Document, 38, 55, 56, 58, 108, 111, 113–119, 134, 141, 144, 145, 169–171, 174, 175, 177, 187, 188, 192, 213, 262, 266–268, 322, 440

Effects of the contract, 410
Employment, 73, 125, 202
employee, 14, 81, 85, 164, 217, 251, 276, 316, 333, 361, 371, 376, 384
employer, 14, 81, 164, 217, 230, 316, 332–334, 361, 376
Enrichment without cause, 93, 94
Equity, 240, 244
Evidence, 142, 154, 155 (*see also* Formalities)
Exceptio non adimpleti contractus (defence or plea of non-performance), 60, 324, 399, 410, 448–450
Exchange, 144
Exemption clause, 49, 246–253, 290, 399, 408, 446
Express terms, 243, 244
Extinction (of an obligation), 382
Extinctive prescription, 382–385

Fault, 36, 37, 49, 50, 77, 78, 81, 82, 84, 86, 90, 92, 112, 115, 129–138, 164, 165, 194, 212, 214, 215, 225, 238, 242, 250, 299, 331, 333, 349, 391–400, 436 (*see also* Tort)
Fiduciary, 99
Force majeure, 400, 401
Foreseeability, 422
Formalities, 54, 55, 139, 140, 297, 364
Frame of contract, 71
Fraud, 145, 251, 253, 301–303, 355
Frustration, 400–409

Generic goods, 34
Gift, 34, 46, 58, 99, 126, 321 (*see also* Gratuitous promise)
Goods, 14, 34, 50, 62, 66, 67, 74, 98, 120, 176, 226, 228, 233, 349, 404, 407, 414
Good faith, 44, 53, 69, 73, 101–105, 107, 112, 117, 118, 209, 230, 245, 253, 265, 305, 323, 324, 346, 387, 407, 432, 437, 441, 449
Gratuitous promise, 127
Gratuitous contract, 62, 127
Guarantee, 290, 293, 420 (*see also* Suretyship)

Hardship, 400–409
Heir, 366
Hire of work and skill, 390
Hire, 67, 73, 106, 125, 390
House, 34, 279, 351

Identity, 65, 145, 148, 172, 384
Implied terms, 244–245
Impossibility400–404
of performance, 402, 403
Independent contractor, 85
Information, 73, 102, 107, 131, 135, 245
Injunction, 413, 420
Instalments, 56, 445
Insurance, 48, 73, 148, 198, 311, 316, 317, 361
Intention (to create legal relations), 30, 173, 338, 410
Interest, 12, 20, 22, 23, 41, 46, 47, 78, 82, 88–90, 92, 102, 104, 138, 145, 148, 175, 180, 205, 206, 258, 259, 297, 312, 341, 342, 351, 354, 355, 365, 366, 383, 412, 414, 423–428
interests of another, 88, 90
public interest, 23, 46
sufficient interest, 22, 104
International, 16, 226, 407
Interpretation, 16, 45, 75, 176, 200, 249, 264–270, 287, 376, 386, 399, 402, 412, 420
Intuitu personae contract, 65, 293, 320, 330, 340, 342

Juridical act, 26, 28–30, 39, 42, 61, 76, 98, 148, 149, 161, 169, 177, 180, 183, 184, 187, 189, 192, 193, 194, 209, 219, 227, 279, 297, 301, 303, 304, 324, 338, 340, 386, 390, 391
Jurisdiction, 22, 100, 107, 142, 262

Laesio, 64, 203, 210, 219–221
Landlord – tenant (*see also* Lease), 320, 432
Land, 64, 290, 366, 400
Lapse of time, 382
Law of property, 96–97
Lease, 233
Letter, 38, 115, 187, 209, 304, 305, 413, 440
  counter letters, 209, 304, 305
  registered letter, 440
  letter of comfort, 38, 115
Liquidated damages (*see also* Damages), 254, 256
Loan, 58, 59, 147, 148, 272, 353, 365, 376

Maintenance (default of), 38, 86
Marriage, 140, 276
Mentally disordered person, 206
Minor (*see also* Child), 77, 200–205, 219, 385
Mistake, 181, 210–212, 284, 290
Morals, 38, 46, 115, 188, 216, 217, 220
Mortgage, 58, 70, 97, 140, 141, 279, 284, 324, 358, 364, 366, 372

Napoleonic code, 3, 15, 43
Natural obligation, 38, 94, 371
Negligence, 30, 76, 77, 86, 90, 134, 249, 251, 253, 291, 292, 346
Negotiable instrument, 146, 321
Negotiation, 73, 111–119, 129–138, 407
Negotiorum gestio, 31, 87–90, 341
Nemo plus iuris, 324
Nominate contract, 66
Non-pecuniary loss, 421
Notary, 58, 143–148, 172, 188, 356, 365
Notice (to terminate a contract)
  notice of the assignment, 323
  notice (‘*mise en demeure*’), 411
Novation, 324, 335, 370–372
Nullity, 46, 47, 50, 129, 131, 156, 175, 203, 204, 210, 212, 213, 215, 217, 218, 223–225, 232, 234–242, 257, 317, 335

Object of the obligation, 37, 227, 349, 375, 391
Object of the contract, 58, 227
Obligation de résultat, 394, 397
Oblique action, 318
Offer, 29, 40, 50, 74, 111, 120
Option, 14, 116, 410, 432, 433

Parol evidence rule, 142
Partnership, 219
Patrimony, 25, 26, 93, 97, 98, 202, 216, 217, 220, 279, 293, 303, 313, 318, 322, 358
Paulian action (*actio Pauliana*), 289, 301–303
Payment, 91–92, 336–369, 423–428
Penalty clause, 105, 119, 254–261, 371, 408, 424, 433, 446
Performance, 331, 335–399, 415–428, 431–432 (*see also* Specific performance)
Performance (Partial), 260–261
Pledge, 58, 59, 70
Policy-contract, 23
Precontractual fault, 112, 131, 133–136, 212, 214, 215, 238, 242
Prescription, 78, 82, 335, 371, 382–385
Principal and agent (*see also* Agency)
Procedure, 6, 44, 154, 172, 178, 180, 182, 236
Promise, 29, 38, 71, 116, 124–127, 307, 308, 311, 324, 327, 360
Proof, 149–192, 397–398 *see also* Burden of proof; Beginning of written proof, Evidence
Property, 14, 15, 25, 34, 96–98, 144, 146, 147, 229, 279, 284
Property (transfer of), 34, 284
Public law, 23
Public service, 23, 420
Public policy, 383

Quality (of the goods), 349
Quasi contract, 28, 31, 87–95

Real contract, 54, 58
Real right, 384
Rechtsverwerking, 386–387
Registration, 173
Release, 112, 329, 338, 380, 438
Remedy, 37, 64, 331, 397, 410–451
Renunciation, 123, 380, 386–387
Representation, 12, 100, 243, 292

Index

Rescission, 64, 68, 408
Restitution, 87, 91–92, 221, 225, 235, 241, 376, 445
Rights in personam, 27, 96, 384
Rights in rem, 27, 39, 42, 96–98
Road traffic accident, 316
Roman law, 301

Saisie, 344
Sale, 56, 62, 66, 67, 71, 97, 123, 141, 146, 147, 219, 290, 297, 308, 321, 366, 407, 414
Sale of goods, 62, 66, 67, 207, 228
Sale of goods (International), 407
Seal, 139
Secret contract, 209, 304
Set-off, 373–378
Settlement, 140, 180, 351, 353, 356
Ship, 125
Signature, 108, 169–171, 173–177
Silence, 121, 386
Solemn contract, 54, 58, 140–141
Specific performance, 415
Statute, 48, 66, 68, 73
Subcontractor, 316, 330–334
Subrogation, 92, 319, 337, 341, 343, 357–376
Successive contracts, 445
Suretyship, 70

Tenant, 432
Termination, 255, 388–390, 431–432, 434–447
Term, 11, 67–69, 102, 139, 207, 245, 246, 254, 255, 271, 272, 284, 388
Three-party contract, 326, 328, 329
Title, 10, 25, 82, 146, 199, 279, 321, 359
Tort (and contract), 76–95 *see also* Cumul
Tort, 28, 30, 76–95, 137, 218, 221, 240, 332, 384
Trade Unions, 14
Transfer of property, 34, 284
Transfer of the property rented, 34
Trust, 98–100, 104

Ultra vires, 22
Unilateral contract, 39, 60, 61, 222, 438
Unilateral juridical act, 28, 29, 338, 386
Unilateral promise, 29, 327
Usage (custom), 390
Usage, 58, 188, 244, 390

Void, 70, 204, 259, 273, 282, 371

Warranty, 226, 243
Work, 6, 14, 23, 32, 125, 147, 197, 198, 334, 361, 390, 444
Writing, 56, 113, 126, 194, 262
Writ, 146

www.ingramcontent.com/pod-product-compliance
Ingram Content Group UK Ltd.
Pitfield, Milton Keynes, MK11 3LW, UK
UKHW020143290926
15471UKWH00004B/680